We Are Not Alone - Part 1

A Challenging Reinterpretation of Human History

D1495273

By

Endall Beall

First Edition

Dedication

This work is dedicated to all the researchers into human history and their continued efforts to remove the blinders of our conscious awareness.

Table of Contents

ACKNOWLEDGMENTS

I wish to thank Richard Redhawk once again for the awesome cover art and also for his continued support in presenting these books.

Foreword

The world owes a debt of gratitude to the author Zechariah Sitchin for making the existence of the ancient Sumerian gods, the Anunnaki, known to the public at large. Prior to his presentation of the ancient Sumerian, Babylonian and Assyrian texts about the Anunnaki gods in his *Earth Chronicles* series of books, the Anunnaki were generally unknown to the public and the texts remained primarily in the realm of the academics and archaeologists. His works have laid the foundation for a public dialogue that sorely needs to be engaged and the mysteries about the Anunnaki and their intervention with our species needs to be solved once and for all. The constant denial of their physical existence by our academic and religious authorities prevents this dialogue from taking place, and in that regard, all of our mainstream academics are doing humanity a vast disservice through their tacit negligence.

Despite Sitchin making the public aware of the ancient gods as real beings from another world whose planet orbits in our solar system, many of his conclusions missed the mark where the interpretations he made about the ancient texts are concerned. He made his own translations of the texts that go against modern scholarship on the subject of the ancient tablets, and despite his efforts, in many respects he did more harm than good in putting his spin on the ancient texts. These mistranslations in no way belittle what he was attempting to do, for his work is part of what laid the foundation for the work you hold in your hands. Without his efforts to make the public aware of the existence of the Anunnaki as real living beings who called themselves gods, this author would probably never have endeavored to solve the mysteries revealed in this book.

In the realm of the academics, the Anunnaki are simply another set of mythical gods that are found all across the ancient world, from Egypt to India and beyond. Modern scholars perceive them to be nothing more than religious superstitious beliefs made up by the people who worshipped them. In this regard, the academics utterly missed the point of our ancient ancestors cataloging of the affairs of the gods. Where Sitchin differed from the mainstream academics is that he had the insight to view them as actual physical beings, not just as religio-superstitious nonsense dreamed up by powerful priesthoods of the ancient past.

The greatest error that Sitchin made in his interpretations was through his assumption that the stories left by these ancient civilizations were fully truthful. He accepted too many of the tales of the gods at face value, and thereby failed to perceive a different story that is presented when one views their stories in an alternative light. In one sense, Sitchin developed a form of Anunnaki tunnel vision which blinded him from seeing a greater, uglier truth behind the stories about the Anunna gods of

Mesopotamia. Sitchin also took too many liberties through his own retranslations and interpretations, which is the main reason that mainstream Sumerologists totally discounted his work.

We only have to look at the Greek religion about the gods of Olympus to see that many of the stories concocted about the ancient gods were a lot of propaganda and fanciful stories designed to misdirect the followers of the religion from the ultimate truth. The same viewpoint has to be taken when reading between the lines of the ancient texts about the Anunnaki, the Egyptian gods, the Hindu gods and ultimately the god of the Bible. What we find in those texts is an admixture of certain partial historical accountings coupled with a lot of intentional misdirection and propaganda designed to glorify certain gods of the Sumerian pantheon, in particular, the Anunnaki god Enki and his sister Ninhursag.

The clues about the absolute truth of our past have been intentionally obscured by these two Anunnaki gods and their created priesthoods so they could be perceived as the ultimate creators of humanity on this planet and be perceived as benevolent in their natures. Many researchers have come behind Sitchin and have unquestionably accepted his interpretation of the benevolence of Enki as the truth without doing any deeper research into Sitchin's theories on their own. Few indeed have challenged this perception of benevolence and, as such, they have all missed the real story hidden behind the self-glorifying tales of Enki and Ninhursag. This book tells the hidden story that we were never meant to see.

Introduction

The book you have in your hands is volume 6 in The Evolution of Consciousness series. The previous books in this series focused on personal spirit work and what one is generally required to do in order to advance one's own cognitive awareness. This volume diverges from the first volumes of this series and focuses on presenting explanations about ancient historical aspects of our past that many have expressed an interest in understanding, to wit, solving the many mysteries of our history.

All the books in this series are controversial simply for the fact that they challenge the status quo where our cognitive awareness and our perception of *reality* is currently focused. This book focuses on the perception of our ancient history in the first cognition. Much of the historical information provided in this book will be unverifiable simply because there are few if any remaining sources of the information that can directly validate much of what is revealed herein. Many of these ancient sources have either been lost or destroyed, or lie sequestered away in

1

libraries that are intentionally unavailable to the public - if they ever existed at all.

What is presented in the following pages is going be challenged by modern authorities as being non-credible, whether they are mainstream deniers or those who have adopted Zechariah Sitchin's interpretations as being wholly correct. The information challenges all our currently held belief systems and misconceptions about human history. I am not asking the reader to believe what follows simply because I wrote it, nor am I peddling beliefs at all. I am asking the reader to view the evidence presented and give it a fair hearing before reaching any final conclusions on the matter. This requires critical thinking, despite how it challenges our current perception of reality.

As with all the material I present, it is purely on a take it or leave it basis. Those with advancing cognitive abilities will be able to verify what they want to know with their own sources, or they will be able to feel the correctness of the information from an intuitive standpoint. Ultimately, I present the information and appeal to the reader's logic to glean understanding from the material and sources provided.

Due to copyright constraints in manners of quotes as well as through the usage of copyrighted pictures, the author will provide the reader with modalities of search through Google to find the illustrations that support the author's contentions throughout this book. In many respects, where these images are concerned, seeing is believing. The author will resort to ancient texts and their standard translations as the major references to many of the ideas presented, for it is through these ancient stories and writings that I will paint the picture that we have all either been intentionally led away from, interpret incorrectly, or simply refuse to see.

This book is going to discuss energy and energy manipulation, what some refer to as magic, but it is not magic at all. Throughout the ages it has been perceived as magic by our species because the truth of it has never been shared in full by those who were experts in such energy manipulation. We were never meant to figure out what will be revealed in the pages of this book, although this type of energy manipulation has been used against Earth humanity by both otherworldly entities as well as certain human organizations that use the same magical traditions that have been passed down to them by the so-called gods, and have existed on this planet for thousands of years. These ancient traditions of energy manipulation have survived into modern times.

This volume is not going to be a 'how to' manual for energy manipulation for the simple reason that there are too many eager egos wanting to be Harry Potter-ish type magicians. These personalities abound in the Neo-Pagan traditions and the religion of Wicca, as well as individuals pursuing the path to learning "High Magic", without having any understanding what High Magic really is. I am not in the business of providing them any information that will advance their ego greed to learn how to manipulate energies.

This volume is going to endeavor to explain how these energies have been manipulated and abused in order to keep all of humanity under a hidden tyrannical control, energetically

3

speaking, by using energy manipulation as a form of control over our consciousness, and exposing those who have worked over the centuries to impede the rest of humanity for their own selfish goals. As with all the other volumes in this series, this book is an exposé that certain parties on this planet would rather have remained unknown to the general public. Many of the accusations about black magic practices leveled against these organizations are already in the public arena, yet even those raising the accusations about its usage have not figured out just exactly what it is or why it works, nor can most of them get past their own shortsighted religious paranoia to see it as anything but the work of the Devil.

Most of what is presented in this book regarding energy manipulation will be focused on the negative aspects of abusing energies for control and power. Again, this is *not* an instructional manual on how to program energy. As one moves into the second cognition they can discover it for themselves or not. It is not my place to provide anything more than select examples for the sake of illustrating certain points - the potential for abuse is too high to share the information with selfish egos who can't get past the personal ego need to gratify themselves by performing feats of energetic magic. I am not going into an in depth presentation about spellcasting, so those who want to practice such things will find no advantage in this volume. This is a work focused on providing explanations to the processes used against humanity since our species began, as well as shedding light on a hidden history that some of us are only now starting to vaguely perceive.

This book will also cover hidden aspects of human history that only a few select individuals on the planet have been privy to over the ages of mankind. The information provided is meant to serve as an alternative source of information for personal understanding and consciousness advancement. The historical material in this book is already being sold to the masses in different forms, none of which are accurately portraying the ultimate facts, either by academic sources or lay researchers. This book is designed to clear up those fallacies and let the reader know where the rubber hits the road in regard to human history in many respects. As with the other books in this series, this volume is designed to set the record straight and remove the misconceptions and many unanswered questions from the public domain, thereby initiating a new, more honest public dialogue into these matters.

Composing this particular body of work has been a challenge, to say the very least. There is a vast amount of information that this book presents in more of a reporting format than as an extensive scholarly analysis on singular events or ancient belief systems. The author had to unravel the mysteries of our ancient past, then reweave the seemingly disparate threads into a new, more cohesive tapestry for the reader's understanding. The picture this book reveals will challenge the reader and their perceptions of our human past, as well as explain why our world is in the shape it is in the present.

The reader is going to find that the snapshots of information provided in this book require more extensive research on the part of the reader if they desire to know more than the overview presented herein. There is no shortage of scholarly works on ancient texts, myths and legends that had to be pored over in order to assemble the pieces provided in this volume to make it remotely comprehensible to the general reader. This book provides a broad spectrum overview of historical events that have been classified as mythology, mysticism and religion, and as such, the real story behind these things has been misinterpreted by those scholars who have delved into it over the centuries.

The reader is going to encounter names of the ancient gods with which they may be familiar, along with other gods that are more obscure to their knowledge. I ask the reader's patience as this massive story unfolds, for what it reveals in the end is nothing short of shocking.

In writing this series of books, we are presenting a systematic sequence of information designed to remove the perceptual illusions of the first cognition that blind us all. We are seeking to expose as many lies to that perception as possible. In reference to lying, Friedrich Nietzsche wrote in § 55 of *The Antichrist*:

> *"I call it lying to refuse to see what one sees, or refuse to see it **as** it is: whether the lie be uttered before witnesses or not before witnesses is inconsequential. The most common sort of lie is that by which man deceives himself. . . "*

Our entire perception of history has been a massive lie. Many times we have been presented with certain truths and we deny those truths because they disagree with our own perceptual self-deception. Many readers are going to continue to lie to themselves about the information in this book, claiming that it is invalid because it challenges the very foundation of their perceptual reality. This book is an invitation for the reader to see certain aspects of our history *as it is,* not what we wish it was or currently believe it to be. The information in this book is going to be a very large and bitter pill to swallow, but if the reader is diligent in their research, I think they will not be able to deny the truth of what this book contains and still be completely honest with themselves.

There is information provided in the following pages that is going to challenge credulity where our normal perception of reality is concerned. Our system of thinking and definitions of reality are what keeps us controlled by those who would rather we didn't know these things. You are going to be challenged with ideas and concepts that go beyond your wildest imaginings, yet that doesn't make the information false. It only means that our definition of reality on this planet does not extend far enough to truly comprehend the universe at large, the varied number of species that inhabit it, and how much interplay these varied races and species had on this planet throughout all of human history.

Much of the information in this book has been intentionally covered up by agencies on this planet who have a vested interest in keeping this information secret. They have used every weapon in their arsenals to keep this truth from coming to light. If the reader wants explanations about why this story hasn't been told, they have to go to their authority figures to get those answers. These authority figures are the academic scholars, archaeologists, paleontologists, religious authorities, governments and certain secret societies who have a vested interest in keeping this information tightly under wraps and strictly under their control. It is not this author who is answerable for revealing what this book contains, but it is our presumed authorities in these matters that owe the global public a massive amount of explanations for why they have not revealed it. It is well past time for what is revealed in these pages to be put before the jury of public opinion where these matters are concerned. All of these authorities are the ones who have some serious explaining to do. They are, after all, the *experts* in their respective fields of knowledge.

As I have stated in the previous works, I am not a lettered man. I claim no authority as an academic or anything other than a layman scholar. The question every reader has to ask themselves as they digest and come to terms with the information in this book is why, if these other people are such touted authorities, they have never put the pieces of this puzzle together? If this layman author can figure this out, why haven't our professed authorities? Or maybe, they not only figured it out, but have known about it all along. It is up to the reader to make that ultimate determination.

Solving these mysteries is like a detective solving a cold case. In this volume the reader is going to be hit with a gigantic pile of coincidences which, at some point, we have to admit that there is more than just coincidence going on by finding the correlations provided in this book. Sometimes we only have circumstantial evidence on which to build a case. The information in this book is that pile of circumstantial evidence accumulated by investigating just too damn many coincidences to ignore.

Due to the scale of historical time that has to be covered in discussing these matters, as well as the huge amount of information to be revealed, I have to break this down into separate volumes. If I were to try and contain all this information in one volume, the picture that the author is working to reveal would be even more confusing than just this one volume will be. As it is, with all the information put forth in this book, the reader is very likely going to find themselves confused, possibly even frightened at certain points, simply because what is revealed shocks our conscious and our perceptions so drastically. I have done my best to alleviate this confusing concatenation of facts by writing the explanations necessary to put all the jigsaw pieces of this massive puzzle together. I just hope you have a strong stomach, because this book is not going to be remotely easy to digest.

1. Throwing Down the Gauntlet

We live in a world controlled by authority and authorities. This is the world of the ego. The ego is all about relinquishing responsibility to others to think for us, govern us, lead us in our religious practices and even to dictate to us what is real and what is not real, predicated on the acceptable boundaries of our cultures and our perceptual reality. These boundaries that rigidly define what reality is presumed to be are most often left in the hands of our academic scholars to determine, ever since the scientific revolution occurred in response to a religion that stopped genuine inquiry into anything that the church disagreed with. Once science stretched its legs and got comfortable as the accepted authority in opposition to religion, science got complacent and empirical and eventually ossified in its own iconic strictures just as religion had done before it. The age of exciting scientific discovery has now devolved into coloring within preset boundaries, intellectual territorial disputes, ego-oriented vindictiveness, and tactics used to excommunicate anyone from the scientific community who dares to challenge the accepted party line of dictated reality. For proof of these contentions we only need to look as far as the treatment handed to any innovator over the last century and a half - people like Tesla and Einstein to name just two of the most prominent figures who butted heads with the ossified religion of science - and who also happened to be right in their theoretical projections, to the dismay of the gatekeepers of the scientific realm of rigid thinking.

Both religious institutions as well as academic institutions are equally guilty of suppressing knowledge where matters that challenge their own defined borders of reality are concerned. Where academia was once the realm for challenging ideas and stretching boundaries of knowledge, it has now become an elitist, ego-driven cloistered society of intellectuals closed to any innovator who pushes the envelope of its accepted doctrinal norms. Administrators in universities and other teaching institutions make policies to insure the standard line of acceptability is adhered to in their arenas of teaching and published studies. Being controversial in one's academic ideas is acceptable, provided the controversy stays within the borders of a pre-accepted and stiffly-defined reality. What most of the public at large is unaware of is the fact that a lot of information and data that concerns human history has been intentionally buried and ignored by modern academics in the store rooms of museums around the world, because if they were to admit the truth the evidence that has been discovered presents in a fair and honest analysis, the academic's cherished *beliefs* would go down the toilet just as quickly as the beliefs of all followers of every religion on the planet.

As related in the first books in this series, no matter where we turn in the first cognition we are met with stone walls erected by egos, and those walls are the thickest and highest where academic and religious beliefs are concerned. Religionists still insist on the idea of creationism by some fabulous concept of god, and science utterly denies anything that disagrees with Darwin's unproven, yet widely accepted Theory of Evolution as scientific gospel. Both sides of this equation fervently defend their positions and anyone who disagrees with either assessment where human origins is concerned is vilified, run out of town on a rail, ridiculed, black-balled and in the case of academics, their very livelihood is threatened if they move against the boundaries of the first cognition perceptual machine. If a dangerous enough controversy is introduced, the messenger is often outright murdered by forces who have an express need to keep their secrets secret and far away from public awareness.

I am fortunate in the regard that I can raise the extreme controversies that arise in all the books of this series, for my livelihood is not predicated on toeing the party line to either side of this equation - religion and science. The ideas in this volume and the one to follow are going to challenge our very perception of reality. It is my sincere desire that scholars who are experts in their fields will give these books at least a fair hearing based on the evidence presented before passing final judgment on the information. It is not the messenger who is relating these new interpretations of information that is important as much our experts doing an honest and fair reassessment of where the evidence leads us in regard to what these ancient texts and archaeological digs are showing us. The ancient texts and the sites being unearthed around the planet are telling us a story that, for the most part, has been overlooked or strictly ignored by most of our academic community. What the reader is going to encounter in these two volumes is nothing short of astounding, yet very disconcerting at the same time, because it opens a Pandora's Box to our past that few of us have remotely considered as a possibility, and which very few of us indeed can comfortably acknowledge. Those who have read the works of Zechariah Sitchin are probably going to be more able to deal with the information in these two volumes than those who persistently maintain the mainstream illusion of reality.

Most academics are going to immediately discount what is presented in this book as soon as they see the word aliens, rushing to denial in order to discount what their current perceptual belief system refuses to entertain as an alternative truth to their rigid perspective of reality. To any scholar who may be reading this book, I ask the same opportunity to be heard as you expect others to listen to your own theories. There can be no active discussion if information is simply denied because it goes up against one's on personal *beliefs or disbeliefs.* What is contained in the pages of this book is not the author's *beliefs.* This presentation provides an immense trail of evidence that tells us a completely different story than our current level of perception allows or is willing to immediately admit. They are not speculative presentations founded on nothing but fanciful ideas. This book contains no shortage of evidence where the scientific and academic community have utterly failed to date to connect the dots, yet the clues to solve this puzzle are all around this planet.

These books are going to shock the conscious due to the magnitude of cognitive fraud that has been perpetrated against the entire human race on this planet since our very beginnings. Initially, most every reader is going to deny the information presented in these two volumes because coming to terms with the reality of it all is going to make us all very psychologically uncomfortable, to say the least. These books are not written to titillate or frighten people, yet many will feel a visceral fear over the idea that everything presented is remotely possible or true. I am asking the reader to suspend passing judgment until all the evidence is presented. It is easy to disagree with any new idea and deny the possibility of its truthfulness. Our species on this planet has been living in denial for untold ages and our academic institutions are still doing it today. It is time we quit denying what makes our egos uncomfortable and step into a greater cognitive reality. In order for anyone to gain true freedom of consciousness they have to first be aware of the slavery. All of the books in *The Evolution of Consciousness* series are designed to identify what enslaves our perception and how we can free ourselves from these perceptual chains that shackle our consciousness.

This volume and the next are an invitation to all academic experts to use the expertise in their respective fields and re-examine the evidence from the ancient texts, archaeological excavations and geological anomalies that we are aware of in light of the information presented in these books. We live in a world of control where truly free inquiry has rigid boundaries. Our academics these days are more in the business of protecting their perceptual turf to the point of denying everything that conflicts with their own rigid beliefs than they are interested in entertaining any idea that goes against their own chosen dogma. If we are ever to advance as a species, our academics have to stop participating in perpetual pissing matches with each other with stupid and arrogant ego blustering about who is right and who is wrong. In such ego-driven contests, truth is always the casualty. The academics need to stop competing with each other and start working together on collectively finding solutions. No arena of academia is totally needless, and none of them stands as independent or superior over the others, despite what the inflated egos within the selective arenas of academia make themselves believe.

In order to decode our true history it is going to take the combined efforts of the philosophers, the philologists, the archaeologists, the historians and the hard core scientists, as well as those experts in mythology, anthropology, paleontology and comparative religions to put all the seemingly disparate pieces of our past together. The psychologists and psychiatrists need to be involved in order to see how even their soft science of understanding the human psyche is just one more part of the entire global control structure to continually enforce adherence to first cognition thinking. On this path to human cognitive advancement, every academic expert has a role to play to help humanity as a species move forward in consciousness, provided they can find the courage within themselves to make that advancement on a personal basis. We are talking about the evolution of human consciousness - all humanity.

In my treatise *A Philosophy for the Average Man*, I pointed out that all humans, no matter their status or position in life, are average from the standpoint that they all operate in the realm of first cognition awareness and thinking. So long as our lettered academics keep playing the petty ego games they are playing, there will be no advancement in human consciousness because they are the experts to whom people look for guidance, instruction and answers. These days, other than in the classroom or through the efforts of making an ego name for themselves, academics live in a closed world, self-sequestered from the population at large. They live in an Alice in Wonderland environment of their own design and make damn sure that the Mad Hatters of the world, or shall we say the innovators, are never invited to their personal ego-elitist intellectual tea party. They write their papers for peer review in their own closed little networks and few, if any, of their ideas get shared outside that bailiwick. Academic hubris has turned academia as a whole into nothing more than a giant circle jerk with every one of them vying for the position of the pivot man.

Academics demand citations and quotations from their own peer reviewed accepted list of authorities to even be heard, and each branch of academia has a long list of accepted as well as ostracized authorities from which to choose to bolster their own ideas. It is as if no academic is allowed to have any original ideas on their own. They must have 'authoritative' words written by their predecessors before a single new concept or idea can be considered, and even then, the ideas are usually not truly new, they are just more recent spins of what other authorities who came before them authoritatively wrote to their peers. Most of the time the concepts presented are merely a rehashing or refashioning of already accepted beliefs and ideas. If one can't provide such authoritative citations, that person's work is belittled by the mighty egos of our presumed experts. The most succinct and truthful statement I have ever heard from a scientist comes from Michael D. Swords, PhD, Biochemist; Professor Emeritus, W. Michigan University when he said in *UFOs: The Secret History (2010)*:

> *"We in academia have it made, after all, especially scientists in academia. We are kind of at the top of the pecking order, and in order to maintain that illusion, which is what it is, we've got to not appear the fool. So the majority of the scientific community is a non-risk-taking group of people that live in a rather small reality and are in fact scared of things which seems to be outside that reality."*

Although Dr. Swords was speaking in reference to the UFO phenomenon in the film and the utter lack of genuine investigation into the phenomenon, the honest observation he makes applies throughout academia where any new ideas that challenge the accepted norms upsets the apple cart of academic perceptual reality. These books are the invitation for our academic scholars to step outside that cloistered realm of their *'rather small reality'* and stop worrying about *'appearing the fool'*. There is no dishonor in being wrong, only in being negligent and complacent.

The information in this book is real. It is ugly and it is hard to accept, but this author does not feel that he is making himself the fool by presenting it. As an academic, I would feel more the fool if all my lettered degrees were challenged by a layman upstart who happened to come up with an innovative and valid solution to human history- which is exactly what I am doing - through which all your arrogant academic ego bluster within your cloistered reality has blinded you from seeing, especially if you are the *"experts"* in your fields.

So, this author is throwing down the gauntlet to the academic scholars as a challenge to put your money where your expert mouths are. Don't just sit up there in your aeries of intellectual solitude and limited reality continually patting each other on the back over your self-presumed ego greatness, get down here in the trenches where real intuitive research is happening and open your eyes to a new potential for human cognitive reality. Be big enough people to re-examine these ancient texts and reassess the information from archaeological digs in a new light. Start doing honest genetic testing on the enigmatic elongated skulls unearthed all around the planet. For Pete's sake, quit lying to yourselves and to the world at large simply because the evidence doesn't happen to agree with your comfortable perceptual reality, particularly Darwinism. You academics are the intellectuals that hold all the keys to philosophy, archaeology, history, philology, comparative religion, anthropology, mythology, psychology and, most of all, scientific *inquiry*. This book is an invitation to reinvigorate the spirit of inquiry in academia, to work towards co-operation and not compartmentalization of academic pursuits predicated on foolish ego turf wars.

This author is challenging all the academic experts to start *inquiring* once more and stop resting on your laurels just to prove your individual intellectual superiority in your own exclusive little peer groups. Become leaders for the advancement of human understanding instead of being ego-driven, petty, arrogant intellectual tyrants who are only defending their intellectual and specialized turf and their own scientific *faith*. If you don't accept this challenge, if you continue to deny and ignore what the evidence tells us, your careers as '*experts*' will be as worthless as the paper degrees you hang on your walls to measure the extent of your over-inflated egos.

Another aspect of the current system of cognitive tyranny resides in the usage of copyrighted material, especially by academic scholars. Too many of these academics think way too much of their work and price their books at exorbitant prices, thereby removing access to the information they posses from the general public. No one I know can afford two to three hundred dollars or more for a book written by certain experts. Such pricing removes academic works from the public at large due to the simple rule of economics. This amounts to nothing more that financially suppressing information. It makes one wonder whether academia is afraid of a challenge to their sacred dogmatic positions by a lowly layman researcher - of which I am only one of a multitude.

I understand the need to protect one's intellectual property and protecting against blatant plagiarism, but if someone is doing genuine research into history and other matters, if they are honest and giving credit where credit is due in quoting citations by our paid experts, then one would think the experts need to pay the researcher for advertising their works by citing their authority rather than charging the researcher, sometimes thousands of dollars, to quote their research material. By placing such a high price on the flow of information and the sharing of ideas, even if such ideas conflict with your own, we are closing the door to genuine public discussion, dialogue and honest academic research. I noted in *A Philosophy for the Average Man* how the age of specialization opened the door to compartmentalized knowledge, thereby removing common sense from all of us. By abusing copyright laws and required paid 'permissions' in order to squelch any voice of dissent, are not the academics working just as hard to prevent any contradictions to their own pet theories or valid observations? If it is at the discretion of the publishers of these academic works that such exorbitant fees are charged, then the publishers should be ashamed of these practices, particularly if they are university presses. Such practices fly in the face of genuine research, free speech and expose the system as a form of tyranny hiding behind copyright laws to suppress fair use of information.

Due to such copyright abuses and restrictions of using fair quotation standards in this day and age, I have had to resort to other means to tell the story contained in the pages of this book. It is a truly pathetic statement about our present system of cognition when the mighty dollar and ego superiority of our academic experts work to suppress any real investigative interest in discovering anything new. So, to all the academic authorities who use this system of information repression through the power of the purse, you should all be ashamed of yourselves. You may claim to be experts in your fields, and many of you are genuine inquiring scholars with highly valuable skills, but I think those skills are wasted when you play continual games of academic hubris and refuse to entertain any idea that goes against your own academic *faith*. In this regard, the academics are doing humanity a vast disservice. We have greater expectations of you than most of you are apparently willing to deliver. You are too busy protecting your own dogmatic turf to allow the fresh air of discovery to blow through your stuffy institutions.

Despite the difficulties presented in copyright restrictions, this story is going to be told, with our without the aid of our academics. There is always a workaround for the truth to be presented. It would be better for all humanity to see our academics start to produce scholarship of inquiry rather than playing petty ego games within their own closed circles of associates defending the academic faith, but due to the power of the first cognition, I don't see that happening any time soon - unfortunately.

The history of the progression of the sciences has always been led by the heretics, the innovators to the system, like Copernicus, Galileo, Louis Pasteur, Nikola Tesla, Albert Einstein, Zechariah Sitchin and Friedrich Nietzsche. Were it not for the heretics and innovators, science itself would have withered on the vine shortly after its birth. The high priests of academia protect their limited perceptual domain just as vociferously as any religious priesthood. Color within the lines! Don't make waves! Don't challenge the status quo! Just as with any religion, excommunication is always the best way to repress the heretic, and the academic community is big on excommunicating its own heretics. Academics have lost sight of the truth that it is the heretics themselves who keep academia remotely valid, not the staunch defenders of the dogmatic scientific faith.

This book is an invitation to all of the potential heretics of academia to finally make your voices heard. I am willing to bet there are more heretics within the different fields of academia than there are stalwart defenders of the faith. If all the academic heretics can release themselves from the shackles of the current system of repressing information, then it may be realized by the gatekeepers that they can't fire all of you and keep their elitist system in place. The universities would collapse. They would be seen for exactly what they currently are, temples to the religion of dogmatic, close-minded academia, which chooses to ossify rather than advance. Fear and the power of the purse control this rigid system, and fear is the mindkiller for all human consciousness. Copernicus and Galileo went up against the most powerful institution in the western world when they brought forth their ideas. That took great courage, which I see greatly lacking in most academics these days.

As stated above, there is no foul in being wrong. No one ever gets it right the first time. There is more fault in not trying at all through negligent bending of the knees at the temple of your academic altars of dogma. If we do not, as a species, start addressing these areas of understanding, despite the pressure of the religionists of all stripes, and I include modern academia as part of that same religious structure, then we are most likely doomed as a species. We will continue to color within the same repetitive and tiresome patterns as our predecessors and we will only make minor advances from time to time, provided the ego program doesn't make us all destroy ourselves in the offing.

This planet needs a revolution, but not a revolution of violence. We need a revolution in the advancement of our consciousness, and that advancement can't take place so long as continually we pay homage at the altars of the accepted perceptions of our current reality, whether it is in relying on ancient scriptures, or depending on peer-accepted authorities from which we must qualify any new idea that presents itself to our consciousness. We are slaves to a system of cognition that must be overturned if we are ever to advance our cognitive abilities and mature as a species.

Many scholars make their living out of contradicting and killing the messages of the heretics. Most of the time, they simply disagree and can offer nothing in the alternative as a solution except providing the same tiresome polemical dogmatic diatribe, and they launch their assaults hiding behind the length of letters behind their names to stand as the enforcers of accepted academic faith. Ridicule and scorn are their weapons, yet not a one of these detractors ever offers anything new to counter the heretics except polemics and threats of excommunication from the academic club. They offer no inventiveness for they are merely the prison guards of academic consciousness, the enforcers of the dogma, the defenders of the faith, and in that regard, no different than any priest that ever lived. They are simply petty tyrants.

As I write these words, the voices of the scholars over the past two centuries in reference to archaeological interpretation as well as textual and historical interpretations have all been heard, and everywhere their voices are raised we find mystery, denial and confounding discoveries that go against the accepted norms. The realm of the academics of the world is exactly the same world for everyone else operating in the first cognition. Each academic division has a predetermined box of perception into which any idea must be made to conform. It is specifically due to such constraints that all of our experts have completely overlooked, or chosen to deny what the evidence in this book portrays. As I wrote in *Willful Evolution,* you can't put 100 pounds of sugar in a 1 pound container. This book, like all the others in this series, is an invitation to tear down the walls of our perceptual boxes and make something truly new and exciting for humanity as a whole. The question is whether academia has the courage and the stomach to help pave that road to human cognitive advancement, or whether our academics are going to continue to be the roadblock to discovery, which is, unfortunately, already too apparent.

2. The Alien Factor

Before I delve too deeply into the explanations about energy manipulation, we have to cover the historical aspect of where it originated on this planet and by whom. I will state categorically that I am not a UFO nut or one of the fringe elements that puts faith in the saucer jockeys to come save us from ourselves. This is not to say that we may not have had certain entities screwing around with Earth humans in the recent past, but I am not a fan of MUFON or any of the other alien chasers that are famous for their infamous tinfoil hats. I find that most of these people are misdirected at best, or people looking for a belief in something outside themselves at worst. The other factor at play in the whole alien thing is what I think is a very directed source of disinformation aimed at the public at large by certain elements that want our consciousness controlled by such limited ideas and fear. The same factions who control all this alien malarkey are intimately tied into peddling the mystical hornswoggle from ancient Egypt and elsewhere. Both areas will be put under the microscope in this book, and I have little doubt that, as with my previous works, I am going to mightily piss off a lot people. Harsh truth has a tendency to do that to people. On one hand, there are millions of people who have been trying to solve this mystery for years who will walk away from this book armed with a deeper understanding of why they couldn't seem to put the pieces of the puzzle together. On the other hand, we find all the deniers who want to stay safely wrapped in their first cognition security blanket and refuse to see the truth for what it is.

The media is controlled in all aspects where television and the news is concerned. It is also controlled through publication and stringent copyright laws. Nothing gets aired that isn't approved by the network heads. All the shows being aired about the Freemasons, the Vatican, aliens and ancient civilizations is contrived pap delivered to an audience that is either too lazy or too ill informed to know any better. It seems that almost everywhere you turn in film media we find ourselves bombarded with symbols from ancient Egypt or Freemasonry. These propagandist themes portraying the Freemasons as nothing more than a bunch of swell guys are illustrated in such films and *Laura Croft: Tomb Raider* or *National Treasure.* Other symbols of Freemasonry show up 'haphazardly' in multitudes of other film media releases and only the keenest observers are aware of this subtle programming. More of this will be discussed in depth in later chapters, but I make mention of it here because its applications go far back in human history.

There is no shortage of ancient texts from many lands that tell us specifically that human beings on Earth were created by the *gods*. Even the Old Testament uses the term *Elohim*, which specifically denotes multiple gods involved in the creation story of man. I am going to use the term gods in this books as it specifically applies to certain groups of entities that were by no means anything godlike as first cognition humans perceive god, but who have continually played the creator god card against humanity, and whose religions still play that card to this day. With the advent of organized Judaism, Christianity and Islam in the West, the gods of old disappeared and the new invisible, monotheistic God of the Jews took the place of the old gods. It is because of this concept of the invisible almighty God that the ancient tales of the many gods were deemed to be mythology, when the fact is their existence is not myth at all.

We have TV shows like *Ancient Aliens* that have run for years pumping people full of all sorts of speculative ideas, the most pernicious of which is that these ancient gods are always interpreted as being higher level intelligences compared to us lowly humans, or they are deemed somehow divine, usually both. It is the constant saturation about divinity and mysticism, linking the two traditions under the banner of ancient alien visitation where we find the real agenda, which is keeping humans on this planet continually sold on the idea that we are lesser beings. I ask the reader to take note if they ever watch those episodes to pay particular attention to how they are linking the aliens with supernatural or mystical traditions. This all serves a specific agenda of which most people are blissfully unaware.

I noted in both volumes 3 and 4 of this series how Alice Bailey, and her variations on Madame Helena Blavatsky's Theosophy had political affiliations, and that much of modern New Age spirituality has a hidden political agenda behind it. The fact is that all traditions of mysticism or the supernatural, whether religious or otherwise, find their origins with those who genetically created humans as their slaves and as a food source. There have been a few books over the years that have recognized this information about humans being created as a slave race, but I found that their authors' ultimate interpretations were off the mark where reality is concerned, particularly when they interpreted who these gods were or what they were like.

The fact is that we had many physical races from *out there* that interacted on this planet since the creation of the human species here. We all keep getting bombarded specifically with ideas about the Greys, the shape-shifting lizards from Draco, or the blond-haired blue-eyed race of aliens that were somehow associated with the Nazis. Through all this hype, the real truth gets lost in the propaganda. It is from the advent of the religions touting the invisible God that the tales of the ancient physical gods got turned into *mythology*. The fanciful dramatic tales of the Greek gods of Olympus and the Egyptian gods served very well to categorize all stories of the ancient gods as fanciful and mythical, and supported the transition to the modern religious concept of the all-powerful invisible creator God of Western religions.

As Mrs. Beall explained in *The Energy Experience*, many of our predecessors from the stars are built in the same, or similar human form that we are. We are *not* unique in that regard. The human genetic *template* is ancient and extends far beyond our known universe. Where the human species on this planet is concerned, Darwinian theory is a dead letter box. There was no gradual linear rise from protozoa to apes into modern humans. We were manufactured in a genetic laboratory by master geneticists of an alien race using their own genes as the master code, possibly combined with certain hominid species on this planet. As hard a pill as that is to swallow, that is the way it is, and even the talking heads on *Ancient Aliens* admit the strong possibility of this based on many of our most ancient texts. This truth is one of the things Zechariah Sitchin figured out, although the ultimate designers of humanity were *not* the Anunnaki.

A few other authors other than Sitchin have correctly seen the influence of the ancient gods using the human race as their slaves - William Bramley's *Gods of Eden,* published in 1993, and Michael Tellinger's *Slave Species of the Gods*, published in 2012 to name just two. Of these two works, I find Tellinger had a more correct interpretation about the nature of the Anunnaki gods, but he still relied too much on Sitchin's interpretations to reach his own expanded conclusions. I feel Bramley reached too far in his conclusions overall, attributing too many human events as alien interventions, and I find substantially less value in his presentation.

The realm of studying ancient aliens and their interaction with humans on this planet is as speculative as anything else in the first cognition. From a scientific point of view, they claim there is no 'hard evidence' that proves the theory (meaning we haven't found any real remnants of their technology). We have the mainstream academic naysayers calling it all twaddle and those professing the ideas of alien intervention playing guessing games at what might actually have happened, without wanting to upset the viewing public with too much information. The thing that bugs me the most is how they often bolster the Bible as their indisputable source, which keeps the religious believers happy. It is this validating such sources that shows they are catering to first cognition religious sensibilities more than they are trying to get at the real hard truth. They are working to keep everyone happy in their games of speculation and not upset any religious apple carts. The constant vacillating and equivocating by the regular hosts of *Ancient Aliens* in order to not upset anyone is just one more example of first cognition concern about hurting some ego's feelings or exposing their beliefs to be an utter falsehood. Certain researchers have accurately noticed this constant sourcing of the Bible as a ploy by the hosts of *Ancient Aliens* to keep the Bible intact as a real source of valid information and history. If the reader wants a real eye-opening lesson, watch the Youtube video called *Ancient Aliens Debunked.*

In all honesty, I will be referring to certain passages from the Bible as well, but not to be supporting it as a pre-existing religious document or valid history of the Hebrew people. This body of work is going to illustrate to the reader that the whole book is a fabricated history of relatively recent design, and the proof of this contention will be made based on the evidence at hand, or more accurately, the lack of evidence to supports its alleged antiquity. Many researchers into comparative religion have already seen that the Bible is a concatenation of stories from more ancient sources in the region, Mesopotamian and Egyptian sources in particular.

The race that created the human species on this planet was based in the Orion constellation on a planet orbiting the star Betelgeuse. There are people who are in the know about the truth of this on this planet. We get our noses rubbed in it with films like *Betelgeuse* where the main character is an evil trickster. We have all sorts of more subtle aspects of Orion put in our faces with Orion Pictures, and even early symbols of NASA with the Orion Constellation on mission patches. Granted, Orion is the largest constellation in the night sky, but at some point we just plain have to admit that there is more than simple coincidence at work here with all this Orion symbolism appearing in as many places as it does. I ask the reader to pay attention to the movies they watch and observe just how often Orion works its way into the films, whether its films like *The Orion Project,* or the reference to the 'Galaxy on Orion's belt' in *Men in Black.*

The evidence for the presence of these beings from Orion is to be found in references to Orion in ancient religious and mythical texts of a number of different peoples. Because these stories have been deemed *mythical,* the actual truth has been overlooked or simply ignored as mythical stories. The Great God of Sumerian legend was known as An or Anu, from which we get the word Anunnaki. In the more ancient texts, all of the gods were submissive to the power of Anu. In many traditions, Anu is associated with creating the universe itself, but that claim is simply a boast. Anu was, however, responsible for creating the circumstances in our local area of space, as will be revealed as we continue.

Anu was most often praised with the epithet as the "father of the gods", which gives him supremacy of title over the subsequent usurpers - others his race genetically manufactured, like the Anunnaki. An Orion connection that it seems all researchers have overlooked is that Anu, as the lord over the 'highest' of the three heavens, is that his 'heaven' was said to be made of the reddish *luludānitu* stone. Curiously enough, the star Betelgeuse is a red supergiant and one of the brightest stars in the heavens. Is this simple coincidence, or are we overlooking an important piece of evidence?

This race of beings, who I will simply call the Orioners, were masters not only at genetic manipulation, but were masters at energy manipulation as well. For the most part, the Orioner interface on this planet has been effectively erased except within small circles of knowledgeable people who don't want the public to discover the truth. Call it a conspiracy of silence or whatever makes you comfortable, but the fact is that there are organizations on this planet with people who know this information and are deliberately keeping it from the public at large. The major reason is that if the truth were known on a wide scale, religions would go obsolete in days and our total perception of human history would be shattered. All the mythology about the all powerful invisible creator God would be exposed for the sham that it is, and no one wants to challenge the lucrative businesses of religious mind control - and they especially don't want to confront the Vatican, nor close to 7 billion believers in one form of religion or another all around the planet. This book is going to do exactly that.

Modern man makes the broad, and I think mistaken assumption, that people in the past were somehow lesser intelligent than we are today, that they were somehow more ignorant, and definitely more *superstitious* in their beliefs. I find this form of thinking amusing at best and downright dangerous at worst. Dangerous, because this attitude precludes people from seeing the hidden truths contained in ancient myths, and amusing because we somehow feel that we, ourselves, are superior to ancient peoples simply because of our use of technology and our literacy. I find it quite amusing in fact that, according to our academic scholars, some ancient peoples managed to erect the pyramids in Egypt with alignments to the four cardinal points of the Earth and also positioned to mirror the Orion constellation, that are so exact that we, with our technological skill today, cannot remotely duplicate the feat. Similar structures can also be found in South and Central America. For a bunch of backwards, superstitious peoples, I'd say that's quite a feat!

In the schools of philosophy, Aristotle and Plato still rule the roost. There's not one of the Enlightenment philosophers, that wasn't affected by their writings, and their teachings affect us to this very day. Not bad for a bunch of backwards, dumber-than-modern-man folks, no? In government we have been handed down a combination of democracy designed by the Greek Solon, mixed in with the Roman Republic (starting about

509 BCE), and the vestiges of Pharoanic rule exhibited by the last remnants of some European royal families.

In light of these observations, we are somehow expected to believe that our ancestors were not smart enough to know the difference between up and down, and were therefore too ignorant to know when entities appeared in the skies and landed here proclaiming their godhead over all humanity. We are expected to accept the idea that all the ancient iconography and statuary remnants portraying these gods in their true forms are simply mythological renderings of some kind of religious mass psychosis. We are also expected to believe that the *mythological* tales about these gods, which were just as powerful religious beliefs of ancient cultures as our belief in modern religions is in our time, were all to be utterly ignored because certain modern religious authorities mandated these stories be relegated to the dustbin of mythology.

The Greek, Egyptian, Phrygian, Jewish, Hittite, Assyrian, Babylonian, Hindu and Sumerians gods were all taken as seriously by those peoples in those lands in those times as any modern religionist takes their beliefs just as seriously today. Hinduism is still rife with a huge pantheon of multiple gods. Modern religions, if one were to study them closely and objectively, plainly show that it has been a continual process of cherry picking from more ancient religious 'myths' to come up with modern-day Islam, Christianity, and Judaism—the three major religions of the West. Eastern religions will show similar patterns of deliberate tampering as this story unfolds. Christianity and Islam purportedly arose as offshoots of Judaism, but Judaism itself, upon close objective scrutiny, is not as ancient as we have all been led to believe, which will be explained in later chapters. Jewish mysticism, as its called, is a collection of Zoroastrianism and Babylonian/Sumerian astrology and a number of other previous, more ancient magical belief systems. Judaism itself is a collection of Sumerian and Egyptian religious doctrines, which its defenders vehemently deny when such claims are made. It needs to be emphasized again that if these ancient peoples were as backwards and uninformed as present day man believes them to be, then why is it that we cling so tenaciously to their viewpoints, teachings and beliefs - except where their religious practices and beliefs are concerned? Even more, why is it that we can accept their principles of governmental, philosophical, scientific and mathematical achievements as being the foundations we adhere to, yet we so handily cast aside the *myths* of their gods and goddesses mucking about in the affairs of man, walking among men, and even breeding with man? That is the question that should concern us most. If they were intelligent enough to produce such scholars, then how are we expected to cast out their tales about their gods and the wars initiated by those gods? Are we really expected to believe that this was all just literary folderol, nothing but a joke on future generations?

Why is it that these ancient people had so much on the ball in government, the arts, and the sciences, which we so readily accept and embrace as part of our reality, but we cast aside the tales of their gods and magic as mere superstitious fancy? How could these people be so right in so many areas that affect our daily lives, yet be considered the crazy cousin in the attic that you don't speak about when they talk about their numerous gods?

So, why start with God, or *the gods,* you ask? It is for the very reason that they shrouded themselves in the myths they did that these gods bear closer scrutiny. There are a number of books available in the market today that propose similar "theories" about the gods and their origins. *The Earth Chronicles* series of books by Zechariah Sitchin discussed in detail the Sumerian tales of the gods known as the Anunnaki. *The Sirius Mystery* by Robert K.G. Temple discusses the gods known to the Dogon tribe of Africa as the Nommo, who I will reveal to be one in the same as the Sumerian Anunnaki, and who had their origin in the Sirius star system. Another look towards Sirius as a point of intervention of the ancient gods is found in *The Sirius Connection* by Murray Hope. Graham Hancock and Robert Bauval have presented a number of speculative works, both individually and collectively, in reference to the Egyptian pyramids and their association with the constellation Orion, the premier work on this subject being *The Message of the Sphinx.* Hancock's *Fingerprints of the Gods* is also a must read in this area. *The Orion Mystery* by Robert Bauval (with Adrian Gilbert) further brings in the apparent Orion connection to the ancient gods' presence in Egypt.

What I intend to present in this work is that all of these authors and researchers are correct, *in part.* Each of their viewpoints are valid in many respects, *as far as they go.* I intend to take you further and draw a more complete picture of the gods and what humankind on earth actually is and why we have merited so damned much attention by all these so-called offworld gods. So, let's upset an apple cart or two right here at the beginning.

Every religion on the face of the planet teaches its followers that we are all *less* than God. This God we are "less than" is usually a male God who has his hand on the wheel of our very destiny, the grand architect of all that ever was and all that is to come. In western religion He is a God of love but He is also a terrifying jealous God of vengeance and judgment. All the religions acknowledge that this God gave us free will, but He Himself is thwarting this gift of free will, or free choice, by mandating to us what we can and cannot do by issuing his religious mandates - His "*Thou Shalt Not's*". He tells us that this is a sin or that is a sin, and if you dare to break His rules, (which change very often depending who is running the churches at any given time), then He will cast you into an eternal hell of flames and sulfur with the hateful Satan poking you in the ass with his pitchfork for eternity. When you question the head of a church about this apparent neurotic dichotomy that exists in their God, be He Allah, Yahweh, Brahma or the Nameless One, they all skate around the issue. To them it is a completely acceptable dichotomy. Many skeptics over the ages have delved into why this dichotomy exists, but none of them have come up with the *reason* it exists. The pat explanation is, "The Lord works in mysterious ways," or "It is the will Allah," or "It is the will of the gods," in the case of Hinduism and other ancient religions of the world.

Buddhism probably comes closest to acknowledging the personal power that resides in all of us, but through the centuries and millennia since the Buddha found his enlightenment, men with agendas have corrupted his teachings as much as the organized Christian church has selectively reshaped the teachings of Jesus. The previous volumes in this series should have made these misinterpretations patently obvious.

Churches and religions are not about truth. They are about subservience to ideas that bind and tie one to a limited cognitive perspective. Religions are about re-legioning people into a certain belief structure so they can be more readily controlled. Religion is about creating dependency through fear. On closer inspection, one can readily see a direct correlation of this attitude that is found in churches also exists in most governments. Someone is always telling you what *they* think is best for you. In my estimation, the greatest crime of mankind is that we all too readily fall into the trap of allowing some authority figure or another to dictate to us what is best for us; how we should feel, how we should think, what we should do, when we should do it, how much we should do it, and even if we should do a thing at all. It is truly frightening to realize that societies as a whole on this planet have this same failing, but that is the nature of the first cognition. In the first cognition everyone looks to someone else to be their answer-man rather than finding their answers for themselves. Even our presumed authorities are slaves to their own egos.

If you want to get back to where this whole thought paradigm started you have to go back to the ancient gods. It was they who felt *they* knew best for us what we could and could not do, when to pray, when to make offerings, how the offerings were to be presented, what rituals to use to *serve the gods,* when to plow and toil and sacrifice, how to worship and when to make war. It is to these so-called gods that we must look to understand the mindset of mankind to this very moment in our development. It is from these self-proclaimed gods that the whole concept of a higher authority originated and which plagues our consciousness to this day, and rest assured, a plague it is.

There *were* many so-called gods, evidence of which has been left to us in myths and ancient writings, temple remnants and ancient unearthed statuary. The funny thing is, they weren't gods at all. At least not in the respect as we currently perceive God. They set themselves up as gods because we are, in part, their creations. Contrary to modern Judeo-Christian religious doctrine, the creation was not just an overnight, or seven day production. Creation is an ongoing process. You have to realize that just as our civilization plods ever forward, creating new technology—through evolution—so too does the creation of life plod ever forward. This was discussed in volume three of this series, *Demystifying the Mystical.* If one wants to argue this I will point out the cloning of plants and animals taking place right now on this planet. We are already cloning sheep. If humans can do this, then why is it so hard to accept that ancient alien intelligent species did the same thing using more advanced technological means when it came to creating Earth humans? We are simply walking in the footsteps of our godly predecessors.

The so-called creator gods managed to take pre-existing raw materials - i.e. human genetics from other star systems - manipulated buy their own genetists to ultimately produce what we are today. Disbelieve if you will, (and many of you will choose to because it's just too fantastic an idea, or it cheapens your concept of God, or yourself), but substantial evidence is present if one takes off the blinders intentionally placed on us by these so-called gods, and we take a closer look at the evidence they left behind.

The fact of the matter is that we have been continuously lied to for millennia. The truth has been well hidden in myth and so-called fantasy because the creator gods and their earthly representatives don't want us to figure out what a crass game they have played with their human creations - and what a dastardly game it's been, let me tell you. I hope to make you mad as hell over the deception. I truly do. Maybe then we, as a species, can pull our collective heads out of our asses and step into what we can truly become and not be restricted to a limited existence of limited cognitive awareness placed on us by those who feared what we might become.

Tales have been handed down for generations about how *fickle* the gods were. Have you ever wondered, I mean *really* wondered, why the ancient peoples went to so much trouble to document the affairs of their fickle deities? Why catalog who was the son of Zeus, which god or goddess slept with which human, what their union produced in the form of offspring as represented in the tales of Hercules and others? For the sake of superstitious malarkey, or myth as it is handily labeled today,

41

don't you think it's just a bit too much of an extreme to go to for the sake of formulating a religion? The ancient Sumerians, to whom the creation of writing is attributed, had over three thousand gods in their religious records. Again, doesn't that seem a bit extreme in formulating a religion—unless of course they weren't forming a religion at all, but were in fact relating tales and events of beings who literally came and went from the heavens at will and called themselves gods? Remember, these ancients are the same people that allegedly invented writing, produced Plato, Socrates, Cato, Solon, art, drama and theater and so many more concepts and ideas that affect our lives to this day. Are we then truly expected to chalk up the tales of their gods as nothing more that mass superstitious hysteria? That's what's occurred at the hands of our religious and academic institutions, but I'll tell you what, it makes immensely more sense to accept the fact that the so-called gods actually walked among men, regardless of how that disrupts our species self-image and presumptions about the grand almighty invisible god that created everything in the universe.

In the Bible they are referred to as Nephilim who bred with the daughters of men. Other ancient peoples around the world, people who we presume to never have been in contact with each other, had similar legends and tales about their gods breeding with their human stock to create demigods - i.e. human alien genetic hybrids. Does this therefore establish a global collective consciousness delusion, that somehow all those unrelated peoples around the planet had this brilliant idea about multiple gods walking and talking and eating and having sex with humans, or does it more likely indicate that there were actually beings who called themselves gods and created the fear/dependency syndrome that's called religion? I suggest it's the latter.

So, let's establish a given right now. There *were* real honest to goodness beings who have come to be referred to as the gods in every ancient tradition on the planet, no matter how isolated these people have been. They intruded themselves here, they came from other star systems and planets (the heavens), developed us genetically (created us), repressed our development in many cases, tried to elevate us in other cases, and they have generally mucked about in playground Earth for longer than our history records. I ask the reader to suspend their current beliefs for long enough to let me appeal to your logic. Can you find any other explanation about this global god psychosis that makes more logical sense without relying on the supernatural solution?

I guess we could accept the explanation of the anthropologist Darwinians. Let me see if I can put this in the correct context. According to Darwinist theory, somewhere along the line of its evolutionary track, the hominid brain increased three times in size (for which science can offer no valid explanation other than it just evolved that way). With this expansion of the neocortex, we developed a sense of self-consciousness. Now this is all fine and good, except that with this expanded awareness and self-consciousness, after living for untold generations in the world of nature, knowing about rain and thunderstorms and the natural cycles of the world in which our ancestors lived, they suddenly shifted gears and started fearing nature, so our ancestors tossed everything they knew about the natural world into the trash and started reaching for explanations about why nature was nature. So, as the theory goes, we allegedly concocted the idea about gods who controlled the weather, or the fruitfulness of the plants, etc. It doesn't matter that our species had lived with nature throughout the ages since our proposed coming down from the trees, our intelligence suddenly gave us the means to become neurotic by creating gods and religion.

But then, this theory gets really interesting because this advanced hominid psychosis about the gods advances from the ideas of nature spirits and evolves into a belief in multiple gods who not only lived in the sky, but who actually *came down* from the sky. From a standpoint of even primitive logic, if some shaman told me that the gods were running around and having sex with my neighbors, I think even the primitive brain would have to call bullshit on such a proposition - unless of course, there was some reality behind that claim that could be observed and proven.

At some point, such theoretical surmises run up against a reality that even our ancestors could and would have challenged if there was a basis to disprove such claims. The gods were here, they were physical and they were real. This fact is the singular fact that modern scholars refuse to accept. They would rather concoct some ridiculous theory that humanity developed this god psychosis because our brain capacity increased and we had nothing better to do than tell mystical stories around the cave at night to scare our children with all this god crap.

The reason we have such a neurotic concept about the gods is because the gods were themselves neurotic and fickle. Of course the gods were *fickle*, they're just folks, just like us - at least from the standpoint of first cognition consciousness. They had the same ego foibles, faults and mannerisms as we do in many respects. Why should that be so amazing to conceive? We are a product of their genetics! They *made* us, for heaven's sake, or for their own sake. We have genetic material from Orion, from Sirius, from the Pleiades, from the 12th planet in our solar system, Nibiru, from Lyra, Vega, Arcturus, Andromeda and who knows where else? Earth has not only been a playground and breeding ground for these so-called gods, it has been one of the most contested pieces of real estate in the cosmos.

We, as a species, have the potential to exceed so many of their design specs that they feared the living daylights out of us. They have no concept of what they truly created, but they see its potential grandeur and they are scared to death of just how we will react when the truth is finally known. Unlike the religionists teach us, those ideals that have been passed down to and through the god-created priesthoods from time immemorial, the human beings of good old planet Earth are *not* lesser beings. We are a composite creation made from the combined genetics of all the "gods" that tinkered around here with our genetics. In our genes we contain both the best and the worst of all the races of the so-called gods. In that light, we are not the rust bucket '47 Ford in the universal scheme of things, as we have been intentionally led to believe, we are the Mercedes, or at least we can be if we can pull our heads out of our collective asses and willfully choose advance our species consciousness. We have the potential to surpass these so-called gods and be more than they ever dreamed, even for themselves.

Due to this, and their recognition of this fact early on in our development, we have been intentionally kept in the dark as to our origins, as to the true nature of the gods, as to the real workings of the cosmos, and our place in an ever-expanding *evolving* creation. We *are* the next step in the conscious evolution of the universe, if we can move away from first cognition brainwashing and godly control to become fully functional human beings. We have the combined genetics of all the gods who came before us within the very fiber of our beings. It's in our DNA. The only questions left are if we are going to recognize what we truly are, and what are we going to do about it?

3. <u>The Orion Factor - Solving the Creation Story</u>

Throughout the process of researching history in order to get to the bottom of the millennias-old conspiracy to take over and control the world, I repeatedly ran across many references to the constellation Orion. These references are most particularly found in ancient religions and mythologies. Believe it or not, there are direct references to Orion in the Bible, one short reference found at Job 38:31 (which will be discussed in the next volume), and further references under different topical matters. In this chapter I will try and paint a picture of what is a likely scenario of events that tie directly from the ancient, mostly unrecorded past, to the present world situation, and reveal who has been behind it.

When starting this research into Orion from the biblical standpoint I was amazed to find the definition in *A Dictionary of the Bible* by John B. Davis, published by the Westminster Press,

Philadelphia, 1942 that the word Orion is equated with giants. I was unaware, until twenty years ago when I started this research, of the correlation between Orion and the biblical references to giants. If you look up giants in *Unger's Bible Dictionary*, you find the correlation with the mythical Nephilim who were purportedly the unnatural offspring of sexual unions between the Orion gods and earth women. Just this single revelation, if we take it for the truth it offers, shows direct genetic compatibility between the races of the Orion gods and earth humans. This definition alone not only discusses the nature of crossbreeding between the "sons of God," but also denotes them by their stature, to wit: as giants.

Comparative religion and comparative mythology show a definitive link to the pantheons of ancient gods between many older cultures such as the Sumerians, Egyptians, Greeks, Hindus, Babylonians and others. Although these "gods" may go by different names between the ancient cultures, their individual characteristics are often the same for the major gods as they cross cultural lines, and the stories associated with these diverse gods are very similar. Many scholars attribute these commonalities to cultural cross-contamination, but I think there is a more cogent explanation. Each of these gods has been obscured by myth and legend and it is only natural that word of mouth stories from elder to elder would be corrupted in the telling over the ages, so the acts and deeds of the gods would become more mystical as well as fictional. Aside from the oral traditions being corrupted somewhat, I assert that many tales of the ancient gods were intentionally falsified by certain of the gods themselves so as to glorify them in the eyes of their enslaved peoples, as well as to intentionally obscure their agenda. In other words, these gods used a lot of propaganda to sow the image of themselves to Earth humans as more powerful than they actually were. More on this aspect will be presented as this story unfolds.

The gods from Orion were the primary race of beings that took over this planet in our ancient past. They had control over this planet for hundreds of thousands of years before an Earth human was ever manufactured. The Orioners were a spacefaring race who interfaced with a lot of other races in this universe. The Orioner gods were probably one of the worst examples of ego-driven control freaks we have ever seen. They thrived on warfare and conflict, but they were not warriors. Instead, they were the type of beings that liked to stir up opposition between other parties and sit back and watch the destruction. The point at which both parties had fatigued themselves through the Orioner-instigated wars, they would come in to fill the power vacuum as a result of the wars they instigated. This is how they eventually became controllers and tyrants of our known part of the universe.

The Orioner race of humans paid homage to no higher principle, no higher authority, than their own egos. They did not have an ounce of spirituality or conscience in their breed. They were arrogant controllers who set themselves up as gods over all those they managed to conquer. Their mindset was no different than a spoiled child that will break one of its own toys to prevent another child from playing with it. Their mentality was that corrupted. They were bloodthirsty, avaricious, manipulative, control freak tyrants. Not a single one of their breed had any redeemable qualities. The foundation of this assertion is found in many ancient texts where it plainly states that Orion was the 'father of the gods'. Let's not blow it off as simple myth, but instead accept it for the truth it reveals to us.

In time, this egotistical self-centered race of beings could pretty much do what they wanted to in this end of our universe because they were very technologically advanced and were also master manipulators of universal energies. I am not going into all the deeds they were responsible for over the last million years of their history, but I am narrowing the scope of this presentation to a very short overview of the last half-million years and how it directly applies to this planet and the creation of this species. What follows will be challenged by our scientific physicists, claiming that what I relate is impossible due to its violation of principles of physics. The reader is left to decide who to believe, ancient texts that repeatedly tell this story in many forms, or our modern scientists who think they already have all knowledge figured out.

Today, we know Sirius as the Dog Star, but in many ancient traditions the Sirius constellation was also represented as a serpent. If we view the Sirius star system as the symbol of the serpent, then we can start to unravel one of the major cataclysmic events in our local universe that gives us the foundation of this planet's most recent history. If we look to the ancient Babylonian creation epic, the *Enuma Elish*, when viewed through eyes that go beyond first cognition limitations, we can see how the Earth came to be in this solar system. Contrary to accepted first cognition reckoning, this planet did not always reside in orbit around our present sun. It started out in the Sirius star system orbiting Sirius B, a now collapsed white dwarf star.

The *Enuma Elish* tells us the tale about a war between the ancient Orion gods and the inhabitants of this planet, which the *Enuma Elish* refers to as Tiamat. Although the story recorded in the *Enuma Elish* is retold and propagandized by later gods, the context can be understood when one can access intuitive information beyond what the facial telling the story represents.

Being spacefaring conquerors, the Orioners initially sought uninhabited planets to use as bases to expand their empirical greed. They discovered a seemingly deserted watery world orbiting Sirius B and started building their outpost there. In time, they inhabited large tracts of land and built cities there. The famed Atlantis was built on this watery planet that came to be referred to as Apsu in ancient Sumerian - what is known in common vernacular today as the planet Nibiru. I found it rather exciting to discover, after many years of knowing this, to find that the TV series *Stargate: Atlantis* portrayed the city of Atlantis being located on a watery world other than our planet. Although the story line placed it in a different galaxy altogether, I was elated, to say the least, to see that someone else had reasoned out that the city of Atlantis was never on this planet.

I told you how the Orioners were an avaricious race. After they had established their foothold on the planet Apsu, they decided to expand their territory and claim other planets in the Sirius system, whether inhabited or not. During the period of time they were building their own structures on the Apsu, they discovered an intelligent breed of fish that had telepathic abilities. It was this breed of fish that they combined their own genetics with to create the hybrid race we know as the Anunnaki. This decision to combine genetic stock was a mutual agreement, not one done strictly at the behest of the Orioners. I am well aware that the concept of not only an intelligent fish, but a breed that also had telepathic abilities is very hard to swallow. I remind the reader that the reality of the universe at large is not based solely on our current level of accepted reality. We are only being very human-centric in our thinking if we discount such possibilities. As with all the material in this series, the reader is asked to not only think outside the box, but to utterly destroy the perceptual box of your perceived version of reality. Whether you can accept this or not does not alter the truth of the matter.

Ancient illustrations and idols abound of these hybrid fish-human entities. Modern interpreters claim that they are priests wearing fish skins as a decoration of their offices. I assert that these ancient illustrations are representations of this genetic hybridization of Orioner human genetics and this Nibiruan breed of intelligent fish. Too many images of these beings exist throughout the whole Eastern Mediterranean and Iraq for it to be simply priests wearing fish skins. If the scholarly assessment about the illustrations representing priests wearing fish skins is correct, why would they even choose to do such a thing? To me, it defies logic, especially if you consider how many of these priests were walking around wearing human-sized fish skins that we are expected to believe were so readily available in the rivers of Fertile Crescent of ancient times. I guess they could have come from the ocean, but even then, the idea of wearing holy fish skins defies logic.

Out of this created hybrid race the Orioners, in time, had an army to do their fighting for them and they decided it was time to expand their jurisdiction to claim the other inhabited worlds around Sirius B. Eventually, this led to a major interplanetary war, the results of which are left in the garbled tales of the ancient gods on this planet as our creation tales. One of the inhabited worlds was called Tiamat. Many of you may have read the ancient stories about the serpent Tiamat and the war waged by the elder gods against what we presume to be a mythical beast. All of our scholars count these stories, which appears in many variants throughout world religions, as metaphorical happenings between imaginary primordial gods which are naturally deemed to be mythological.

The Orioners set their greedy eyes on taking possession of the planet Tiamat and the war started. The inhabitants of Tiamat fought the Orioners to a standstill. Being the psychopathic race that they were, when the Orioners figured out that they were not going to win this planet, they decided to try and destroy it to prevent anyone else from having possession of it, including the natural inhabitants living on the planet at that time. Contrary to popular science fiction mythology found in films like *Star Wars* and a multitude of others, space warfare is highly impractical. Most of the ancient wars fought by the spacefaring races were ground wars, and the spaceships were nothing more than transports used to get their armies to the contested territories. The results of this war between the Orioners possessing the planet Apsu and fighting to claim Tiamat are left to us in ancient writings, although the story has never before been interpreted correctly.

Zechariah Sitchin tried to interpret this tale in the first volume of his Earth Chronicles series of books, *The Twelfth Planet,* but his interpretations fall far short of the mark and his interpretation collapses due to his narrow reckoning. The *Enuma Elish* relates that two primordial 'gods', Tiamat and Apsu, had their waters 'mingled'. The reference to these two 'primordial' gods represent two planets, not human-like gods. The fact that their waters were mingled in the story represents that they were two planets orbiting the same sun, to wit, Sirius B. The story tells of a great "to-ing and fro-ing" with the great serpent Tiamat, signifying this war with the Orioner faction. Ultimately, one of the gods fired an 'evil wind' into the belly of Tiamat tearing her asunder. This evil wind is allegorically representative of some kind of weapon fired into the sun Sirius B to cause it to artificially go supernova. Sirius is the fifth closest star to Earth, being 8.6 light years in distance from our planet. Sirius is a binary star system comprised of Sirius A and a now white dwarf star, Sirius B.

As the story goes, in its allegorical telling, the head of Tiamat was placed in parts unknown, and out of Absu they made a watchman over the heavens, or the 'hammered bracelet'. Sitchin interpreted the term 'hammered bracelet' to mean the asteroid belt in this solar system. With that one assumption, his whole interpretive theory falls apart. In the most simple of terms, Earth (Tiamat) was placed in orbit around this sun, and the other larger, watery world, Apsu, was left to orbit between our sun and Sirius B. The 'hammered bracelet' is an allusion to the orbit of Nibiru between here and Sirius B.

Many readers are familiar with the symbol of the Ouroboros worm, or the serpent that ever swallows its tail. This symbol represents the orbit of the Apsu, also known and the planet Nibiru in ancient Sumerian textual references. The serpent swallowing its tail is simply an allegorical symbol representing the orbit of Nibiru always returning to the 'serpent' star Sirius B in its long orbital cycle. In at least one of his books, Sitchin relates that Nibiru orbits to a 'station' in the heavens. Unfortunately, he never picked up on the meaning of this key clue to figure out that the 'station' that Nibiru orbited to was in fact another sun - to wit, Sirius B. For a more concise explanation of this story I suggest the reader take the time to look up the *Enuma Elish* on the internet and read the lengthy story for themselves with this new perspective.

For the sake of a different reference, I offer a brief interpretation of the Babylonian creation epic as analyzed by the early 20th century scholar, Donald A, Mackenzie from his work *Myths of Babylon and Assyria:*

> "The Babylonian Creation Myth, for instance, can be shown to be a localized and glorified legend in which the hero and his tribe are displaced by the war god and his fellow deities whose welfare depends on his prowess. Merodach kills the dragon, Tiamat, as the heroes of Eur-Asian folk

stories kill grisly hags, by casting his weapon down her throat.

He severed her inward parts, he pierced her heart,
He overcame her and cut off her life;
He cast down her body and stood upon it . . .
And with merciless club he smashed her skull.
He cut through the channels of her blood,
And he made the north wind to bear it away into secret places.
Afterwards He divided the flesh of the Ku-pu and devised a cunning plan.

Mr. L. W. King, from whose scholarly Seven Tablets of Creation these lines are quoted, notes that "Ku-pu" is a word of uncertain meaning. Jensen suggests "trunk, body". Apparently Merodach obtained special knowledge after dividing, and perhaps eating, the "Ku-pu". His "cunning plan" is set forth in detail: he cut up the dragon's body:

He split her up like a flat fish into two halves.
He formed the heavens with one half and the earth with the other, and then set the universe in order. His power and wisdom as the Demiurge

56

were derived from the fierce and powerful Great Mother, Tiamat."

Mr. Mackenzie's interpretations of the myth are still found as the predicate belief system with modern academics. They view this whole story as simple myth, and completely overlook what the story is telling. Although the hero of the Babylonian tale is the god Marduk (Merodach), the core elements of the story survive. If we view this brief translation in the context which I provide, we find the full story of the destruction of a sun and the moving of two planets. When the story claims to have severed the inward parts of Tiamat, it is an allusion to the causing Sirius B to go artificially supernova, for every planet revolves around a sun, which is also its heart. As the story relates, Marduk made the north wind bear the head of Tiamat 'into secret places'. As the second stanza relates, with one half he formed the heavens (i.e. Absu) and the earth with the other.

We find a similar creation tale in the Hindu mythology where Brahma was conceived when Vishnu laid on the water, and Brahma lay in a golden egg for 1000 years. When Brahma came out of the egg, he split the egg in two and heaven was made from one half of the shell and earth was made from the other half. There will be more such references from other regions and other religions as this story unfolds.

As I said, our physicists will totally refute what I just related because it goes against the laws of physics as they currently understand them. The story doesn't jive with what their physics tells them is possible and what is not, so I will simply be labeled a quack by putting forth these ideas. Although I feel Zechariah Sitchin's interpretations were insufficient in solving this particular mystery, he at least took a shot at it, which is more than I can say for our mainstream academics. Where Sitchin failed was by focusing his interpretations about the creation story of Apsu and Tiamat occurring strictly within the limits this solar system, in other words, he did not expand his imagination enough to encompass a more meaningful interpretation. As such, he failed to see the larger picture. His interpretive conjecture dealt specifically with a collision of planets in this solar system that resulted in the creation of the asteroid belt, not the artificial destruction of a sun. This is not to say that some kind of collision between planets did not occur as a result of this planetary perfidy, I only state that his interpretation of the myth was incorrect. This mythology will be discussed in more depth later.

To further expand on my contentions that this planet once orbited Sirius B and that it was artificially induced to go supernova, we need to examine whether there is any evidence on this planet that might scientifically support this. I think we need look no further than what is known as the 'iridium anomaly', which is a layer of iridium deposit found everywhere on the planet. Since iridium is an extremely rare element found on Earth, there is no real reason for this band of iridium deposits to be on this planet unless there was some external event that brought that iridium here.

Science theorizes that the existence of this enigmatic layer of iridium that surrounds the planet provides the explanation for the extinction of the dinosaurs some 66 million years ago, and they theorize that this iridium came in when a large asteroid hit our planet, thereby releasing iridium into the planet's atmosphere. Overall, this is not a bad theory so long as you are only considering such a possibility as the only solution. I will put forth another theory based on the destruction of Sirius B scenario.

When Sirius B collapsed, the force of the explosion caused the supercontinent of Pangaea on this planet to split, thereby resulting in the eastern and western hemispheric continents today. Not only was the blast of the sun going supernova the cause of the breaking up of the supercontinent, the tremendous amount of radiation that this planet was bombarded with before the shock wave also saturated the atmosphere with iridium and other radioactive waves like gamma rays and xrays, thereby creating the iridium anomaly which is found in a layer of iridium present everywhere on the planet.

Initially, scientists and geologists may protest at such an idea, especially since I project this event occurred only 500,000 years ago. Scientists are firmly convinced that it was 66 million years ago that the iridium deposit occurred, but here is where scientists and geologists make their error. Every science on this planet operates from the incorrect assumption that this planet has always been in this solar system since its beginning. All of their theories of geology and evolution are predicated on the foundation of this assumed uninterrupted linearity and stability of this planet always residing in this orbit around our present sun. Any scientific theory developed on a false foundation will always, *always,* deliver false conclusions. This is where we find ourselves today with the vast majority of scientific theoretical conjecture. It is all predicated on a false presumption of an uninterrupted linearity of events that shaped this planet. With this primary assumption as the foundation of their theories, they also rely on the approach that these things all occurred gradually, over millions of years. It is through this assumption of evolutionary gradualism, that everything has always been the same as it is now where this planet's assumed unchanging stability is concerned, that they miss other possibilities. In light of that, I challenge all scientists with this question. If what I am relating is true, then where does that leave Darwinism and the linear progression of evolution of the species when every species on this planet was destroyed from a supernova event in another star system that destroyed *all* life on this planet a mere 500,000 years ago? Where does that leave the leave the science of geology and its theories of the gradual geological formation of this planet?

It may well have been an asteroid hit that destroyed the dinosaurs 66 million years ago, but if that is true, it didn't happen in this solar system. Further, the crater found in the Yucatan peninsula to which science attributes this event had to occur *after* the continents were separated as a result of the Sirius B event, which means that impact also had to have occurred in the last half million years and probably didn't have a thing to do with the extinction of the dinosaurs, despite how sound the theory may appear.

It is because science embraces the idea of gradual linearity in all its theoretical projections about this planet that we can't make heads or tails out of the iridium anomaly. Science can only theorize when and why the continents separated. Scientists can point to no specific event that divided the continents except the theory of continental drift. If continental drift were the only factor to be considered in the separation of the continents, then their timeline projections might pan out, but if we take a singular cataclysmic event that has not yet even been considered by modern science, to wit the artificial inducement of a star to go supernova, then all of their conjecture about the gradualism of continental drift goes down the same drain as Darwinist evolutionary theory.

Despite scientific conjecture that the iridium anomaly is a result of an asteroid impact, we have to look at the amount of iridium there is that layers this *entire* planet. Even a 30 mile wide asteroid could not deposit the amount of iridium found in the iridium layer even if it were made totally of iridium. That being the case, we have to look at some larger source to explain the amount of iridium that coats this planet, and the Sirius B event explains it all. It explains the separation of the continents, it explains the iridium anomaly, and it is the explanation found in all the creations myths, no matter how much they are garbled, found everywhere around the world. These myths will be presented over and over throughout this book.

Aside from just splitting the continents and saturating the atmosphere with high amounts of iridium, it put this planet into a geological age of turmoil that lasted for somewhere between 50-

100 thousand years after the event before things geologically stabilized. This being true, then every calculation made by geologists on the age of geological structures also comes into question. Where geologists forecast millions of years of gradual alteration of the Earth's surface after the iridium anomaly, their calculations based on linear gradualism all come into question. This planet went through a geological upheaval beyond what science has yet imagined after the Sirius B event. What they think took millions of years to take place geologically, actually occurred in roughly 100,000 years or less after that cataclysm.

With the iridium anomaly, science admits that pretty much all life had to be removed from this planet as a result of the high levels of radioactivity as well as what could be considered a nuclear winter scenario. If all life was destroyed as a result of this cataclysmic event, and the earth became barren as a result of this, the next logical conclusion is that all the life on this planet had to be seeded here by other agencies starting roughly 400,000 years ago, give or take a few millennia. This state of evolutionary interruption as a result of the Sirius B incident means that the concept of evolution from dinosaurs into mammals could not and did not happen, regardless of the discoveries we have made about fossilized dinosaurs. Any evolutionary cycle occurring on this planet before it was forcibly removed from the Sirius star system would have come to an abrupt and immediate end.

Many dinosaur fossils that have been unearthed and placed in museums were radioactive and had to be coated with a special lead paint in order for the fossilized skeletons to even be put on display. Academics wonder how these skeletons became radioactive. It may have been a result of the iridium soaking into the ground long after their demise, or it could be a result of other more penetrating forms of exotic radiation emitted in the minutes after Sirius B went supernova. I can offer no sound explanation for irradiated dinosaur fossils, but since our science has absolutely no experience with a supernova, we also have no information on the numerous types of radioactive waves that may result on a planet in proximity to such an event, even if only briefly, nor how deeply penetrating these radioactive rays might be.

The astrophysicists are going to challenge this event predicated on the knowledge they possess. But the fact is that all our physicists possess in the way of knowledge about the cosmos at large is based upon observations within our local solar system. They presume that, because this is how it works here in this solar system, that their rules of physics must apply everywhere. What they are not considering is that we are only seeing and making our calculations from a very limited 3D material perspective. They have yet to advance their science to consider the frequencies of other dimensions and other-dimensional impact on time and space. The universe is vast and it doesn't operate strictly from our limited understanding with purely 3D material science.

The other factor that science has yet to consider is the facts related in this story about the Orioners. They were already traveling between universes when they arrived in our universe a million years ago. This means that they had technology at their disposal that is over a million years older than anything we can remotely comprehend at the young age of our current science. If that race had the capability to artificially induce a star to go supernova, then why should we think they wouldn't have the capability to move this planet and Nibiru safely away from the full repercussion of the blast moments after the primary radiation wave hit the planets and before the full impact blast of the supernova gravity wave tore the planets apart? As the mythology tells us, "*he made the north wind to bear it away into secret places*". If they could jump universes with their space traveling capabilities, then relocating a planet should not seem too far outside their technological capabilities. We can only wonder what this allegorical '*north wind*' is that was used to move this planet to this solar system.

Of course this sounds fantastic beyond the wildest science fiction, but that is because we have not stretched our imagination to even ponder such an event taking place. I can tell the reader this, I am not so imaginative as to think this up on my own or I would be a screenwriter. All I have done is look at the evidence presented all throughout this book to reach the conclusions the ancient stories tell. All I am asking academics to do is compare notes on all the areas discussed in this book and the one that follows it and see if you can come up with a more rational explanation without binding yourselves to your limited strictures of acceptability or simply denying the possibility because it makes you psychologically uncomfortable, or challenges the limits of your scientific knowledge.

We are going to skip forward tens of thousands of years from the creation of the Anunnaki to how that breed of hybrids was used as slave labor for their Orioner creators to start building bases and mining on this planet once things settled down, geologically speaking. The Sumerian texts tell the tale of a revolt by the Anunnaki against their own creator gods after being used as slave labor for tens of thousands of years. The stories left to us by the Anunnaki have been intentionally tainted, and what we are left with is a corrupted version of the full story found in the *Epic of Atrahasis* text.

Although the Orioners were in fact their genetic creators, the name Orion has been intentionally removed from these later Sumerian textual references. The primary Orioner overseer on this planet was the god Enlil, although the difference in breed between the Orioners and the Anunnaki was left intentionally vague in the Mesopotamian written accounts for reasons that will be explained shortly. In the Sumerian tablets, Enlil was lord of the Earth, and Ea, or Enki, was lord of the watery Apsu. Enlil is often referred to as 'father Enlil', and although other Sumerian texts refer to these entities at brothers, there was no racial or blood lineage involved between them. The term brother was more a term of patronage used amongst all the gods than anything familial, not that much different than Catholics or Masons using the term brother or sister with each other in their own organizations. When Sitchin composed his work, he made the assumption that Enlil was an Anunnaki specifically because his Orioner association had been conveniently left out of the story. The Anunnaki, who were themselves created by the

Orioner geneticists, got tired of doing the slave labor for the Orioners and apparently there was some kind of revolt where the Anunnaki insisted that their Orioner masters manufacture another worker so they would no longer have to be the labor force of the Orioners' gold mining operations. Sitchin covers this in depth in his books and, based on the Sumerian tablets, I think his portrayal is generally accurate, except that it wasn't the Anunnaki who created the human species on this planet, it was the Orioners. The Anunnaki convinced the Orioners to make a new worker so they wouldn't be doing all the grunt mining labor for the Orioners, and that new replacement work force was the human race. This story is found in the Sumerian *Epic of Atrahasis* and can be easily found online by searching by that text title.

To refute the claims of subsequent Anunnaki gods that they were the creators of mankind, this appeal to a higher authority god in the person of Enlil, pretty much proves that the Anunnaki themselves were slave subjects to another more powerful race of beings - i.e. their own creator gods who were the Orioners, the Elder Gods. This is one of those clues that has to be read between the lines to see, and which Zechariah Sitchin completely overlooked with his primary focus on the Anunnaki gods themselves.

Modern researcher Michael Tellinger has brought forth the theory that millions of stone edifices found all over South Africa are in fact the remnants of habitations for ancient mining operations of the Anunnaki, accurately predicted by Zechariah Sitchin in *The Twelfth Planet,* and that they date back at least

200,000 years. Mainstream scholars are actively denying Tellinger's theory because it throws Darwinism out the window if he is correct. Academic denial will not alter the existence of these ancient structures, and simply refuting Tellinger without offering any type of explanation to the contrary only shows the disingenuousness of the academics. Google 'stone structures of South Africa' for still photos of a few of these structures.

These structures, which have for over a century simply been called *kralls* (South African for corrals) have no entryways at all. They are circular enclosures, often within other circular enclosures, and they are connected by what I think Tellinger accurately calls 'channels'. What Tellinger has failed to recognize is that these stone, high-walled enclosures were never inhabited nor built by Earth humans. They were filled with water to house a semi-aquatic race of beings, a human-fish hybrid race called the Anunnaki. I ask the reader to go to Youtube and watch some of the videos on these ancient sites in light of what I am presenting as this book unfolds, and reach your own conclusions. The channels, as Tellinger calls them, link many of these circular structures, which I will refer to as large Absu tanks, and were in fact the roadways between these structures for a water-borne species called the Anunnaki.

In the 1920's, once aviation came into being, remnants of similar stone structures were discovered in the Middle East. There are thousands of these structural remnants that are currently known to exist from Jordan to Saudi Arabia, and I will predict that we will find more throughout other regions of the Middle East further east. Do a Google search for *'ancient stone structures of Jordan - pictures*' to see the remnants of these stone structures. You will see that they are very similar to those found in South Africa. Just as with the South African structures, there are no doors or entryways into the structures that are still raised enough above ground to make such a determination. One has to climb over the low walls to get inside the structures that are still evident. Most of the structures are worn down and unnoticeable from the ground, unlike the structures in South Africa which are plainly evident. What is left more closely resembles the Nazca lines in Peru inasmuch that they can't really be perceived from ground level and can only really be defined from the air.

One can tell by the manner of construction that the remnants in the Middle East are eerily reminiscent of those from South Africa. The major difference in their condition most likely can be attributed to the wear and tear of sandstorms over tens of thousands of years which has eroded the Middle Eastern sites into obscurity. There is no way one can compare these structures and think that they are not related, nor possibly built by the same race of beings - which were not Earth human beings.

Earth human beings were designed and manufactured to be a slave race as well as a dual type of food supply for all the gods who preceded us. I hate to tell you folks, but that is the origin of Earth humans on this planet. We started out as slaves and we are still slaves to our creators' whims and the religions their usurpers created to this day, so long as we stay firmly rooted in the first cognition systems of beliefs the gods created for us.

When the Orioners created our race on this planet, they intentionally made us of a smaller stature than they were, feeling that their size gave them an edge for more easily intimidating and controlling our species. This variance in stature can be seen in ancient illustrations where the gods depicted on their thrones are about twice the height of their human subjects. This height difference, portrayed in many ancient pictures and carvings, is an actual portrayal. Scholars choose to define these illustrations as simply being a metaphorical illustration to signify the gods. I choose to interpret the images literally, simply because it makes the most sense when all the evidence is weighed together. Remember the passages about the race of giants and this explanation makes the most logical sense. Yes, it may seem fanciful, but as this book unfolds, you are going to see how these literal interpretations make more sense than scholarly refusal to see the truth or simply rely on metaphor to interpret these images.

The Orioners also hampered our genetics and turned off many of the internal DNA switches they possessed in their own genetics in order to prevent us from ever attaining the abilities they had. This is what our modern geneticists call junk DNA. The Anunnaki had revolted, and other genetic hybrids the Orioners had created elsewhere had also rebelled against them in other parts of this universe, so they did their utmost to handicap our race in many different forms to insure that as a species we would never have the power to buck their control. They not only wanted to use us as slaves, they wanted to insure that we would always *remain* slaves. Until this moment in our history, they have totally succeeded in that endeavor.

Once the Orioners came up with the Earth human compact-model replica of our genetic design, they placed specific programming in the sub-genetic level that was undetectable to other geneticists from other races who experimented on our species, but only worked on a physical genetic level, much like our modern geneticists. This sub-genetic programming meant that the Orioners would always have a direct connection to energetically feeding off humans. It also had a more sinister agenda that will probably be discussed in the next volume of this series. Once they set this programming in place, in time they invited many other races from out there to come and genetically play with these new human lab rats. As shocking as this may be, and as much as our ego sense of self rebels at such an idea, the human race on this planet has been little more than a Petri dish genetic experiment for older stellar races since our creation.

Through the course of time, there were more wars between the ancient gods on this planet that will be discussed in the next volume in this series, but for now I am only going to make note of what the Greeks referred to as the War of the Titans. In that war, the lesser gods, read that to mean the Anunnaki, overthrew the elder gods (the Orioners and others) and took over the planet for themselves. Since that war, it was the Anunnaki who have directly controlled the direction of mankind over about the last five to six thousand years. Although the Orioners were technologically advanced and knew about energy manipulation, the Anunnaki race were more adept at certain forms of energetic manipulation than their creators based on their hybrid genetics. This will be covered more in depth as we continue.

There are any number of researchers who are aware of the Orion connection in our ancient past, but most of them are coming up with false conclusions. There is too much presumption that the popular shape-shifting lizards are somehow affiliated with Orion, yet are also associated with Draco. I'm here to bust that myth about shape-shifting lizards having anything to do with the Orioners, or that such beings exist at all. Through all my years of research and probing out there, I have yet to encounter any kind of shape-shifting lizard of the type used to hype fear on this planet at this time as certain promoters of the subject persistently do. They don't exist. Although there is a race that closely fits that description, which will be explained in the latter chapters of this book.

I realize that what I cover in this chapter defies first cognition logic, but as I said in volume 4 of this series, I am making no apologies for the information provided herein. The reader can either take it or leave it. I told the readers in the previous volumes that they do not know how weird the universe at large gets, that no matter what we may think reality is from our limited perception, that it goes far beyond what we currently know and are often even willing to acknowledge. There is no information that I am providing that is untrue based on my own experiences and the evidence available to us, and the reader is invited to judge this information through instinctual intuitive reckoning more than simple first cognition thinking. I will, however, continue to present a trail of evidence that the reader is encouraged to investigate further that supports my contentions.

To put the final cap on this chapter, I mentioned previously about some of the Dogon teachings about Sirius. The Dogon tribe of Mali had knowledge about the Sirius star system from their ancient lore that was only discovered by science using telescopes in the 19th century - for instance, the existence of Sirius B, and possibly a Sirius C. The one point I want to offer in reference to the Dogon traditional teaching is where they state that, "*Where our sun is, Sirius was.*" This particular reference was reported by Robert K. G. Temple in his book *The Sirius Mystery.* Absent the explanation provided in this chapter about our planet originally orbiting Sirius B, what kind of sense does that statement by the Dogon make? Even from a mystical standpoint such a statement has no validity. The only logical explanation is the one offered in this chapter and alluded to in the *Enuma Elish* texts. I have never seen any other suggestion as to how to remotely interpret that particular statement by the Dogon tribal elders. From the standpoint of logic, my explanation makes perfect sense, despite its contradiction to our current understanding of the laws of physics.

4. The Anunnaki

There is no shortage of speculative information in the public arena about the Anunnaki. Much of this is misconstrued information, but there are other researchers besides this author who have figured out that the Anunnaki were a race of fish-human hybrids and have come to some cogent realizations on their own. Although pictures go a long way in relating this information, due to copyright constraints and paid permissions, this author is not going to provide the reader the with illustrations that could more easily paint the picture for understanding. Finding the relevant images are the responsibility of the reader and they are easy to find through internet searches using *'Oannes'*, *'fish-humans'* or other search variants on Google. As this book progresses, I will provide other areas of research through internet search links to Wikipedia and other look-ups. Although many academics choose to disparage Wikipedia, the references I provide for look up are referenced with scholarly works and are not simply unsupported conjecture. Despite its critics, Wikipedia is one of the best sources of public domain information for the serious researcher.

There are those sources of disinformation that would have us believe that the Anunnaki were human in form just like we are. Zechariah Sitchin, the primary revealer of the Anunnaki to the public at large through his own books, either failed to recognize the Anunnaki as the hybrid race they were, or intentionally overlooked what the evidence showed him. He left his readers to reach their own conclusions in that regard rather than explaining what the ancient Sumerian illustrations showed about them. It is through his own omissions that many people came away with the idea that the Anunnaki hybrids were simply another race of human-like beings from outer space. Our own human-centric perspective also would have us believe those assumptions because the actual truth scares the crap out of us. It is also this misconception that leads many of the sources of disinformation to lay claim to some distant Anunnaki heritage in their royal bloodlines.

I realize the idea that seemingly incompatible species could be genetically manipulated into a homogenous, viable life form is hard to accept, but let me take this a step further and see if I can promote more understanding. As humans, we judge every type of intelligence based on its usage of tools. This focus on tool usage is a direct result of our manipulation of materials to make and use tools, but this is a very techno-human-centric perspective. We know that dolphins have larger brains than humans and we have seen that they are very smart, yet we have no more idea of how their intelligence operates than they do ours. Dolphins are also mammals like human beings. We know they use a form of sonar to find their food sources and that they also hunt in packs, but we have no idea about how they communicate between themselves to co-ordinate their pack hunting or anything of that nature. Is it such a far stretch of the imagination to consider the possibility of psychic or telepathic communication in them about which we know absolutely nothing? If we can give credence to this idea, then the concept of an intelligent telepathic breed of fish born on another planet should not be that hard to digest. Yes, its stretches our sense of credibility, but human scholars do not know as much as they think they know.

I want to offer some information on these fish gods through numerous references found on the internet using 'Berossus' as the search word. I want to first reference part of the history of Berossus in regard to the origin of Babylonia. His description follows:

> *"But, in the first year appeared an animal endowed with human reason, named Oannes, who rose from out of the Erythrian Sea, at the point where it borders Babylonia. He had the whole body of a fish, but underneath and attached to the head of the fish there was another head, human, and joined to the tail of the fish, feet, like those of a man, and it had a human voice. Its form has been preserved in sculpture to this day."*

The Erythrian Sea is that area of the northwest Indian Ocean that borders southern Arabia. To see exact replicas of these beings carved in stone, do a google search for *'fish god images - Jeremy Green'*. The images you will find exactly correlate to Berossus' description of them. Berossus was a Babylonian priest to the god Bel-Marduk and wrote his works (which are lost) during the 3rd century BCE. As such, his story is retrieved from later references to his works. See 'Berossus' on Wikipedia for more information.

Having Berossus' description in hand, let's now take a look at what the Dogon tradition has to say about the Nommos. The following quotes can be found on Wikipedia using the search word 'Nommo':

"The Nommos are usually described as amphibious, hermaphroditic, fish-like creatures. Folk art depictions of the Nommos show creatures with humanoid upper torsos, legs/feet, and a fish-like lower torso and tail. The Nommos are also referred to as "Masters of the Water", "the Monitors", and "the Teachers".

"In the latter part of the 1940s, the French anthropologists Marcel Griaule and Germaine Dieterlen (who has been working with the Dogon since 1931) were the recipients of additional secret mythologies, concerning the Nommo. The

Dogon reportedly related to Griaule and Dieterlen a belief that the Nommos were inhabitants of a world circling the star Sirius. The Nommos descended from the sky in a vessel accompanied by fire and thunder. After arriving, the Nommos created a reservoir of water and subsequently dove into the water. The Dogon legends state that the Nommos required a watery environment in which to live. "

I first became aware of the tradition of the Dogon people in Robert K.G. Temple's book *The Sirius Mystery.* Since its publication there has been contention by other scholars that the Dogon held any such beliefs based on subsequent research that purportedly refutes what Griaule and Dieterlen related in their studies. Griaule and Dieterlen had spent close to ten years working with the Dogon in their anthropological studies, and the most logical explanations of why these particular stories were shared with them by the tribal elders and mostly denied to subsequent researchers is that they had earned enough trust to allow the sharing of these secrets, where the later researchers were not trusted enough to share that information.

I ask the reader to ponder on my interpretation of the *Enuma Elish* in light of the traditional Dogon teachings and realize they had no reason to concoct such a story about hybrid fish-human gods who originated from and whose planet orbited the star Sirius. Is this just another one of those odd coincidences that we will continue to encounter as this book progresses?

As this story unfolds, the reader is going to see how legitimate the Dogon teachings actually are, and how they are not fictional as later authorities like Walter Van Beek and Carl Sagan tried to refute. I want to share another aspect of the Dogon teachings that sort of echoes what I related about Sirius B and the displacement of our planet and Nibiru. Although I think their version is corrupted, it comes close to my solution to the *Enuma Elish*. This passage can also be found on Wikipedia under "Nommo":

> *"Dogon mythology says that **Nommo was the first living creature created by the sky god Amma.** Shortly after his creation, Nommo underwent a transformation and multiplied into four pairs of twins. **One of the twins rebelled against the universal order created by Amma. To restore order to his creation, Amma sacrificed another of the Nommo progeny, whose body was dismembered and scattered throughout the universe."**

[Bold emphasis mine]

What we are seeing here is two different stories combined into one. In the first highlighted portion we find that the Nommos (Anunnaki) were created by the sky god Amma, which resembles the Sumerian Anu, the ruler of the Orioner creator gods. The second highlighted portion I feel is completely representative of the destruction of Sirius B as I interpreted from the *Enuma Elish,* about the war against the Sirius star system. If we look at the part about *"one of the twins who rebelled against the universal order by Amma"* equating with the rebellious planet Tiamat orbiting Sirius B (which is a twin, or binary star) rebelling against Orioner tyranny , then the part related by the Dogon about the twin *"whose body was dismembered and scattered throughout the universe"* makes perfect sense and perfectly mirrors the story in the *Enuma Elish.* Through their handing down of certain oral traditions, the Dogon have lost the original meaning of the actual story.

Temple gave credence to an amphibious race from Sirius, in *The Sirius Mystery,* but his conclusions ultimately fail because he relied on first cognition thinking that they had to get here by traversing that 8.6 light years from Sirius by spaceship. *The Sirius Mystery* was published in 1976, two years before Sitchin published his first book about the Anunnaki, *The Twelfth Planet,* in 1978. It's too bad that these two researchers did not work together because they might have ultimately solved the riddles I am revealing in this book.

To further emphasize the fishy characteristics of the Anunnaki, we only need to look at one of the ancient Sumerian stories called *Inanna and Enki.* The translation of this story can be viewed by searching that title through Google, and it is from that translation we find the following brief passages. The story revolves around how the Anunnaki goddess Inanna got Enki drunk and stole his instruments of power, what the ancient Sumerians called a *Me* (pronounced may). Me's will be discussed in more depth in a later chapter. Anyway, Inanna stole the me's from Enki and once he sobered up and realized what had happened he sent search parties after Inanna to reclaim his goods. Part of his instructions are as follows:

"Go now! <u>All the great fish together</u> ...... are to take the Boat of Heaven away from her!"

"Now as these words were still in her mouth, <u>he got all the great fish together</u> ...... to seize hold of the Boat of Heaven."

[Underlines mine]

From an ancient text called *The Erra Epic,* which can also be viewed online by searching for that particular text, we find the following passage:

"Where are the seven sages <u>of the depths</u>, those <u>sacred fish, who, like Ea their lord</u>, are perfect in sublime wisdom, the ones who cleansed my person?"

[Underlines mine]

If my explanation about the Anunnaki being fish-human hybrids exactly as they are portrayed in ancient illustrations is remotely in error, then I challenge the reader and all of our scholarly academics to provide a more cogent explanation of what these textual passages mean. If we interpret the *"great fish",* or *"the seven sages of the depths, those sacred fish"* to simply

80

mean ordinary fish, then the text is substantially more ludicrous than what I propose. How are we expected to believe that a normal fish can catch any kind of boat? Only the interpretation I offer makes any sense. The seven sages of Sumerian origin is the word Abgal, but you can find reference to the seven fishy sages by looking at Wikipedia under Apkallu, the Akkadian variant of the word. As Wikipedia relates about the Sumerian legend, these seven fishy sages came from the *'sweet waters of the Absu'*.

I discussed in the last chapter the avaricious nature of the Orioners and how they recognized no higher source of authority than their own arrogance and ego superiority. The Anunnaki were no different in that regard. Once they purportedly vanquished their Orioner controllers from this planet, they took on exactly the same roles of god as their predecessors, with substantial alterations. For all intents and purposes, from the standpoint of Earth humans, it was simply a change in management, with the new bosses being little better than the previous owners.

Although Sitchin went to great lengths to sort of glorify the Anunnaki god Enki, mostly based on the ancient propaganda painting him in a benevolent light found in the Sumerian and later Babylonian and Assyrian writings, Enki was far from a sweetheart. The name Enki is translated by Sitchin from the Sumerian EN.KI, meaning Lord Earth. The Sumerian term EN translates to mean Lord and KI means Earth. Enki's name went through many transitions. In the *Enuma Elish* he was originally called Nuddimud, who became the ruler of the watery Apsu, or Nibiru. Later he was called E.A, generally meaning *'he whose house is water'*, then later changed again after the Anunnaki expelled the Orioners, to Enki, which means *'lord of the Earth'*. The word for Nibiru can be spelled either Apsu, Absu or Abzu. I have seen all three renderings used depending on the source. So if you see me shift from one spelling to the other within this text, understand that they are all legitimate renderings that can mean the same thing. You may also see me switching from Ea to Enki in the same manner, as they are the same entity.

For a more in depth study of the Anunnaki, although certain conclusions are erroneous in many places, Sitchin's books are a wealth of information where the story line of the Anunnaki is concerned. During my own years of research, I made a habit of challenging sources. I eventually spent a princely sum purchasing James B. Pritchard's *Ancient Near Eastern texts Relating to the Old Testament,* which is a huge compendium of translated texts from ancient Mesopotamia, Egypt, Assyria, Babylonia and other Near Eastern sites. I was not content to just take Sitchin's word for everything. I also read other books by Samuel Noah Kramer in regard to ancient Sumerian culture, so don't think for a minute I didn't do my homework. If the reader finds this an area of interest, then these books may be helpful to you. Many of the texts referenced in these two volumes can be viewed online as well.

Sitchin came up with the erroneous conclusion that the Anunnaki were here mining gold here to sustain the atmosphere of their planet, Nibiru. I have no idea where Sitchin came up with this particular concept, and there is nothing in his body of work or elsewhere that remotely substantiates such a claim about their planet's atmosphere. It is simply an unsupported bald face assertion supported by nothing more that Sitchin's conclusions about why the ancient gods had such a greed for gold. There is absolutely nothing in the ancient textual evidence that remotely intimates such an idea. The concept simply sprang from Sitchin's fertile imagination.

You will see no shortage of theorizers about the Anunnaki story alleged by Sitchin being preached as gospel in New Age books, on radio talk shows and in articles or Youtube videos. The simple fact is that the Anunnaki miners, working for their Orioner creators, were mining gold out of pure greed for the costly metal just like we do. What puts Sitchin's theory as a lie is found in the recording of the wealth of the temples of the ancient world. If the Anunnaki were so desperately dependent on gold to sustain their planet's atmosphere, then why was there so much gold and silver in their temples, on their statues and in their counting houses? I illustrate this point to emphasize discernment when doing any of this research.

It was the Orioners, in their own arrogant laziness, who created priesthoods at the suggestion of the Anunnaki. The major difference between the Orioners and the subsequent Anunnaki overlords was the fact that the Orioners were so superior in their arrogance they cared nothing about a 'public image' from their slave races. The Orioners didn't give a whit about what their creations thought of them, so long as they were feared, whereas the Anunnaki were very image conscious, which explains why all the writings about them serve to glorify them as 'good gods or goddesses'. This image consciousness is one of the major ways to follow Enki and his sister Ninhursag as they migrated into different regions of the world and assumed the many names they hid behind in the many religions they created and controlled. A leopard can't change its spots, and neither could Enki nor Ninhursag change their personalities and dispositions, despite the many roles they played in different lands. Knowing this one fact alone is what led to many of the discoveries about them I am sharing in this book.

There is a major distinction between the rulership of the Orioners and the later rule under Anunnaki domination. The Orioners didn't care at all about the human race they created on this planet except as a labor pool and another animal food source. They had greater focus and paid greater attention to their hybrid genetic creations, exhibiting a scientific curiosity into how animal genetics mixed with their own genetics produced certain cultural results. To the Orioners, humans on this planet were below notice. We were utterly disposable.

The rituals of human sacrifice, which later devolved into animal sacrifice, were initiated by the Orioners. We were simply two-legged quasi-intelligent cattle to them. The Orioners didn't care about providing any semblance of freedom to any of their creations. For them, 'my way or the highway' was the manner in which they ruled the universe. This attitude was especially pronounced with their genetic creations. Earth humans were completely below their notice and they cared nothing about this species from any kind of intellectual standpoint.

When the Anunnaki eventually revolted against the tyranny of their own creators, wanting freedom from the Orioner yoke, they had already learned some valuable lessons about the human psyche, which would set the tone of their rule over humanity on this planet since that time. The Anunnaki learned that it is easier to control people if you give them a little bit of presumed freedom. The appearance of being free makes more ready slaves, so when they took the reins of power, they allowed more freedoms for their human slaves than the Orioners ever would, but they also kept a very tight psychological rein on their behavior through the cults and religions they created. Despite the semblance of freedom, the human race was still their slaves. The Anunnaki learned how to sow more devotion for themselves from certain humans by providing favors in both status and wealth, which is why the priestly classes and kings were always better off than the general populations.

The greatest lesson the Anunnaki learned over their Orioner predecessors is this; under Orioner rule, every one of their creations was simply a lab experiment and fodder warriors for the Orioner's incessant wars. I am going to use the example of a dog that has been continually abused to the point that it cowers and wets itself when a human comes near it to explain the mindset of the pathological Orioners. To treat any creature that way only generates a certain amount and certain type of energy. In time, the original fear energy tapers off and the only increase in an energetic food supply is through breeding more slaves that one can terrorize in the same fashion. In contradistinction to this, the Anunnaki noticed that the various emotional energies emitted by humans provided a smorgasbord of different energetic flavors. They discovered that the energies generated by our emotions provided a 'spice' to the energies that the Orioners never cared about. The Anunnaki realized that there was a much greater food supply to be harvested by fluctuating the emotions of their human slaves. Since the Orioners cared nothing about humans in any sense other than as cattle, the Anunnaki were able to tap this energetic food supply without notice of the Orioners and thereby started increasing their own strength unbeknownst to their Orioner overlords. Through this subversive means of co-opting human energies, Enki and Ninhursag were able to make themselves energetically stronger, and eventually challenge the Orioners, which will be covered in depth in Part 2.

We are all familiar with the energies associated with elation and joy, just as much as we are aware of the negative energies of fear, depression, dread and guilt. Each human emotion provided a different 'flavor' of energy that the Anunnaki relished and gained strength from, where the Orioners had no interest to curry or harvest such a wealth of energies from our species. The Orioners were the dog-kickers, continually lording it over an ever-diminishing energetic food supply where Earth humans were concerned. Whenever they felt the need to increase the fear factor amongst either humans of gods, they would literally go off on a murderous rampage without cause to generate their energetic food supply of fear. The Anunnaki were wiser tyrants than their masters and realized that humans provided an abundant source of energetic food, especially when they could manipulate human emotions to their wills. This same practice of directing the human race through emotional manipulation continues to this day with the manipulation of our perceptions and emotions by the mass media. This is not accidental.

To remotely understand all of this this, we only have to look at popular figures who revel at the adoration of the crowds, whether they be Popes or politicians, actors or rock stars. They thrive on the adoration of the masses. The adulation gives them a high. The Anunnaki were no different in that regard, except that the energies of adoration were as appealing to them as a food source as were the energies of fear over their presence if someone raised their displeasure. Behind all of this we have to imagine a twisted psyche that generally goes beyond human understanding. The Anunnaki became experts at manipulating human emotional responses because they fully understood the nature of human ego psyche and how easy we are to manipulate emotionally as a species. Both breeds, the Orioners and the Anunnaki, were sadists beyond human imagining. To complete this understanding of the Anunnaki gods, couple all this knowledge on how to emotionally manipulate humans with the power of a god who is either a psychopath or an utter sociopath with an extreme narcissistic misogynist superiority complex, and you come away with an accurate picture of their true natures.

If you read much about the ancient Sumerian culture, and pay attention to reports about the tens of thousands of unreleased translations of Sumerian tablets, you also discover that the Anunnaki were greedy bean counters. A large majority of the hundreds of thousands of Sumerian tablets are temple inventories, lists of the goods, bills of sale and legal documents of the gods and the humans they ruled. The priesthoods were set up as their accountants! This 'holy' system of accounting still drives religions to this day. It brings to mind the Frank Zappa song, "Heavenly Bank Account". It's all about the law and the *profits*. The Roman Church is the richest and most powerful institution on the planet, with national leaders from around the world going to Rome to kiss the Papal ring. From the standpoint of political protocol, the sovereign never visits the vassal, the vassal always goes to the sovereign. As this story unfolds, you will fully understand why 'all roads lead to Rome' to this day.

When we can finally come to terms with the reality of who the Anunnaki were and what their physical characteristics were as a fish-human hybrid race of genetically manipulated species, then we can ultimately start to decipher many references using the fish symbol, not just in Christianity but in other cultures. In ancient Egypt, the hieroglyphic symbol for an administrator was a fish, not unlike the representation found on Christian bumper stickers. The inquiring mind has to ask why a fish was used as a symbol for an administrator in the sandy regions of Egypt? The logical conclusion points us to Anunnaki control of the region during that time in history.

In time, through interbreeding with humans by some of the Anunnaki, the fish genetics of the Anunnaki started being overridden by the more dominant mammalian genes of the humans. They lost their scaly characteristics, but the genetic transitional period spawned a different breed of humans, the evidence of which has been found the world over, of a human race of long-skulled individuals. Modern scholars would have us believe that all these elongated skulls can be attributed to a process of skull-binding, performed by certain societies around the world in order to emulate their gods. I have read reports of Peruvian mummies that have been discovered with these long-skulled fetuses still inside the mother, which puts the whole skull-binding theory into question as the only solution about these skulls. The question has to be asked why humans would do that, unless they were in fact emulating a species that had those specific characteristics and called themselves gods? The next question is that if they were binding the skulls of their children to emulate these gods, who were the models they were emulating?

The transitional hybrids were these long-skulled individuals whose bones have been dug up in Peru and as far away as Russia and China. Illustrations of the Pharaoh Akhenaton and his family, along with certain surviving statuary busts of them, illustrate this hybrid breed. Although the claim that these skulls are all a result of head-binding, the cranial capacities of most of these ancient skulls is larger than the human skull, which is highly indicative of a different species of humans entirely. Modern medical science apologizes over these physical characteristics claiming that Akhenaton suffered from two types of definable physical disorders, Froehlich's Syndrome or Marfan's Syndrome. They are simply refusing the acknowledge the truth that will continue to be revealed in this volume.

I personally went to a Peruvian exhibit many years ago specifically to see some of these skulls on display. I don't care what any of the scholars say, those skulls are not all strictly of human origin. For one thing, most of the skulls had an additional suture, or seam, running from the bridge of the nose upward to the crown. This suture is not present in human skull composition. This anatomical structural anomaly alone proves that these skulls are not simply human skulls subject to the binding rituals performed by many cultures around the planet, yet this anatomic anomaly is persistently overlooked by our authoritative scientific figures because it throws a huge wrench into the whole Darwinian theory of human evolution. Further information in regard to these elongated skulls reveals that many of them had no cranial suture lines whatsoever, which is also glaring proof that they are not wholly human. These skulls obviously represent some type of human hybrid. The inquiring individual wants to understand why the scientists and geneticists of the world won't honestly address this fact without fabricating suppositions rather than admitting the truth the evidence reveals?

The scientific community blusters that there is no evidence of alien intervention on this planet in order to preserve its human-centric first cognition perceptual world of Darwinism, and yet these skulls are all part of the *hard evidence* we need for proof of other-than-human species living on this planet for a long, long time. If I'm smart enough to recognize this anatomical anomaly, then surely our scientific and medical *authorities* are smart enough to see it too. So why are they so vehemently denying such evidence exists and who, or what, are they protecting by doing so? For an example of these skulls, just do a Google search for *"long skulls"* or *"elongated skulls"*.

If you view some of these elongated skulls you will see some of them with very large circular eye sockets. The UFO crowd persistently overlays images of the Grey aliens claiming these skulls are theirs. I will offer an alternative perspective to skulls with those large round eye sockets. They were not the eyes of the Greys, they are round eye sockets that held fish eyes, which as anyone familiar with fish knows, are all round. Yes, this is a shocking interpretation, but if we are looking at progressive generations of genetic manipulation and hybrid breeding, why should we not assume that characteristics of the fish genetics would not appear as genetic throwback recessive genes, even if the rest of the form was human? If you look at those large round eye sockets, it takes little imagination to fill them with round fish eyes, creepy as it makes your feel in your guts.

If one looks at the tall crowns of the pharaohs from ancient Egypt, as well as the Papal mitre, illustrations of the ancient Hittite gods and multitudes of others, they are all indicative of the ancient Anunnaki and their subsequent genetic corruption by interbreeding with Earth humans, creating these long-skulled hybrids who served as rulers in every land they inhabited. One only has to look at the ancient portrayals of the fish hybrids and compare them to the Pope's headdress over the ages of the church to see the direct correlation. They put it right in front of our eyes, yet most of us refuse to see what it means. Many people on this planet have already discovered these correlations without having the complete picture that this book will unfold. Just do a google search on *'fish creatures - papal mitre'* to see all the pictorial comparisons you need to realize this fact. or is this all just another *coincidence* that we are expected to ignore because our authorities don't agree with the truth the pictures tell us?

Because of the weakening of their fish genetics, and presumably a notable loss in many of their telepathic abilities, these Anunnaki hybrids started breeding with their own kin in order to preserve the telepathic talents they were losing by breeding with humans. We see this attempt to maintain their psychic abilities in the practice of the ancient pharaohs marrying their sisters and daughters. Such marriages had less to do with the succession of royal lines as it did with preserving the abilities of their fishy progenitors. Due to this type of continual incestuous inbreeding, this race of beings bred itself out of existence by the 17th century CE. It is common knowledge that continual inbreeding causes all sorts of health issues, hemophilia being one of the best known due to royal inbreeding in Europe. In the Anunnaki-human hybrids, it also led to shorter lifespans and many birth defects.

Through my own research, another cogent point that Sitchin made was the orbital cycle of Nibiru being roughly 3,600 years, what the Sumerians called a *sar*. Sitchin was generally correct when he projected those orbital swings of Nibiru through our solar system at roughly 11000 BC, 7400 BC and 3800 BC. Where Sitchin totally failed the readers of his works was in not projecting that orbital cycle to the next orbital rotation around our sun, which would have occurred near *Year 0* of our current calendar, or 200 BC. Calculating Nibiru's orbital cycle from 3800 BC forward to the next orbital cycle raises too many uncomfortable questions, and that is probably why Sitchin didn't take his study that far forward. This places Nibiru in our solar system exactly at the time of the rise of the Caesars, Christianity and the Roman Catholic Church. To me, this is a little bit more than coincidence given the history of western religions since that time, and the Pandora's Box it opens is also why Sitchin probably never ventured there when presenting his books. *It is a very dangerous subject.*

I want to take a moment to explode this whole Planet X mythology that has so many gullible people spooked at this time. There is no shortage of ill informed people, or agents of disinformation, predicting the return of Nibiru into our solar system any day now. Nibiru is the mysterious Planet X. Apparently, those putting out this hogwash have either not read Sitchin's works or, being agents of fear-mongering disinformation (or simply fools), they think that the public is just too gullible to not question the swill they are pumping out. If we take Sitchin's orbital timetable as being remotely correct, and I do, then one only has to do the math to expose this whole Planet X thing as total bullshit. Let's do the math using that 3,600 year progression suggested by Sitchin. 7400 BC to 3800 BC to 200 BC to, um, 3400 AD. Following this logic and using simple addition, Nibiru is out at the far end of is orbital swing having circumnavigated Sirius B a mere 200 years ago, give or take a century. It is not going to appear in our solar system again for at least another 1400 years! So let's put all this Planet X malarkey to rest.

There is a wealth of information on the internet about the Anunnaki. I am not going to provide exhaustive information on them in this chapter. The main foundation I wanted to establish is the fact that we have not been 'visited' by alien races in the cosmos as the *Ancient Alien* TV hosts repeatedly intimate. This planet has been a place of alien intervention since before we were created as a species to inhabit it. The most erroneous assumption is the belief in Darwin's theory of evolution and that this planet has always been 'ours'. I hate to break it to you, but nothing could be further from the truth.

5. Recalibrating History

I have to take this opportunity to explain something to the reader. I have been working for well over two decades on trying to solve the riddles of our history. Much of that research has been done strictly through the limited textual references we have about our ancient history available to us on this planet. While I was working to solve riddles and find supporting information from earthly sources, I was also working with my partners gathering information from other intelligent sources in our universe. Many of the ancient gods are still alive and kicking, as hard as that is to imagine. Not all of them were total tyrants, or at least they no longer remain so. Some of these ancient entities have provided a lot of information to me over the years, many times verifiable through ancient texts interpreted in the correct manner without all the mystical overlays.

I know there are a lot of readers who are going to balk at such a claim and who will choose to disbelieve it altogether. I have no control over what the reader accepts or doesn't accept. Your acceptance or denial will not alter the information I have in my head through these decades of deep research and personal experiences. The problem both my wife and I have is that the more we learn, the harder it is to find a starting point to even begin to relate all the information we possess to other human beings on this planet. There have been so many offworld players on this planet that each of them is a history in themselves. Trying to come up with a way to remotely tell these stories is like watching a Quentin Tarantino movie, where a bunch of seemingly unrelated pieces have to be addressed before we can begin to see the overall story line. Our history is the same way, too many disparate pieces have to be presented in order to come to any major understanding of the overall tapestry.

What I am delivering in these books is a mere snapshot of a vast library of information which I could easily write about for the next ten years or more. Most of the supporting information presented in this book comes from earthly sources and from intuitive reasoning based on the conclusions the evidence presents. My focus in these presentations at this time is on showing the influence of the worst perpetrators of tyranny Earth humans have ever known. Their physical presence may be removed, but the after-effects of what they did to our species still causes fear in us to this day on a very visceral, almost genetic level. As with the previous volumes in this series, by both myself and my wife, we are here to set the record straight. Whether certain readers want to accept this truth or not, this history needs to be known and exposed.

Our past, especially how the world was 2,000 years ago, or just before, is not what we have come to believe it is. We have accepted a superficial illusion intentionally designed to keep our consciousness enslaved and trapped in living a massive perceptual lie. From the standpoint of our first cognition ego-centric view of the world, we are always at the center of our own perceptual universe. As I wrote in previous volumes, we are very human-centric in all of our perceptual interpretations. All of our history is about *us* and our presumed advance towards civilization starting with the theoretical progression of humans from our alleged ancestors hanging in the trees to who we are today (if you believe Darwin), or that some singular god created us just so he could be worshipped. In the grand cosmic scheme of things, for tens of thousands of years after we were created in an Orioner laboratory, we were not even a footnote. We were cattle in the most literal sense of the word. Many of these creator gods literally feasted on us as a two-legged food source. In Egyptian religious legends, it was claimed that Osiris and Isis stopped the practice of cannibalism. Whether they did or not is questionable, but the fact that it is mentioned at all should serve as notification that such practices were widespread, as horrifying as that idea is to our psyche. The Rakshasas of Hindu mythology were rabid cannibals, but then we can protect our cognitive sensitivity through denial, and accept the idea that all such stories are mythical make believe, and never really happened.

If we look into the ancient Vedic texts of the Hindus, we find many wars fought between their gods over one god stealing another god's cattle or *kine*. From our modern perspective we automatically think of 4-legged bovines when we read these stories about wars over stolen cattle, but this is where we make our perceptual mistake. Earth humans were not only a food supply to certain alien races, they were also a workforce. If you can alter your thinking to perceive these Hindu gods going to war using their flying vehicles, their *Vimanas,* over simple cattle rustling, it really doesn't make a lot of sense. If, however, you interpret the cattle being stolen as the human cattle of their workforces, their man-*kine,* then the stories take on a completely different meaning, and their grand wars over their stolen cattle makes tremendously more sense. Our species was nothing but a valuable commodity to our alien overlords from many different worlds, just as any slave is a commodity to its owner. I am only citing this one example in an effort to help you alter your thinking from first cognition interpretations into a broader perception of reality.

Most of this work is going to be focused on Western history since that is the place the Anunnaki held the most sway, although their control did eventually reach into the East through proxy rulers from other star systems, and their ultimate religious control expanded everywhere. By the West, I mean anything west of India. The gods of India will be covered in more depth in the next installment of this series.

We have many blanks in our history. Too many records have either been totally destroyed or intentionally sequestered away to prevent detection by powerful institutions who want to keep these stories hidden from public knowledge. I want to provide one example in passing at this time. If we look into our history, we are instructed that the Library at Alexandria, Egypt, was the greatest repository of knowledge in the western world. If we can believe the historical accountings, the Alexandrian Library was allegedly burned at least four times, possibly more, before it ultimately disappeared - once when Julius Caesar invaded Egypt in 48 BCE, once again by Aurelius between 270-275 CE, again when the Coptic Pope Theophilus ordered its destruction in 391 CE. Another story tells of the Christian prefect Cyril ordering the Jews to leave Alexandria in 415 CE, and the renowned teacher at the library, Hypatia, protested the expulsion, for which she was executed. The Muslims allegedly burned the library again in 639 CE. The Christian destruction of 415 CE is presented in the modern movie *Agora*. It is a truly heartbreaking film to watch and probably comes close to illustrating the Christian religious frenzy and fanaticism of that time. It is no different than Muslim extremism in this day and age.

Although it is reported that Julius Caesar had the Alexandrian library burned during the civil war in 48 BC, a general who was leading Caesar's army in Alexandria wrote his own autobiography after the civil war, and there was absolutely no mention of the library being burned by Caesar during that revolt. I have no documented source that can verify what I am about to posit, but here is what I see in regard to Caesar's invasion. The Alexandrian Library possessed the greatest amount of history and knowledge of the ancient world. It was a treasure that even Julius Caesar should have been able to see. I suggest that, rather than burning the library, for which there is no real substantiating information other than legend, Caesar took most of the library back to Rome as a war prize after the civil war. This theory makes more sense than the senseless burning of the greatest repository of knowledge in the Western world at that time. Chances are that the Library contents were taken back to Rome as a war prize and most likely stored in the Temple of the Vestals, which is also where many Roman legal documents were stored, like the wills of the Caesars, or possibly in the Temple to Jupiter. The fictional story of the fire was told by later historical redactors to cover up the real reason the books in the library disappeared. I will discuss more on this Alexandrian Library accumulation of knowledge in later chapters.

I mentioned in the last chapter about the orbital cycle of Nibiru and how by simply doing the math, using Sitchin's general timetable, it places Nibiru in our solar system roughly near Year 0. As with any numbers of the nature projected by Sitchin, they are rounded off to be generally close to true, meaning that the year dates he provided are not necessarily wholly accurate on the specific years he suggested. In order to see if I could find any enigmatic events that might remotely support Sitchin's projected timeframes, I found two events that appear to support his rough timeframe in regard to that 3,600 year orbital cycle and what seems to place Nibiru in our solar system near 3,800 BC.

In reading H.G. Wells *The Outline of History* I came across a chart in the book that shows the appearance of the mysterious Aryans, noted by a large question mark, appearing on the scene of history out of nowhere some unknown time prior to 3,000 BC. The origin of the so-called Aryans is a mystery to this day and will be covered at length in the next volume. The other factor that played into giving credence to that rough time frame for the orbital cycle is the start date of the Jewish calendar at 3760 BC. These two discoveries made me wonder if there is some kind of connection between the two, but either way, they are events that occurred close to that orbital cycle near 3800 BC projected by Sitchin, so I give his projected dates of Nibiru's drift through our solar system some credence based on these two enigmatic events alone. Although this may seem like a weak linkage at the moment, when the rest of the story is told in Part 2, these factors will prove to not be as tenuous as they currently may appear.

If we can accept that the 3,600 year orbital cycle placed Nibiru in our solar system around 3800 BC, based on the start date of the Jewish calendar and the mysterious appearance of the Aryans onto the historical scene at roughly the same time, then we can move forward 3,600 years to find Nibiru once again in our solar system about 200 BC, give or take a century or so. So in order to better understand our own history, we have to make a projection of Western societies before the arrival of Nibiru and the direct influence of the Anunnaki returning *en masse* to Earth.

Before the arrival of the Anunnaki, the Roman Republic was still in place. Although Rome was an expansionist society, and it had no shortage of ills that history can complain about, the Roman Republic created civilization in the areas into which it expanded. It brought roads and building, indoor plumbing, baths and education. Schools opened to teach on a tuition basis modeled on the Greek system of education. Rome brought literacy, the arts and a sense of refinement to the tribal peoples it conquered. Granted, the manner in which it brought civilization can be questioned when compared to our current standards, but civilization *was* advancing and humankind was moving forward from tribal backwardness into more civilizing practices. In truth, the subsequent expansionist policies of all Western governments were pretty bloody when is came to placing indigenous peoples under subjugation, but in Rome, it was a more brutal time in human history.

Now, let's factor in the arrival of Nibiru and the Anunnaki onto the world stage. As with all things, there are certain time lapses to keep in mind as the Anunnaki have to get reacquainted with human affairs before they start exerting their control when their planet arrives in our solar system. Within about 150 years after their arrival, provided the date of 200 BC I provided is remotely accurate, the Roman Republic started to dissolve when the Senate gave dictatorial power to Julius Caesar and the bloody reigns of the Caesars began. I will assert that the Anunnaki, Enki in particular, had a major hand in the political swing from the Republic to the Empire under control of the Caesars. This political move from a Republic to a quasi-hereditary dictatorship of Caesars eventually led to the destruction of Rome as a civilizing factor in the world.

Before continuing, I have to add one other important Anunnaki player into this scenario for global control, and that was Enki's sister Ninhursag. If Enki was evil, Ninhursag was evil incarnate, as I think the reader will agree after reading this first volume. There is so much depth to this tale that I will leave it for now to just tell the reader that there was an extreme competition between Enki and Ninhursag over who was going to win over and ultimately control the minds of humans where religion came into play.

Ninhursag, at that point in time was more popularly referred to as Isis in the Mediterranean regions. Where Enki was pushing for control under total patriarchal rule, Ninhursag was pushing her own agenda for goddess worship under the name of Isis. I will probably also lapse into referring to her as Isis given the role of the Isis cult during those few centuries before and after Year 0. I will make the distinction now that Ninhursag was not the original person of Isis, but that the identity of the real Isis was co-opted and overlaid, and her name and image were heavily tarnished at the hands of Ninhursag over our most recent history. This will be explained in depth in the subsequent chapters of this book.

To continue with the timeframe of the Anunnaki revisitation around Year 0, Caesar was assassinated in 44 BC on the steps of the Roman Senate. After his assassination, the Roman Senate created a legal triumvirate, what is historically known as the second triumvirate. This triumvirate was made up of Gaius Octavius (later Caesar Augustus), Marcus Antonius (Mark Antony), and Marcus Aemilius Lepidus. After fighting a civil war with Julius's assassins, the triumvirate divided up the empire, with Octavius taking Rome and Italy, Antony taking control of the Eastern provinces and Lepidus controlling Gaul and Spain in the west. This triumvirate fell apart in time, with Lepidus making a faulty political move against Octavius, which gave Octavius the means to remove him from the triumvirate and take control of the western provinces. Ultimately, Lepidus was exiled in 36 BC.

This left Antony and Octavius to compete for control of the Roman empire. Because of the friction between these two men, Antony stayed mainly in the East. Skipping most of the details that the reader is invited to look up if they are interested, Mark Antony eventually deserted his wife, Octavius' sister, and hooked up with Cleopatra. From our historical accounting we are left simply with the idea that these were human participants occupied in human affairs. But when we interject the power struggle going on between Enki and Nin, a different picture emerges.

Antony and Cleopatra were reported to have often appeared together dressed as Osiris and Isis, indicating that they were supporters of the Isis cult, which was in direct competition with the patriarchal system developing in Rome under Enki's specific guidance. In Israel at this time, we see the compiling the Dead Sea Scrolls fully in motion, which I will discuss more fully later on. Most people do not see these events as being related, but they are more intimately entwined than our historical scholars have realized, or are willing to admit. Octavius, even after he came to power as Augustus Caesar, was a patriarchal conservative where the gods of Rome were concerned. As the leader of the Roman empire, he was also the chief priest of the cult of Jupiter and, along with the title of Caesar, he also carried the title of *Pontifex Maximus* as the high priest of the religion of Jupiter - the same title every Pope of the Catholic Church has carried since the church was created. Augustus didn't want that religious applecart overturned by a foreign Eastern religion of goddess worship that had its origins in Egypt. This war of the patriarchal system, primarily worshipping Jupiter as the senior god of Rome, against matriarchal Isis worship from Egypt has continued into the present day, although in a more subliminal manner.

With the defeat and death of Antony and Cleopatra at Actium in 31 BC, the pathway of the *divine* Caesars was set in motion, based on the system that Julius himself started as the first god king of Rome, following in the steps of the Egyptian pharaohs. Over the next few centuries, this struggle between Enki and Nin did not die down. The purported history of *The Twelve Caesars* by Seutonius focuses on the fact that the Caesars who got the worst press and were called the worst of the Caesars by Seutonius, were all followers of the Isis cult or other Eastern-influenced religious cult practices. Both Caligula and Nero, and a number of other more denigrated Caesars in Seutonius, were followers of Isis in one form or another. Caligula built a Temple to Isis in Rome during his short reign. If any reader cares to review Seutonius's works, I'm sure they will see the same trend that I do when reading the material when it comes to vilifying the worshippers of Isis in the Roman royal house. These may seem to be inconsequential facts at the moment, but before this book is finished, the reader will see the relevance of all of it.

6. From Civilization to the Dark Ages

We are most all familiar with the decadent period of Rome under the Caesars and how the Roman empire became more violent and degraded as it declined under their rule. As civic Rome was weakening, the stage was being set for the patriarchal Christians to eventually move in and take over Rome. As the Roman Church started advancing, it subsumed and adopted many pagan belief systems under its umbrella in order to woo pagans to this new religion. I will offer just a few of these sycretisms as example. A more comprehensive study of this religious syncretism can be found through studying books on ancient Roman Pagan religious practices as well as other Pagan cultic practices.

The Roman holiday for celebrating the Birth of the Unconquerable Sun, *natalis Invicti*, was an annual celebration in Pagan Rome on December 25th. This tradition was altered from the birth of the sun, to the birth of the Son of God in Christian tradition. This holiday is generally accepted to celebrate the solstice shift where the sun alters it course from the short days of winter and starts its progression to the longer days of spring and summer.

Just as Christians use the rite of baptism in varying practices, the Isis cult also practiced baptism, which substantially predates the practice of baptism adopted by Christians. There will be more on these water rituals later in this volume when I start explaining energy manipulation.

Like Pauline Christianity, the Isis cult also used eternal salvation as one of the primary selling points of its religion - literally. One had to pay for salvation to be initiated into the Isis cult. Isis was known for helping in people's lives, just as Catholics pray to the Virgin Mary to intervene in their lives. This correlation is by no means accidental, as will be revealed in subsequent chapters when I provide a closer examination of Ninhursag's role during this time period.

In ancient Roman Pagan religious festivals, the priests and priestesses of the temples, along with their followers, would parade statues of their gods carried on litters through the streets as a form of celebration on the respective holy days of their pantheon. This same practice is utilized by Catholics to this day, especially in Latin America. The origin of this practice will be covered later.

The Roman Pagans had the practice of worshipping what are known as household gods, called lares, usually associated with their dead ancestors. The lares were usually set up on an altar on the hearth in the home for private worship. The practice of worshipping household gods finally disappears around the early 5th century CE. The Roman Church effectively replaced the lares with statuettes of the Saints and the practice of idol worship continued with a new wardrobe called Christianity. Although many lares were worshipped at the hearth in the home, other lares had more power, being lares over roadways, seaways, livestock and in other areas. This concept of a lare with greater 'jurisdiction' is little removed from one wearing a St. Christopher medallion as the Saint that protects travelers, and also protects against storms and plagues.

Ninhursag as Isis was known as the Queen of Heaven. This title was rolled over to the Virgin Mary in Catholic tradition, with Mary also still referred to as the Queen of Heaven. As Isis, Ninhursag was the Virgin Mother, exactly like Mary in Catholic tradition, and this Virgin Mother aspect tracks all the way back to ancient Sumeria.

I could go on about these Pagan adaptations into the Roman Church, but these examples should be substantial enough to make my point. Given all that I have written about the second cognition, it should be even more readily apparent that the man we know as Jesus had nothing to do with the either the foundation of, or the religion spawned in that name.

Due to the adaptability of the emerging Christian religion by adopting and subsuming older Pagan traditions, the religion started taking root in places where the old religions of the Pagan practices previously thrived. As Christianity advanced in financial strength and power, they converted ancient Pagan temple sites to their own usage, but more often built new houses of worship where Pagan temples previously stood. The advance of Christianity operated through the systematic erasure of all that came before it, either through assimilating Pagan doctrines that the Church found suitable to its needs, or through outright destruction of their temples and outlawing their means of worship. There was also a systematic erasure of ancient documentary evidence that it seems many of the early Church fathers had access to, but that have now conveniently disappeared or become 'lost'.

With the advancement of this new religious doctrine, which I claim was directly influenced and driven by the Anunnaki presence, we see the systematic removal of information from our historical background. From ancient Mesopotamia archaeologists have unearthed statuettes of the Anunnaki in all their hybrid glory. We know the cult of Dagon existed in the ancient Near East and had found its way into the region called Israel. Dagon was another hybrid fish god of the Anunnaki variety. Dagon was the chief god of the Philistines and his name goes back as far as ancient Mesopotamia as Dagan.

We know that idol worship was the thing in the ancient temples. The question one has to raise is that if these Anunnaki were worshipped and revered in so many places, especially the homage paid to idols in most ancient Pagan traditions, where have all these idols disappeared? If their worship was as prevalent as even non-biblical texts indicate, where are the fish idols? Are we simply supposed to accept the idea that the rising Christian sect was so far ranging as to be able to destroy all this historical evidence? The images of the Anunnaki abound in ancient Sumerian texts, which lay buried for thousands of years until they were rediscovered in the 19th century. Without our discovery of these images, and what few remaining carvings of their imagery still exist, we would not know a thing about them. What I assert is that there was a systematic removal of all such idols and images, dictated and driven by the Anunnaki themselves, in order to hide the truth of their existence from humanity. This is the origin and the basis of the biblical prohibition that "there shall be no graven images."

Before the reader dismisses such a possibility, it needs to be pointed out that the systematic removal of historical information is still alive and well in the modern day. From the times of the pharaohs in ancient Egypt, the systematic erasure of the faces and names of previous pharaohs was a regular practice. The existence of the pharaoh Akhenaton was entirely removed from the historical record and his city destroyed, not to be rediscovered for almost 2,600 years after he ruled in Egypt. Libraries have been burned, tombs have been robbed, and entire civilizations have disappeared. The records held in the Mayan codexs by the Catholic invaders into Central America are another prime example of such erasure of cultural histories, where the Spanish Conquistadors burned hundreds, possibly thousands of the Mayan codexs. Book burnings have taken place worldwide over the centuries when any ruling party designates certain writings to be illegal, especially when they challenge the new party line and the fabricated history these governments weave around themselves. What we are talking about in reference to the planet Nibiru being in our local solar proximity the few centuries preceding and following Year 0 is an entire planet of hybrid beings making a systematic effort to expunge the knowledge of their existence from human memory, all so their leaders could fabricate a new religion about an invisible God and cast mankind into a cognitive dark age. If any imagery in carvings or idols from that time had been left in place, there would be too much room to question the new religious paradigm, so all traces of the Anunnaki had to be removed from our historical record, especially since the agenda in the West was a shift to the new invisible god of Judaism and Christianity.

What was put in place by the Caesars and the corruption of that system of government led to the weakening of an empire and gave Christianity the opportunity to take over. Where before, many of the Pagan practices were only available to the educated classes who could afford to purchase their way into the mystery schools of the time, Enki, through his religious proselytizers, created a religion that was available to all classes, especially the slave classes, capitalizing on a system that had already been started by Ninhursag posing as Isis. Salvation was no longer restricted to the well to do as with the initiates into the Isis cult. Salvation was now in everybody's grasp, and this created one of the greatest mind-control, energy-harnessing programs to ever plague mankind. Contrary to popular belief, this religion could not have taken hold in the manner it did without a lot of help from sources with serious influence, and those sources were the Anunnaki themselves.

Enki's new religion was a religion of subjugation and intolerance. Once the religion gained enough strength in followers, systematic wars were waged against all traditions and peoples that disagreed with or challenged the new doctrine and they were eradicated or driven underground. Those deemed heretics were killed if they did not submit to the will of this new church. For a time, so long as certain factions like the Gnostics gave lip service to the doctrine of Jesus, they were allowed to play the game. But as the doctrine of the Church of Rome solidified and became more rigid, it also became more intolerant of objections to its patriarchal doctrine. This homogenization of doctrines into an accepted solidified whole was finally achieved in the First Council of Nicea in 325 CE. It was during this first ecumenical council that what was considered as acceptable writings and what was not, was decided by the voting members in attendance. The council was so fraught with emotion that actual fist fights broke out among the members fighting for their own doctrinal superiority. We inherited Christian doctrine by majority vote.

It was out of this council that the doctrine of acceptable religious canons came into being - i.e. the Bible. The books of the Bible were voted on and other doctrinal issues settled, like agreement upon when to celebrate Easter. As Rome had conquered other nations and brought foreign people's under their control, they already had a tradition of folding foreign gods and goddesses into their pantheon of gods based on Alexander's system of religious syncretism. This same tradition of assimilation was continued with the formation of Christianity.

I wrote about Alexander the Great's plan for religious syncretism in *Demystifying the Mystical*, and also how the formation of the Catholic religion was just a furtherance of that agenda. With the final subsuming of Pagan religious practices and the solidification of its doctrines, under the supervision of the Roman Emperor Constantine the Great, the road was paved for centuries of societal degradation at the hands of the new elite class of Enki-controlled priests. With the establishment of the Roman Church, all serious pursuits of knowledge were considered heretical unless they could be proven to be of value to the doctrine of the Church. Religion became the focus of this tyranny, not the cultural or conscious advancement of the human race. Mental slavery to the principles of these religions, Judaism and Christianity, was the mandate. With the creation of Islam, this same mindset of cultural religious conquest continued under a different guise.

With the lessening of Roman military power and the focus more on evangelizing and converting the world to the new doctrine of docility and priestly subjugation, it only took a few invasions by barbarians like Attila the Hun and the subsequent invasions of the Vandals, Goths and Visigoths to kill off the cultural advancements made by the Roman Republic. After these invasions, civilization cratered and we were left with the world that Enki and his Anunnaki associates demanded - a world of harsh poverty, ignorance, illiteracy and fear, with his corrupt priesthood dictating the affairs of man for centuries - the period we now know as the Dark Ages.

7. Tangential Observations

I illustrated how the Anunnaki were a hybrid race of combined fish and human genetics created in a laboratory by Orioner geneticists. I want to cover some ground here for other aspects that have been overlooked in this historical redirecting of the reader's perception. I am not asking you to believe what I present out of hand. Most people are going to balk at most all of this information anyway because it so severely challenges their perceptual world, not just the religious adherents. What I am providing to the reader is a new perspective by providing information that few outside the realm of academia are even aware. Archaeologists are aware of a lot of this information, but because of first cognition limited perception being totally human-centric, they have missed what the evidence that has been unearthed reveals. They have often reached conclusions in error because their perceptual boundaries would be challenged too much if they admitted what the evidence actually shows, provided they could make the leap of consciousness necessary to reach these conclusions.

This book is ultimately going to reveal many aspects of energy manipulation, what some call magic, but a historical framework must be presented in order to interpret certain aspects of the information in a different light. This chapter will be a transitional chapter where I start to link the historical with the magical. The two will most likely be interwoven throughout the rest of the book in order to maintain a consistency of understanding.

Everything we think we know is based upon human first cognition reckoning from that human-centric point of view. Modern scholars have a very bad habit of projecting our level of understanding backwards into the past in order to try and understand ancient civilizations. We have no real understanding of those civilizations beyond what our current perceptual interpretive system makes us believe we *think* we know about them. We project our own modern system of cognition onto our ancient ancestors, yet we have no real way to understand either them or the world in which they lived. Most of these interpretations wind up being in error due to this perceptual misjudgment.

Archaeologists have unearthed many items from the Iraqi and Iranian deserts over the past few centuries through excavating ancient Babylonian, Assyrian and Sumerian civilizations. One of the items I want to focus on at the moment is what is known as an abzu tank. The illustration of an abzu tank that I have seen was in the book *Gods, Demons and Symbols of Ancient Mesopotamia* by Jeremy Black and Anthony Green. I have found this particular book very valuable in my research over the years. It is not very large, but is an illustrated dictionary that provides a wealth of definitions and pictures from the aforementioned ancient civilizations.

The abzu tank pictured in the book was an ornately carved stone bathtub, for all intents and purposes. I don't know the size of the tank as I don't remember if the book provides the dimensions or not. I want to share a little bit of the information about the abzu, Enki and abzu tanks from *Wikipedia.com*:

> *"In the city of Eridu, Enki's temple was know as the E2-abzu (house of the <u>cosmic waters</u>) and was located at the edge of a swamp, an abzu. Certain tanks of holy water in Babylonian and Assyrian temple courtyards were also called abzu (apsû). <u>Typical in religious washing, these tanks were similar to the washing pools of Islamic mosques, or the baptismal font in Christian churches.</u>"*
>
> [Underlined emphasis mine]

The first thing I want to point out to the reader about scholarly misinterpretations is the conclusion that the tanks were filled with holy water. How did the researchers reach this conclusion? Were the abzu tanks actually filled with holy water, or is that just an assumption of our modern perception casting that interpretation onto ancient societies about which we have no real understanding, using the religions we know as a basis for comparison? Also pay attention to the interpretation that Enki's abzu temple was the 'house of *cosmic* waters."

If we take what I have written about the Anunnaki being hybrid fish-human creatures, and if we take the surviving imagery of their form to be remotely accurate, then we have to naturally assume that they needed water to keep themselves functioning at their best. Remember what I related in regard to the Nommos of the Dogon traditions building a reservoir upon their arrival and that they needed water to survive. The Middle East provides a very dry climate, one that would seem to be totally inhospitable to such semi-aquatic, amphibious beings. So what would their alternative be to surviving such arid climates when they were not near water? The solution is found with the numbers of absu tanks unearthed in the region. The absu tanks were not filled with 'holy water', they were more likely places for refreshing dry, parched fishy-skinned beings who needed water to stay functional and be remotely comfortable for long durations on the land. Logic dictates this solution and the concept of the tanks being filled with 'holy water' is simply a human misconception based on modern religious beliefs being cast backwards into a past we do not understand.

All of the ancient Sumerian cities are found in what is known as the Fertile Crescent, and are located between the Tigris and Euphrates rivers, with most of their cities being built next to the rivers. Being semi-aquatic hybrid beings, they would have to have water, and even as the Wikipedia description says in regard to Enki, his temple in Eridu was built next to a swamp. So, I am asking the reader to make a cognitive leap and see these abzu tanks as not something necessarily filled with holy water, as the modern scholars suggest, but were instead a necessity of life for amphibious beings with a regular need to immerse themselves in water. I will make a further suggestion that those abzu tanks found in temple courtyards were for public use by all the Anunnaki whenever needed in order to wet their fishy skin, much like towns used to use public watering troughs or fountains to provide their general water needs. From our human-centric perspective, we automatically make the false assumption that the abzu tanks had to do with human affairs and how our religions today use such things, i.e. as baptismal fonts, etc.

If we take the ancient *myths* about the Anunnaki gods and translate them in a more literal sense, then things such as abzu tanks can be readily and logically explained, without having to resort to ideas about them being filled with holy water. It is through centuries of indoctrination by the Catholic religion that the idea of holy water even enters into the interpretive equation. If the water was so holy, as scholars assume, then why are the abzu tanks located in public temple courtyards? Wouldn't such public access run the risk of the water becoming somehow unpurified by the profane, especially given the purification demands of so many ancient religions? These are all cogent questions that I ask the reader, and especially the academic experts to ponder, for they have merit. It is no coincidence that abzu tanks have found their way into Islamic mosques, Roman baths and Christian baptismal fonts. Baptism and other water rituals are one of the most pernicious abuses of energy manipulation perpetrated by the Anunnaki against humanity on this planet.

Since one of the contributing species to the genetic pool of the Anunnaki were types of intelligent fish that inhabited Nibiru at the time the Orioners claimed that planet, those intelligent fish species had learned ways to work with water energy based on their environmental surroundings no differently than we humans utilize our environments to harness energy technologically. I know I am asking the reader to challenge their acceptable levels of cognition when I make these observations, but I ask for your patience long enough for this whole thing to reveal itself before passing judgment.

In the opening stanzas of the *Enuma Elish*, Wikipedia.com provides the following passages under the definition abzu:

> *"Abzu (apsû) is depicted as a deity only in the Babylonian creation epic, the Enûma Elish, taken from the library of Assurbanipal (c 630 BCE) but which is about 500 years older. In this story, he was a primal being made of fresh water and a lover to another primal deity, Tiamat, who was a creature of salt water. The Enuma Elish begins:*

> *When above the heavens did not yet exist nor the earth below, Apsu the freshwater ocean was there, the first, the begetter, and Tiamat, the saltwater sea, she who bore them all; they were*

still mixing their waters, and no pasture land had yet been formed, nor even a reed marsh..."

From this brief description we discover that the Apsu (Nibiru) is a fresh water planet in contradistinction to our planet Tiamat, which is primarily a salt water world. This description in itself should be supportive of my earlier contention about this planet being joined as a partner planet with Nibiru in the Sirius B star system. Being a fresh water planet, it is also indicative that the fish providers of the Anunnaki genetics were fresh water fishes. Being fresh water inhabitants, I propose they learned how to energetically manipulate their watery environment on Nibiru well before the Orioner race ever showed up on that planet.

In light of this information, let's take a moment to revisit Rome near Year 0. The tradition of bath houses in Rome was adopted from the Greeks, but there is a difference in the two systems. The Greeks employed a system of hip-baths, where the Romans went full blown with large edifices for their bath houses, including heated floors and heated pools. It is very striking to realize that wherever the Romans took their civilization, they erected bath houses. Naturally, we could chalk this up simply to a matter of human cleanliness, civilization and leisure, but let's look at it another way. With the arrival of the Anunnaki on this planet *en masse* once again around Year 0, there would be a great need for abzu tanks - umm, let's call them Roman bath houses. This expansion of bath houses into all the conquered Roman territories starts to take on a completely different and more sinister flavor when viewed in this aspect.

The Anunnaki were of greater stature than humans. The need for higher ceilings and larger facilities was a mandate in order to cater to their comfort, especially if they were expected to handle more than one or two random Anunnaki at a time. So, let's look at the aspect of the bath houses being heated and having heated water. In my research over the years, I noticed that the Anunnaki seemed to stay located in regions of warmer temperatures. This need for warmer temperatures led me to the conclusion that they did not do well in colder climates. Despite the fact that their genetic predecessors were fish, once they were genetically manipulated into warm-blooded quasi-human creatures, any tolerance they may have had for the cold probably disappeared with their genetic hybridization. We see no archaeological evidence of their presence in their more fish-related forms where colder winters prevail. I suggest that in colder climates they grew torpid and moved slower, meaning that the cold handicapped them. If this assessment is true, then there is a very good reason the Roman baths were heated, especially as the Roman empire expanded into the colder climes of northern Europe.

If we take all these collective observations combined, then I think we can start to see another piece of circumstantial evidence being built to point to Anunnaki presence on our planet during that critical point in our history. In uncovering our past, and it is greatly covered up, it is like a detective solving a cold case. Often times cold cases are solved when a new set of eyes can view the evidence in a new light, bringing a new perspective to the case in order to solve it. Granted, the evidence is scanty and is intentionally veiled in a lot of mystery, but I think with the correct interpretive tools this cold case can still be solved. It is going to take the efforts of academic innovators who are experts in their respective fields to further resolve the issues of our ancient past, and this is why I made my entreaty to their expertise in the first chapter in this book. With new perspective comes new insights and new directions in which they can focus their attention to solve this multitude of ancient riddles. No single individual can do it alone.

During my research over the years I studied many different subjects. I mentioned in previous works that I had read *The Nag Hammadi Library.* It was through studying the translated Gnostic texts that I found one of my most important revelations in regard to this chapter's presentation. *The Paraphrase of Shem,* translated by Frederick Wisse is but one of the philosophically confusing texts of those collected writings by the Gnostics, but amidst the philosophy contained in the work we find a serious diatribe against baptism in more than one location in the text. There was one brief segment in particular that eventually led to the revelation I am going to share in this chapter.

> *"O Shem, they are deceived by manifold demons, thinking that through baptism with the uncleanness of water, that which is dark, feeble, idle, (and) disturbing, he will take away the sins. And they do not know **that from the water to the water there is bondage,** and error and unchastity,*

envy, murder, adultery, false witness, heresies, robberies, lusts, babblings, wrath, bitterness, great . . ."

[Bold emphasis mine]

The part of this passage that troubled me was the emphasized reference, *"that from the water to the water there is bondage."* The composer of the *Paraphrase* definitely railed against what he called 'impure baptism' in several locations in the text, but what puzzled me most was in trying to solve this riddle of water going under the bondage of water, especially when speaking particularly about baptism. Since I had studied and experienced energy work, and had to ultimately give some credence to certain traditions of magic masking true energy work, the solution finally came to me.

Human beings are made up of mostly water. Babies have the highest percentage of water when they are born, about 78% according to Dr. Jeffrey Utz, Neuroscience, pediatrics, Allegheny University, and adult males drop to maybe 60% water in later life. We are, for all intents and purposes, water - walking. To solve the riddle of impure baptism and the mystery of water going under the bondage of water as related in the *Paraphrase of Shem*, I finally realized that the Anunnaki were using a form of what I call hydromancy, or energetic water magic, utilized in all religions under their designs. Now, if you look up a definition for hydromancy, it goes back to the ancient Greek study of divination using the activity or actions of water to allegedly make prophecies. The hydromancy I am referring to amounts to

123

using water as a binding agent through a process of energetically programming water. I am going to use the terms spellcasting and programming interchangeably from here forward, because for all intents and purposes, magical spellcasting is nothing more than programming energies through intent. When I state that water is a *binding* agent, I am using the term in reference to harnessing energy into a certain purpose and using it as an element to *bind* those who come under its influence, directly the same premise as the word is used in spellbinding. This binding concept is no different than the principle of *bondage* related in the *Parapharase of Shem*.

I am going to use holy water as an example of programming water. As most people know, the only difference between regular water and holy water is that a priest 'blesses' holy water, although in light of what follows, we must severely question what these purported 'blessings' actually entail. What we all have to realize is that it was the Anunnaki who introduced priestcraft to humans on this planet. Every form of priestly function originated with the Anunnaki. If we take the ancient Sumerian literature correctly, then we had priests for a lot longer than we've had kings. Everything about priestly rituals, including 'blessing' holy water, has its origins with the Anunnaki and their "magical" energy manipulation. Given the deceitful nature of the Anunnaki, every reader should question anything that remotely deals with any kind of priestcraft, regardless of the religion.

Since magic is nothing more than programming energies through intent to do either good or bad, it is not that far a stretch of the imagination to picture the fishy hybrid Anunnaki using a form of water magic to bind their earthly slaves to their religious beliefs. They used programmed 'holy' water to bind the water in the human form as a type of energetic tyranny to control us. You could call this a form of sympathetic magic, or programmed energy controlling through the factor of elemental resonance.

Virtually every religion is wrapped in certain ritualistic practices. One of the most common practices across the board is the use of water. Buddhists, Muslims and others are required to wash their feet and hands before going to temple or prayer call. These rituals serve the same purpose of 'binding' in those different religions that baptism does in the Christian religion. The water serves as a binding agent, creating a form of energetic bondage of Enki's God-spell over those who practice it. One studied in the metaphysics of Eastern thought understands the chakras, or power centers of the body. There are primarily seven of these chakra points; the root or genitals, the solar plexus, the heart, the throat, the third eye at the forehead, the fifth eye, and the crown chakra. Notice that when a Catholic priest baptizes a newborn that he sprinkles holy water on the baby's third eye and crown chakras, thereby effectively sealing off access to these spiritual energy conduits with Enki's hydromantic God-spell.

The human body is like a walking bio-electrical circuit with a positive and a negative side, or a receiving and transmitting side. Water is a great conductor of electricity. Catholics dip their fingers at the font in the front of the nave of the church and cross themselves when they enter. This font is in actuality a stylized Anunnaki *apsu* tank. It is through this act of 'crossing' themselves with fingers dipped in priestly-blessed holy water that the believers ultimately give up their own personal energies to Enki through a form of hidden energetic tyranny. The original binding spell of baptism, *water going under the bondage of water*, occurs with Catholics when babies are christened, or when they are baptized into the church. Given the physiological fact that newborns contain more water in their bodies, then Christening ceremonies for newborns takes on a very sinister meaning indeed when we introduce the use of hydromancy into the equation. The ritualistic requirement of the dipping of fingers in the holy water in the font (apsu) of the church is a continual reinforcement of that original spellbinding that occurred at birth, or after taking on the faith, and is perpetuated through all the years they practice the ritual.

In most of the Protestant breakaway religions from Catholicism, full emersion baptism is more the rule and rarely used more than once unless someone wants to 'rededicate their life to Christ'. The act of crossing oneself is little different than Reiki practitioners tracing Reiki symbols in the air. The pattern in and of itself, combined with having holy water on the fingers, is an energy trap that keeps human energy bound and feeds that energy to their unknown God. When one does this with the holy water, it delivers sort of a double type of enspellment, the crossing is one type of programmed energy and the energetically charged holy water delivers a secondary punch to the program.

The tyrannical and energy-thieving nature of the Anunnaki gods is everywhere to be seen in the religions of the world if one has the eyes to see the truth of it. Enki and Ninhursag's hydromancy is in virtually every major religion in the West in one form or another, and every time some religious adherent bathes his hands and feet, or is baptized, they fall further under the energetic God-spell of the Anunnaki. Communion and other similar rituals serve to further steal personal power and energy, which keeps them from truly realizing true spiritual growth. It is a secret metaphysical, or magical war that we have been involved in and the adversary hasn't even had the courage to tell us that we are at war. We truly are at war for our very souls.

As much as Christians deny this observation, the ritual of communion is reminiscent of the cannibalistic practices utilized against humans since we were created as two-legged livestock to feed our creator gods. The former Catholic mandate of eating fish on Friday served as another form of binding magic through hydromancy to the followers of the religion, with the fish being associated with both water and the Anunnaki fish hybrids. The practice was nothing more than a variant form of hydromantic enspellment delivered through eating aquatic cuisine as a mandate of their religion.

8. Temples and Other Energetic Structures

When we look at the ancient temples around the world, aside from being used as meeting places and literal homes to the gods in the ancient past, the question arises as to just how the Anunnaki were able to effect such power over mankind for as long as they have. Certainly, it could be attributed to a certain amount of technological superiority in some cases, but the more powerful answer lies in Anunnaki capability to program energies of the elements and the cosmos to strengthen their hold over mankind. To verify this assertion the clues are found in ancient temple ruins in the Middle East and even in the Bible.

This cognizance of universal energies is prevalent in the Buddhist religion with the definition of a number of types of energies, *prana* and *buddha* energies just to name a couple. The Far East also recognizes this use of energies and is easily illustrated in the art of *Tai-Chi*. *Chi* or *qi* is the name of the energy being used in that art. There are numbers of defined energies in the Eastern philosophies, so the concept, or principle, of using and directing energies is not new—except to the western mind. Aside from using these energies for maintaining health and well-being, all energies can be used to program certain outcomes, influences and cast 'spells'.

There are plenty of ancient tablets and manuscripts telling the story of the Anunnaki giving instructions on the building of temples to their servant vassals on Earth. The Bible offers explicit instructions to the Children of Israel as to the construction of Solomon's temple. I leave it to the curious reader to read the three chapters in Ezekiel that describe its construction. Similar instructions are found left in ancient Sumerian and Assyrian tablets to kings of that time. To emphasize the fact that the Anunnaki knew about universal or cosmic energies and how to harness their power, one need only read the tale of Gudea, the king of Lagash, who was instructed in a dream to build a temple to be called E.Ninnu, or "The House of Fifty". From his dream, it is reported, he awoke with a lapis lazuli stone, etched with the instructions on how to build the temple, resting in his lap. Gudea was instructed to start building his temple on the "day of the new moon." The first question one might ask is why start the temple construction on the day of the new moon? Why not any other day?

Many people in agriculture know that you get stronger plants when the seeds are sown on the new moon. There is an energy portal that exists four days prior and four days after the new moon phase during which one can plant their seeds to get the most benefit from their crops. Taking into consideration that the "gods" wanted their temples started on a new moon, the only logical explanation that comes to mind about why they demanded their temples be started on the new moon is that the Anunnaki knew full well the energies associated with the moon. They had the knowledge of "portal" energies, if you will, associated with the different phases of the moon. They knew the ebb and flow of lunar energies to the planet. The new moon is a powerful phase for incoming energies. My assertion is that the Anunnaki gods knew full well about these energies and utilized them in their temple constructions in order to exercise a controlling tyranny over the minds of mankind. Just as a farmer knows that he will get a stronger yield by planting seeds on the new moon, the ancient gods (not just the Anunnaki) planted the 'seeds' of their temples on the new moon. These 'seeds' are what is commonly known as the cornerstone.

This may be a rather ludicrous idea at first glance, but I hope to prove otherwise before the chapter is complete. So, what more can I offer to bolster my assessment? In temple ruins in Sumeria and elsewhere, bricks or stones have been found with inscriptions on them. Some of these inscribed stones were dedication stones by kings who rebuilt the temples. There are, however, other inscribed stones associated with temple building. These stones and bricks are in fact the magical spells, the written programs, that bind the power brought in on the new moon, combined with the personal energies of the specific gods, into the completed temple complex to hold this energy within their temples. These stones or bricks served as the energetic focal containers, or catalysts for the *shem*. The generally accepted translation of the word *shem* means 'name'. Sitchin tried to retranslate the word to mean spaceship or rocket ship. I offer a different, more valid interpretation of the word *shem* as it is used in ancient magical temple traditions.

Every temple is designed to harness energy in one form or another. It doesn't matter if it is an ancient Hindu temple, an ancient Anunnaki temple, the ancient temples of Egypt, the Vatican, or a Masonic Temple. Every temple is an edifice that ultimately houses an energetic interior, sort of an energetic temple erected within a physical temple. Following certain prescriptions passed down to the priesthoods of old by their gods, every temple had a specific design structure created to house certain energies. A *shem* is a form of energy, what some in our world might call divinity, but is has absolutely nothing to do with the divine as we currently understand it. *Shem* as divinity is more along the lines of the specific energy signature of the particular god or goddess who was having the temple built in his or her name and for their purposes.

I propose that the ancient temples were started, and probably consecrated, on the new moon phases of the lunar orbit in order to harness that lunar energy for 'new growth'. In essence, by *planting* their cornerstones on the new moon, they sought the same larger harvest that farmers did, only that harvest was the energies of the followers of the particular cult involved who met in their temples. The Anunnaki wanted to control people, first with their priesthoods, then later through the aegis of vassal kings—who were usually subservient to the priestly class. The priesthoods, even through the establishment of the kingdom of Israel, were trained and well versed in the "secrets" of the temple. These "secrets" were the knowledge and workings of harnessing energy, at least the knowledge that their power was supported by the "blessing" of their god in the form of a stone, magically inscribed to store and hold the *shem* energy of each individual god. This gave both the kings and the priests an unnatural form of energetic control over their subjects and parishioners. The power that encoded these stones and bricks was the *shem*—the *focusing point* of the harnessed energies within each temple. No temple was built without its *shem* stone.

When one reads the *Temple Scroll* found in the caves at Qumran, just one text of the Dead Sea Scrolls, you wonder just why there are so many preclusions about the "do's" and "don'ts" of the temple passed down by Yahweh to his priests. Could it be that in order for the harnessed energy to remain pure and strong, and that Yahweh's *shem* remained uncorrupted, that the Jewish purity laws, insofar as the temple and its practices are concerned, are nothing more than insuring that Yahweh's *shem* could be not be weakened?

Modern Freemasonry claims its origin dates back to ancient Egypt or maybe even further. The instructions of the gods in reference to building their temples, in many cases, specifically called for the masons to be involved in the project and the placement of the *"shem"* stone in a certain specific place. Instructions given by Babylonian god Marduk in reference to the building of the temple of Esagil read in part:

> Let its brickwork be fashioned
> Its *Shem* shall be in the designated place.

By this passage it is revealed that the *shem* stone is placed in a "designated place". In the *Temple Scroll* Yahweh instructs his priests on every minute aspect of the temple; the type of wood, the number of stones, the number of doors, altar construction, everything. This type of micro-management by a god seems rather tedious and somehow below the interest of a god who only wishes to be worshipped. Why is it that all these minute instructions are given, unless the construction is designed as an energy generator of some kind? Just as we design different motors, generators and engines to fulfill specific tasks in our material world, I assert that the temple construction served as an energy generator, or enhancer, for the energy bound by the gods' *shems* to amplify the worship energies of their followers to feed to the gods. Ceremonies prescribed to be performed on certain days of the month were most likely associated with certain stellar or lunar energetic alignments in order to harvest more power for control over humans and feeding energies to the gods. This idea is given particular relevance when one realizes that the Jewish calendar is still based upon the lunar and solar cycles.

In reference to the Masonic connection to building the temples, one might argue the obvious and claim that only the masons knew how to construct buildings, but given the fact that the Masonic Rites have been secret for god knows how long, and given the fact that there have been allegations and books written about the freemasonic conspiracy for centuries, I think there is substantially more to the story than their just being simple bricklayers or stone carvers.

Most of the readers are familiar with the term "cornerstone" in reference to buildings. The *planting* of the cornerstone is usually accompanied by ritual and ceremony. David Ovason, in his book *The Secret Architecture of Our Nation's Capitol,* provides a wealth of information about the American Masonic forefathers and their planting cornerstones for certain buildings in Washington, D.C.. He provides a lot of relevant information about their consulting astrological charts and planting the cornerstones according to specific planetary and celestial alignments, a goodly percentage of them associated with the constellation Virgo, and most pointedly, an association with the star Sirius. Naturally, the Masons have attacked his presentation on their websites claiming that his work is all speculation, but all they offer to counter his material is simple denials of his claims. The potential Virgo connection is found with the consistent association with Ninhursag as the Virgin Mother Goddess wherever she held power, which will be discussed in more depth in later chapters.

That the Anunnaki gods were control-freak tyrants is of little doubt. We only have to look to their legacy of tyranny to accept that. So while they were away on their long orbit between our sun and Sirius B, how were they able to "keep watch" over their human "flock" as the hidden rulers? Let's see what the Bible has to say about that:

> *"And Yahweh said to him: I have heard*
> *thy prayer and thy supplications that thou hast*
> *made before me, and have sanctified this House*

that thou hast built, to place my Shem in it forever, so that my eyes and my heart shall be there in perpetuity."

In this passage, neither the interpretation of "name" nor "rocket ship" for the word *shem* make much sense, unless the Anunnaki Yahweh intended to use the temple in Jerusalem to park his "rocket ship' there "in perpetuity". But if Yahweh (aka Ea or Enki), as I assert, meant to strengthen his control over the people of Israel and all those they came in contact with, by use of that energy embedded in the *shem* stone in his temple, then things start to make sense. All one has to do is look at the hold that organized religion, no matter which faith, has on the minds of mankind, and how long such a hold has been there. This is especially curious when each religion contains so many obvious contradictions embedded within them—contradictions that theological scholars still haven't reconciled after centuries of research and incessant arguing and apologetics over interpretation.

I know there are many that will disagree with this proposal, particularly academics, so what further indicators are there about the power I claim is embedded in the temples? The best answers are found in the Sumerian and other Near Eastern texts where utterly razing a foreign god's temple to the ground was the norm. When the alleged temple of the Jews was destroyed, it was also razed to the ground.

We have to ask why wasn't it good enough to just kill the enemy priests and burn or partially destroy their temples? Why was it necessary to totally raze temples to the ground unless there was power in the temple structure itself? For information's sake, it wasn't just the Hebrews that utilized this practice of destroying temples and razing them to the ground. It was common practice all across the Middle East and Egypt, as noted with the temple of Akhenaton earlier. The reason for total, razing destruction of the temples of the Anunnaki gods, "leaving no stone unturned," was precisely because my assertions are correct. The ancient peoples knew about the power of the temple structures, or at least their gods did. They knew that they were places of tyrannical energetic control by both the gods and their priests. Just for the sake of pondering this thing further, why were the temples due such special attention? Why aren't other buildings as pointedly defined in the plan of the ancient gods' instructions for vanquishing an enemy? This is a strong point to ponder, in my thinking.

Have you ever heard the term "cast in stone"? Have you ever considered that what it actually means is a *spell*-cast in stone? When we view the interpretation of the word *shem* by the definition I offer, then this seemingly harmless saying takes on a darker meaning. Is there any historical evidence that there might be power in stones and that moving them also moves the power they contain with them? How about when the Caesars moved the obelisks out of Egypt to Rome, where they still stand today, one right in front of the Vatican, and what about that obelisk in our nation's capitol called the Washington Monument, which is a copy of an Egyptian obelisk? We have to wonder just where, or to what, these obelisks might be energetically linked to with manipulated and harnessed energies.

As another factor to consider, there have been measurements made at Stonehenge and other dolmen sites around the world that emit electromagnetic energies. Some researcher refer to these emanations as subtle energies. If these dolmen circles and other stone structures emit electromagnetic energy that we are yet to understand, then is it such a far reach to think that ancient temples were any less energetic in their designs?

Mainstream academia needs to expand its horizons beyond its first cognition materialist worldview and help support research into these other areas already being investigated by the heretics of the industry. Scholars like Anthony West, Robert Bauval, Carmen Boulter and the geologist Robert Schoch are at least on the hunt for answers, despite how far afield some of their conclusions may currently be. As I stated in chapter 1, there is no foul in being wrong, only in being negligent and refusing all possibilities when it comes to archaeological investigative research. Academia does humanity a greater disservice hiding behind their walls of denial than looking for expanded alternative solutions to what the academics think they already know.

If you look at the major temple ruins around the planet, and the awe inspiring churches that still survive, you should now have a greater understanding of why those temples present those feelings of awe. The energy was harnessed to enthrall and cow the worshippers with their cognitive sense of insignificance in the houses of their gods. They were built the way they were to intimidate and make the followers feel small before the energetically manipulated power of their god's house. The energy of the *shem* stones not only focused that energy of the power of the gods to intimidate their worshippers, but also to steal the power of their worshippers. No matter how you view this, it is a form of the most terrible and sublime tyranny imaginable.

The Persians were once well known for their magical practices. In fact, the word Magi originated in ancient Persia, and it is from the word Magi that we have the words magic and magician today. The Magi were most closely associated with Zoroastrianism, of which certain dogmatic traditions got grafted onto the Roman Catholic Church doctrine. How much truth is there to all those old "myths" of magic and alchemy attributed to them? How about Jewish mysticism and their magic book The Kabala, or the hidden rites and rituals of the 33° masons? Secrets, secrets, secrets! I believe I have revealed a key secret within this chapter. What do you think? And how upset do you think certain parties will be because they know what I am revealing *is true*?

Another term many people are familiar with is keystone. In masonry, the keystone is the last stone placed at the top of an arch that locks the arch in place. The arch itself started in construction projects in Mesopotamian brick work as early as 2000 BCE, if not before. Later, the Romans started using arches in many of their building projects. In ancient temple construction, the keystone was placed over the entryway of the temple and, like the shem stone, it was enspelled to serve a dual energetic purpose. When someone entered the temple, it would capture all of their personal energies and prevent them from upsetting the energetic 'purity' of the temple by carrying those energies into the temple precincts upon entering. Upon leaving, the keystone would take away the energy accumulated in the temple to keep it firmly in the temple precincts. There is no earthly public source that can substantiate this claim, but it is nonetheless true.

Once the temples were completed, certain rituals to harness energies were performed by the priests, or in the case of the Masons, the Grand Master. These rituals serve to erect an energetic temple within a temple and gives all their members certain energetic advantages over the rest of human society. It is due to these types of hidden energetic secrets that certain secret societies and priesthoods have held an energetic edge over the rest of humanity throughout the ages. It doesn't matter if you call it magic or energy manipulation, it all amounts to the same thing, one group of people holding a 'magical' energetic advantage over the uninformed, or profane. The tradition is ancient and can be tracked back to the most ancient gods who ruled this planet, the Orioners and their successors, the Anunnaki.

One other thing that needs to be considered where the Anunnaki particularly are concerned is the fact that they used mud bricks in the construction of their temples in ancient Mesopotamia. Contrary to mainstream archaeological conjecture, the Egyptian pyramids are much older and stonemasonry was not unknown to the Anunnaki, so we have to ask why they chose to use mud bricks in their temple construction over stone? The answer lies with their practices of hydromancy described in chapter 6. Mud bricks were made using water. Making bricks with programmed water gave their temples more energetic or magical strength than had they used stone. The aspect of energetic water manipulation is everywhere to be found with the Anunnaki. The reader would be wise to recognize this factor when doing their own research. One surviving example of Anunnaki water works in a stone temple can be found by Googling *'Osirion'*. If you view the pictures you see the inside workings of an Anunnaki temple dedicated to Osiris that to this day fills with the waters of the Nile, making a nice environment for the fish heads. If you check the pictures closely you will find not only two or three square abzu receptacles, but you will find that it is also surrounded by a moat.

This practice of using mud bricks was also utilized in the Indus Valley culture in the 3rd millennium BC, and as will be explained in Part 2, there is a very valid explanation for using mud bricks in that culture and who was ultimately behind using such building materials. In certain Sumerian tales, Enki also had a huge water works facility beneath his temple in the E-Abzu that was ultimately destroyed in a war that will be covered in the next volume of this set.

When one takes into consideration all that's been presented in this chapter about the Anunnaki, their control over our consciousness in their temple cultures of all kinds throughout the ages, it should be patently obvious that the Anunnaki were not nice people. Their human followers into earthly priesthoods and secret societies only makes the tyranny that much more dastardly. Because of these secrets, humanity as a whole has never stood a chance against the energetic tyranny wrought by the gods and their human initiates into these secrets. This is only part of the hidden tyranny as you will discover as this book progresses.

The practitioners of magic at one time used sleight of hand magic. In order to distract people from the truth of energetic magic, these priestly secrets of sleight of hand were made public so they could convince people that magic was all just parlor tricks and therefore had no basis in reality. Academia has accepted this idea hook, line and sinker, and to this day absolutely refutes the possibility of the existence of magic. It is through our collectively accepting the idea that parlor trick magic was all that magic amounted to, that we have since been propagandized into believing that any kind of real magic can't exist. This disbelief in magic, i.e. energetic manipulation, has served the real magicians very well over the centuries. They have the whole world convinced that magic is all smoke and mirrors, all the while they are doing their energetic magic behind closed doors in midnight rituals far away from the public eye. This deception has worked very well for them.

To understand energetic manipulation as a form of magic, we all have to move beyond tales of magic like Harry Potter, for it is in maintaining that intentionally programmed illusion about magic that we completely overlook what it actually is and how it has and continues to be utilized by the priestly adepts worldwide. Lower level Masons have no concept of what is happening behind the closed doors of their highest level adept brothers in the craft. As Albert Pike truthfully noted, the first three degrees of Masonry, the Blue Degrees are simply the outer portico. They are the levels of the benevolent front of Masonry to shield the darker elements of energetic abuse ever being known. The members of the Blue degrees are simply the duped front line defenders of the Masonic faith.

The Catholic and Brahmin priesthoods are equally as steeped in their own forms of Anunnaki magic, and their initiatory rites for their religious priestly candidates are simply mirrors of the Freemasonic traditions. Although Papal magic is more hidden, Hindu magic is right out in the open and found in the Atarva-veda. This is nothing but a compilation of charms and spells to use for its believers. The charms themselves have little real effect, as they are more of a superstitious salve for the believers of the variants of the Hindu faith. The spells to counter sorcerers and demons, on the other hand, are little different than the energetic black magic found in Simon's *Necronomicon*. Anyone remotely sensitive to energy can feel the ugly energies in both of these tomes.

9. The Power Vested in Me

As you've noticed, the priesthood was very important to the Anunnaki gods. The origin of the concept of a priesthood goes back tens of thousands of years to an Anunnaki ruler over Earth found on the Sumerian *King's List* who allegedly ruled here for 21,000 years called Enmedurana. That Anunnaki's name was eventually changed EN.ME.DUR.AN.KI spelled in ancient Sumerian, which translates to mean Lord of the Power that Bonds Heaven and Earth. I will simply spell his name Enmeduranki for convenience.

To further understand the translated name, in ancient Sumerian there is a lot of reference to ME (pronounced may). A *me* was a power designated strictly to the gods. It was part of their energetic powers insofar as the context of this book goes. Enmeduranki was the male Anunnaki who is reported to have proposed the idea for initiating priesthoods on this planet. This particular tale is found in an obscure Sumerian text translated by W.G. Lambert that he called *Enmeduranki and Related Matters*. The text can be looked up online for your reference.

One thing that has to be explained about both the Orioners and the Anunnaki is that they were patriarchal races with a severely male-oriented psyche as well as male-controlled societies. This is one reason that we have so much patriarchy in our first cognition mentality at this time, and also why it is so reinforced through our societies handed down through patriarchal religions. We inherited it from our creators. I bring up this male-superior orientation of both these races because it has a high relevance to this particular aspect of the discussion. In Sumerian titles, a male was generally designated with the term Lord, found in the Sumerian word EN, meaning Lord. Females were designed with the word NIN, meaning Lady. This is one primary way to prove that Enmeduranki was a male Anunnaki.

Although he was a male Anunnaki and he proposed the establishment of priesthoods on Earth, the most telling aspect of the translated text is found where Enmeduranki had to make a pledge to protect the secrets of the gods, but that this benediction was sanctioned and fashioned by Ninhursag. With the interplay of Ninhursag in this whole episode, it leaves me with the idea that she may well have proposed the idea of the priesthood, yet she let Enmeduranki float it for approval because her being female would have precluded its acceptance in a male dominated culture. The misogynistic Orioners never put *any* woman in a position of power.

To understand what the original concept of priesthood was does not relate to what we see as modern priestcraft on this planet today. In ancient times, the Orioner gods were very protective of their energetic knowledge and did everything they could to keep others from accessing that knowledge. The proposal by Enmeduranki to institute a priesthood for their Orioner creators had the singular goal in mind to insert the Anunnaki into Orioner-controlled precincts for the sake of gathering intel against them, to observe what they could of how the Orioners did their magic, and ultimately to try and find a weakness in their tyrannical rule. This initial concept of a priesthood had nothing to do with religion as we currently understand priesthoods, but was probably more closely associated with the early Sumerian priesthood as accountants and bookkeepers. This, then, explains the reasoning behind creating priesthoods at all. The concept was subsequently expanded on and altered into a religious context after the Anunnaki wrested ultimate control of this planet.

Ninhursag was a manipulator and magician beyond Enki's wildest personal imaginings, despite the fact that Enki glorified himself with the title of Lord of Magic. Through our 'external' research, we have learned what a truly filthy being Ninhursag was. She was probably the most adept Anunnaki energy manipulator that ever lived, and her energetic spell work was not only phenomenally complicated, but extremely dastardly and clever. Ninhursag plays a major role in all of these energetic manipulations, and in many cases, it was her work that is behind these designs more than either Enki or Enmeduranki. Make no mistake, though, Enmeduranki was quite the adept in his own right at energy manipulation, as were all the Anunnaki.

In *Gods, Demons and Symbols of Ancient Mesopotamia* by Jeremy Black and Anthony Green, the definition of *me* can be found in items of physical construction, worn, or as objects. It is through the power of the *me* that we discover the hidden energies found in priestly garments. Black and Green's definition further states that a *me* serves as a binding element on a plan, or design, and I re-emphasize that it can be 'worn'.

If we take the meaning of the name Enmeduranki as being the one in charge of the power of the bond between heaven and earth, then one manner in which this energetic bonding takes place for a priest is through his vestments. My assertion that the vestments of priests have power may seem a bit far fetched to most of you, but there is little doubt about the hold that religion has had on the consciousness of mankind operating in the first cognition, and also the presumed power of priesthoods over the ages. Since I've made the assertion that the vestments are a part of what serves as a priestly binding *me* that cloaks a priest in the 'power' of their gods, we have to look at whether there is any evidence that may support this contention. Let's see what *Unger's Bible Dictionary* has to say about priestly garb. Under the header "Priesthood, Hebrew" and the sub-header "Dress" come the following excerpts:

> "The **coat**, enveloping the whole body, woven in one piece without a seam and forming the principal article of dress, indicated spiritual integrity. . . while the four-cornered form of the cloth of which the coat was made was for a sign that the one wearing it belonged to the kingdom of God."

146

I have to make a couple of points here. The primary question is why the cloth had to be *seamless*? Anyone who has looked into the rituals of magic will readily understand that the reason is because there is to be no interruption of the energies flowing around and through the vestment and who wears it. There is additional understanding when we hear the term 'weaving a spell'. Given that the entire priesthood was created as an energetic control mechanism by the ancient gods, then the last part about the four-cornered cloth indicating that the wearer was of the kingdom of God should also be quite revealing if you think about it for a second. The four corners could represent the four cardinal points, or they could associate with the 4-lettered name of god, YHWH, also known in magical terms as the tetragrammaton, or the four corners could represent the four elements, or all of the above. The tetragrammaton can also be spelled as YHVH, JHVH or JHWH. It is the kingdom of the Anunnaki god Ea, (aka Yahweh) and the wearers of the vestments, who weave Yahweh's god spell of enchantment onto their followers, and are most certainly a part of his kingdom. *Unger's* provides this further explanation:

> "**Upper robe**. *Woven of blue yarn and in one piece, this article indicated entireness of spiritual integrity; blue pointing to the heavenly origin and character of the office. As every Israelite was to wear tassels of blue on the hem of his robe, to remind him of the law (Num. 15: 38,*

sq.), we may infer that in the fringe of pomegranates and little bells there also lay some reference to the word and testimony of God; and that the tinkling of the bells were to be heard by the high priest to remind him that his calling was to be the representative, guardian, and promulgator of God's commandments."

No doubt the blue signified the heavenly connection - to Nibiru - but I assert that it is equally illustrative of the connection with the water, over which Ea had such control, on both Earth and Nibiru. Once you understand who the Hebrew, Christian and Islamic 'God' really is, then these powers 'vested' in their leaders by the *mes* of their god have substantially more meaning when the dictionary talks about their roles as illustrated in the last sentence above. Is anyone starting to get a crawly feeling in their guts over this yet?

The ancient Egyptian priesthood had rituals they had to practice, which included taking baths twice a day and twice at night (another hydromancy practice). They also shaved their heads bald and had to be circumcised, along with avoiding certain foods at certain times for purification reasons. There were no animal products allowed to be worn in Egyptian temples so the priests had to always dress in linen. In the Isis cult the chief priests had to be Egyptian and had to have their heads and bodies shaved every three days, according to R.E. Witt in his book *Isis in the Ancient World*. The priests of Isis also had to wear linen.

They could not eat moist foods, but only dry ones, humidity to them was deemed impure.

Now, let's look to the Bible and see if there is anything contained there that suggests that there's power in the vestments. Look in the Old Testament in II Kings chapter 2 where the prophet Elijah is taken up to heaven. I will only quote a few relevant verses and leave it up to the reader to research the rest if they are so inclined.

> *"And it came to pass, when the Lord would take up Elijah into heaven by a whirlwind, that Elijah went with Elisha from Gilgal. . . and they two stood by Jordan. And Elijah **took his mantle, and wrapped it together, and smote the waters, and they were divided hither and thither**, so that they two went over on dry ground. . . And it came to pass, as they still went on, and talked, that, behold, there appeared a chariot of fire, and horses of fire, and parted them both asunder; and Elijah went up by a whirlwind into heaven. . . . He (Elisha) **took up also the mantle of Elijah that fell from him, and went back, and stood by the bank of Jordan; and he took the mantle of Elijah that fell from him, and smote the waters, and said, Where is the Lord God of Elijah? and when he also had smitten the waters, they parted hither and thither:** and Elisha went over."*

[Bold emphasis mine]

Here we see that it was in Elijah's mantle, or robe, that the power lay - if we can give any credence to this story. As the biblical passages clearly show, Elisha, after taking up Elijah's mantle (vestment), was able to perform the same feat of parting the waters of the Jordan as had Elijah. I ask the reader to also note that the power of the *me* contained in the mantle exhibited control over *water*. And let us not forget the magical feat of parting of the Red Sea by Moses, using his 'holy' staff to draw water from a stone or turn from a staff into a serpent and back again. What needs to be noted here is not the validity of the stories themselves, but the role that water plays in all of these tales. Isn't that curious? Or maybe this is all just another coincidence.

Given what I have revealed here, it puts a whole new light on the saying "By the power vested in me," doesn't it? Or maybe, it should be read, "By the power vested in *me*." That there is something special about the vestments and the donning of the vestments can be proven by the fact that the Catholic Church has a special room just for this purpose—the vestry. According to Witt, the priests of Isis also had a vestry in the dark chambers under her temples. Also note how Catholic priests kiss the stole that they hang about their neck before donning it. Is all this ritual for no reason, simply ritualistic exhibition designed to give the followers some sense of the supernatural, or are all these *mes* serving an entirely different and more sinister purpose?

Each of these elements stirs the energies, the power that is contained in the *me* of religious vestments. Black and Green also noted that a *me* could be symbolized by a throne. Isn't it odd that the Pope sits atop the *throne* of St. Peter until the purported return of Christ? Is it just another coincidence that the name Isis means throne. If I'm wrong on all of this, then why is it that the ancient Temples and churches always face east so as to gather the energies of the rising sun? It doesn't matter if they are oriented directly east, or whether they are oriented to sunrise points on the solstices, it still amounts to 'charging' the temple or church with solar energies in order to boost the power of the *shem*. This charging is no different than our using solar batteries in this day and age. The temples opening to the sunrise are used as an energetic form of technology about which only the priestly caste has been informed over the centuries and which modern science has yet to discover.

People, there is a very big, very sinister game afoot on this planet. The 'secrets of heaven', the magic of the Anunnaki and Orioner gods, if you will, are possessed by the priesthoods and the secret societies. It is through their use of programming spells and their knowledge of moving energies around that they keep themselves and their institutions in power. What the Jews from the Qumran community meant when they wrote about them being the 'sons of light' only means that they are privy to the truth about the Anunnaki magic, and the rest of us live in the darkness of ignorance. All I can say is that a vast number of people on this planet better wake up and realize just what is, and has been going on in their temples, churches, mosques and synagogues for thousands of years at the hands of the ancient gods.

By illustrating the use of high magic in the priesthoods—and yes Betsy, the Pope knows all about it—is it then any wonder why the Bible and the Quran place the emphasis on the Christian and Islamic religious adherents to stay away from magic? "Thou shalt not suffer a witch to live." The priesthoods have had the better of us for millennia, and you have the wonderful, tyrannical Anunnaki gods to thank for it all. The vestments are the bond that unites the water the temples and the *mes* straight back to the Anunnaki gods Enki and Ninhursag, and gives religion the strength it has over the minds of mankind.

Another aspect of control through *mes* is found when people wear the symbols of their religions in the form of jewelry. When a Christian wears a cross or the Christian fish symbol on a necklace, or a Jew wears a Star of David, or a Muslim wears the symbol of Islam, they are all carrying around the power of the *me* of their religion on their bodies, thereby further binding them to the magical tyranny. It matters not who manufactured the jewelry, the power of the *me* itself carries with the symbols and the meanings they possess. People are unwittingly and willingly subjecting themselves to this form of tyrannical magic by wearing these symbols, innocently believing that by wearing them they are doing nothing more than making statements of their faith. The exact same thing holds true with Pagans wearing their pentacles. All of these symbols of religious designation only serve to bind the servants more deeply with the harnessing energies of their respective belief system when they wear them.

Since I have established some of the workings of the *mes* in this chapter, I want to cover a few follow up points.

Throughout the ages priests have used any number of provisions provided by their gods as to how they comport themselves; dietary restrictions, the manner of dress and badges of office. Each of these things were a mandate by the gods to keep their temple energies clean and powerful on one hand, but they were also used to instill fear in their priests and followers if they violated any of their god's mandates or commandments.

I related in *Navigating into the Second Cognition* about certain entities feeding off fear energies. The Anunnaki and Orioners both fed on fear energies, and they used every manner of intimidation against their human creations to insure their food supply was uninterrupted. Even though the priests worked for the gods in their temples as accountants and the guardians of their secret magical practices, the priests were by no means remotely considered anywhere near equal partners to the gods in their enterprises. They have all merely been *servants of god* in a very literal sense They were just favored step-and-fetch-its to the gods. The priests were simply their lackeys, and they are all doing the same thing today. They are the 'shepherds' of the human flock created to insure the food supply of the gods stays uninterrupted. Many Protestants are liable to protest that their ministers or pastors are not the same kind of animals as those idolatrous Catholics, but the fact is they're teaching from the same book, no matter how it may be edited and retranslated, and they are feeding the same paradigm of fear and control that sprang from Enki's mind. They stand on their pulpits preaching the last days and the fear of the same God just as much as any Catholic, so they are all part and parcel of perpetuating the same system of tyranny begotten by the Anunnaki when they visited this planet near Year 0, when both Judaism and Christianity had their births.

Although most Protestant religions are not as steeped in ritual as the older faiths, they are all still cut from the same tyrannical piece of cloth because they all buy into the 'God is great we, are nothing mentality', and continually preach that message to their followers. It's like this, you have chocolate, raspberry, cherry, vanilla, rocky road and even Neapolitan ice creams, but when it comes right down to it, its all ice cream. This analogy can be applied to all Protestant breakaway sects from primary Catholicism. Regardless of the apparent dogmatic variances, they are all peddling the same hope and fear paradigm predicated on a book of highly questionable provenance. There is a saying that no Protestant reads his Bible except with Catholic eyes through Jewish spectacles. Unfortunately, this happens to be a truism.

The same principles can be applied to every religion on this planet. Regardless of the doctrinal label and the variances in presentation or ritual, it's all still the same mental tyranny. The fear and guilt preached by every preacher and priest on the planet all goes to feed the same entities at the end of the day, folks. It is the same ice cream that is called the Old Testament from which all three western religions get their flavoring. It is the Vedas from which this tyranny is sown through Hinduism, regardless of how philosophical and mystical the religion may appear on its face. The asceticism demanded of Catholic priests and monks is no different than the asceticism of the Brahmins in India or

Buddhist monks worldwide. The Anunnaki thrived on misery and sacrifice - often times human sacrifice. The purported death of Jesus on the cross was nothing more than a human sacrifice, all the doctrinal son of God malarkey aside.

We use terms in our everyday vocabulary, and most of the time the real meanings of those terms is lost. We have all heard about the trappings of power, for instance. Given what is revealed in this chapter about the power of the *me*s and how that power can be contained, or trapped, in objects and/or vestments, we have a new way to interpret the meaning of the term. Take the phrase 'the trappings of power' and see it for what it really means, energy trapped in clothing, rings, mitres, churches, synagogues, temples, idols, badges of office and mosques. The meaning of 'the power vested in me', would be better interpreted to be 'the power vested in my trappings of power'.

Another term we use without any true understanding is when we say or hear that 'it isn't written in stone'. Given what I revealed in the last chapter about the *shem* stones, this phrase takes on a different meaning. Granted, most people in Western societies think the reference applies to the Ten Commandments being written in stone, but even then, we have to wonder the hidden power behind those commandments written in stone, given the fact that we now know who the Jewish, Christian and Muslim god actually is.

These books are about advancing one's cognitive and perceptual awareness. What is being exposed in this book is just one more chapter in that unfolding of your higher consciousness that is currently bound in a realm of perceptual illusion. As hard as all this information may be to swallow, it is simply revealing more of the illusion that we have allowed ourselves to be controlled by through our own lack of critical investigation and just plain ignorance. As I have repeatedly told the readers throughout this series, nothing is as it appears.

10. Spells and Rituals - Energy Access

In order to further the reader's understanding about energy manipulation, I have to cover the aspect of rituals as a form of either harnessing or accessing pre-created energetic programs. Mrs. Beall discussed many of the ritual practices performed by Wiccans during her year of following those practices herself in the fifth book in this series *The Energy Experience.* I am going to clarify more things in regard to other ritual practices in this chapter.

I explained in the last chapter how the ancient gods manipulated energies in order to advance themselves from an egotistical drive to power as well as a manner to control their human slave creations. Mrs. Beall revealed that virtually all this ritualism was unnecessary where human practices of magic are concerned, that it only takes intent to program energies to be used in one form or another. There were, however, other reasons for establishing rituals by the ancient gods. One of the major reasons they established certain ritual practices was to insure than no one but their initiated priests could access the energy programs of their magic. Rituals were set up in many cases as protective safeguards to insure that the uninitiated couldn't access the harnessed energy programs the gods created for their own select uses.

Another aspect of creating complicated rituals, aside from the protective safeguards (not just safeguarding against men, but also against other gods); many rituals were composed strictly to sow fear in the practitioner. The rituals got very complex at times, with specific things that had to be performed in an exact manner and sequence before the program could be accessed. What follows are a couple of simple examples of ritual requirements from ancient Egypt from the *Demotic Magical Papyrus of London and Leiden* from the Roman period:

"You go to a dark chamber with its [face] open to the South or East in a clean place: you sprinkle it with clean sand brought from the great river; you take a clean bronze cup or a new vessel of pottery and put a lok-measure of water that has settled (?) or of pure water into the [cup] and a lok-measure of real oil pure . . ."

". . . . . you take a vine-shoot before it has ripened grapes, you take it with your left hand, you put it in your right hand - when it has grown seven digits (in length) you carry it [into your] house,

and you take the [fish] out of the oil, and you ties
it by its tail with a strip (?) of flax, you hang it up
to . . . of (?) the vine-wood . . . "

These are only two simple examples of how complex and demanding such rituals could be. I have seen other rituals where the person doing the magic is instructed to soak a dead falcon in milk and eventually drink the milk as part of the ritual. A number of other rituals were required to be performed during certain moon phases, required certain personal purification rituals or fasting, required a special kind of knife with the blood of a sacrificial animal still on the blade, abstinence from sexual contact for a month before the ritual, or any number of different requirements.

I am not in any kind of authoritative position to tell how many such rituals actually opened doors to specific energy programs and how many were simply superstitious nonsense sold as spells by priesthoods to make a fast buck from the gullible public. The ancient priesthoods were big on selling talismans and amulets for protection against certain spells from other people or the gods themselves. Even today, many Muslims buy protective ornaments with a single eye on them to protect them from the 'evil eye' of magic - and all of this superstition is based in fear, which also feeds the Anunnaki gods. This selling of talismans and amulets is absolutely no different than the Catholic church selling slivers of the 'one true cross' or finger bones of the saints. Priestcraft has always been in the business of making a profit through any means it can. Modern religions are no different, only their methods have changed to separate the gullible believers from their hard earned money.

Too many people over the ages fell into the trap of believing that it was certain rituals themselves that were magic. At best, the rituals that actually worked were more like keys that opened an energetic lock. There was no power in the ritual itself, but performing a ritual designed by some god or goddess who knew how to program energy, was a protective measure to accessing the programs they created. Performing the rituals they designed gave the ritual performer access to a pre-existing programmed energy already in place. Because their priests were initiated in order to cater to the desires of their gods, they were given greater access to certain programs that worked. These initiatic programs are why the Jewish, Catholic and Orthodox churches are so steeped in ritual. Their rituals were designed by the Anunnaki to keep people enslaved to their faiths through fear and awe. The flipside of failing in a ritual was the energetic backlash for anyone who missed a step in the ritualistic process, and let me assure you from firsthand experience, getting energetically bitch-slapped is no laughing matter, as discussed in *Navigating into the Second Cognition.*

The Catholic sprinkling of holy water on the crowd during masses increases the power of the *shem* stones in their cathedrals. It also reinforces the god-spell program through hydromancy over the followers as explained earlier. This same practice of ritual sprinkling of the masses in the temple was also practiced in the cult of Isis, where the holy water sprinkled purportedly came from the Nile river. Certain prayers, hymns or chants are also part of this energetic harnessing and spellbinding over the believers. Pick any of the religions you want and you will find some element of ritualistic behavior present in their services or religious practices. The Eastern religious practice of repeating mantras like Om Mani Padme Hum, or others also produces energy traps that steal the energies of the believers. Singing hymns also produce energy waves and evoke emotional discharge in every religion where hymns or chanting are found. Hymns are to be found everywhere from ancient Egypt, Sumeria and Mesopotamia, into India and virtually every religion worldwide. The gods loved to feed on the energies invoked through emotionally moving hymns and prayers, and the practice is alive and well in all religions to this day.

It doesn't matter whether it is lighting candles, praying, baptizing, saying the rosary, praying with prayer beads, or uttering mantras, bobbing back and forth before the Wailing Wall or kneeling and bowing on prayer rugs, all of these rituals are designed to harness the energies of the followers of the religious traditions or keep the priests in line - all so the gods can feed off of humanity's energies. Aside from being energy control traps, they are all traps for our consciousness. The only reason the gods have this power is because we willingly give it to them in our utter ignorance and fear of bad things happening in our lives or to our spirits after our death if we happen to piss off our individual gods. There is nothing any of these ancient gods did that we cannot do ourselves once we advance our cognitive awareness enough to see that the gods were no better than us, except in the scope of their energetic knowledge. From the standpoint of first cognition awareness, they were no better than we are, because they had absolutely no sense of spirit as that being related in these books. They were simply arrogant and tyrannical egotistical assholes that knew how to manipulate energies to take advantage of others, and they have been doing it to us since we were created.

To be utterly and completely honest, in order to remotely understand the nature of the Orioner and Anunnaki gods, we only have to look to the TV series *Stargate SG1.* The adversarial characters in the TV series are called the *goa'uld,* who are a snake-like creature that drills itself into is host carrier then takes over their mind and bodies. The point of correlation between the worst of the real ancient gods and the *Stargate* goa'ulds, is illustrated in their utter arrogance and their continual fighting amongst themselves for overall superiority. I don't know where the creators of the TV series tapped into their information, but it is so close to the truth of the nature of the ancient gods that it is spooky. The major difference between the goa'ulds as portrayed in the TV series and the real ancient gods is that they didn't have to rely strictly on technology to rule over others. There was much more energy work involved as elements of control than there was simply passing off technology as magic to ancient humans.

While we are on the subject of *Stargate SG1,* let me digress briefly and show another aspect that appeared later in the series, and that is with the alien race they encountered called the Ori. The Ori were a group of so-called *ascended* beings who fed off the energies of the people they could trick into believing their faith - not much different than the inorganics and the Orioners and Anunnaki did. The more believers they could attract, the more energy the Ori received in order to gain more power. This is exactly the framework of reality I am presenting to the reader without a science fiction context through which to deliver the message. I related in *Demystifying the Mystical* that we have been receiving many messages over the past few decades in an attempt to wake us up from our cognitive sleep. The *SG1* series has been but one more avenue of that information, provided one has the eyes to see what the message is about. In my own defense, I never watched the series when it was airing because I was too deep into my other research. It is only after I came to the realizations about the things I am sharing in this book and the ones that preceded it that I even bothered to watch the series. You can imagine my utter amazement at how close the series portrays the truth I am sharing when I finally watched it.

Another movie that captures the nature of the Anunnaki tyrants is L. Ron Hubbard's *Battlefield Earth*. L. Ron Hubbard is the creator of Scientology and was purportedly a member of the Ordo Templis Orientis, purported by some to have even been initiated into the order by Aliester Crowley himself, the creator of the organization. Although the movie got terrible reviews, I want to focus on the presentation and character of the alien overlords. All of them had long skulls, much like Akhenaton and those discovered in Peru and elsewhere around the world. The nature of the characters was total avarice and ego self-promotion based on deception with a primary focus on greed. In the story the antagonist aliens, called the Psychlos, were 9 feet tall, hairy and sociopaths. Other than being hairy, it sounds exactly like I have been portraying the Anunnaki. And no, I didn't use this movie as a foundation for this material. I had much of it written 20 years ago before the movie ever came out.

Further comparisons with the Anunnaki can be found in the history of the Psychlos, who were originally non-violent miners who were subjugated by another race and forced into war like activities. The Psychlos had ruled the multiple universes for 100,000 years (eerily similar to the Orioners). By the story in the *Enuma Elish* we know that the Anunnaki were a race of beings created by another race that I identify as the Orioners. The Anunnaki were originally used to mine minerals on this planet for their Orion overlords, not just gold - see the *Atrahasis* tablets. The Psychlos had controlled Earth for 1000 years in the story and were here to specifically mine gold. There are too many coincidental correlations here to simply ignore, even if the movie has been panned as possibly the worst film of all time. We can only wonder what information Hubbard may have been privy to when he created these characters for his book and why they correlate so closely to the Anunnaki.

Let's get back on track about all this ritual stuff. I told you how the ancient gods fed on fear energies. Setting up complex rituals and purity rites were part of manifesting that sense of fear in their priests. If you look at the sacrificial requirements of Judaism, imagine the potential fear or dread of finding out that the red heifer you just sacrificed to your god had a blemish on it. Imagine the fear of not finding such an unblemished animal if a certain ceremonial date was approaching. When we look at the fear programming that pervades our consciousness in the first cognition form of thinking, we are all feeding these self-proclaimed gods and inorganic beings our fear energies all the time. Their priests were in no way exempt from being part of the food supply to the gods. This is why all the believers of the faith are 'god-fearers', or *Hypsistarians.* If a priest screwed up a ritual sacrifice in the ancient world, including Jewish priests, they were killed, pure and simple, despite the lack of reporting such incidents in our religious dogmas.

The fear instilled by making a mistake in a ritual fed the gods as much as using their programmed energies to strike fear into their adversaries and their followers. No matter which side of the coin came up, they got fed. This is why all religions demand that people fear their gods. To keep fearing god, or fearing the devil, is only providing those entities with the energy they required to survive and grow more powerful. This is why every human that advanced into the second cognition taught to fear not. Fear feeds *all* their systems of control, not just the religious bailiwick.

It is presumed by academic scholars that the Sumerians created writing on this planet. What I am about to explain is the bedevilment of writing. First off, I have to explain that I am not preaching for illiteracy in presenting this information, I am sowing awareness. In our most ancient past, the gods used symbols and images to designate not only their properties, but also as a tool to sow fear. Our ancient ancestors were branded with the symbols of their owner gods, just like we brand cattle today. We were, after all, only their property and seen as less important than bovines, which were substantially more rare and precious to the gods than human cattle.

People wore the brands of their owner gods on their foreheads. In later eras, physical branding become unnecessary as our ancestors took to painting certain symbols on their foreheads with ash or ochre. The earliest Christians used to trace the cross on their foreheads before the symbolic practice we know as crossing today was fully initiated into the Catholic faith. The Jews used to paint the *tau* symbol on their foreheads, which was the symbol of the cross more representative of a + sign than the modern portrayal of the Christian cross, and this usage of the *tau* by the Jews substantially predates its adoption by the Roman Church. This symbol was placed in the center of the forehead, right over the third eye. Another simple coincidence?

Using these symbols was as a form of ritual performed out of fear of displeasing their gods, as well as being a property designators as to which god owned them. The same can be said about the ritual of using rosaries or prayer beads by Catholics, Hindus and Muslims. All of these trapping of power were designed to steal energy from the adherents to these varied religions. In modern Wicca, most all of the ritualistic requirements are hollow rituals. The believers are convinced that the rituals work, but even then, we find the presence of fear in not doing the rituals correctly. If anyone reading this book is a Wiccan, I ask you to consider the fear or anxiety you project about doing a ritual wrong, or making a circle that is a little bit out of whack.

Almost all religions contain the proscription against sin in some form or another. The concept of sin and being a sinner sows no little amount of fear and guilt. The Christian recognition, "For we have all sinned and come short of the glory of God," is a tacit admission from first cognition thinking that no matter what you do, you will never measure up to the standards you believe about your god. Given what I have revealed thus far in this book about the Anunnaki gods, I don't see where that is a standard to which any being would wish to aspire.

Although most Protestant Christians have shunned the doctrine of original sin, the concept was not new to the Catholic religion and actually traces back to the Sumerians. Paraphrasing an astute observation made by the noted Sumerian scholar, Samuel Noah Kramer from his book *The Sumerians,* the concept of original sin sprang from the idea that the rulers of the cosmos were evil and their creations were therefore evil because the evil transferred to them from their makers. Given all of what I have revealed about the Orioner overlords creating both the Anunnaki and the human race on this planet, we can only conclude that the only 'sin' humans ever committed was being manufactured by the same gods who created the Anunnaki. The Anunnaki were never able to wreak revenge on their creator overlords (which will be covered in Part 2), so as an older 'sibling' race to humans who had the same 'father', the older child is continually persecuting the younger child because they hated their daddy and couldn't get back at him themselves. I ask the reader to ponder just how psychotic that mindset is, and how utterly petty and depraved any being who might instill such ideas into the psyche of others is. Here we see the Anunnaki gods in all their splendent glory. Shall we now pray for their forgiveness?

I wrote in this series about how the world of the first cognition is a world of definitions and inventories, and how it is virtually impossible to describe second cognition awareness using first cognition tools for explanation. This is particularly true when it comes to the written word. Based on the development of alphabets and written language by the Anunnaki, we have all become slaves to the written word as our primary means of education. So let's look at the written word and see what we can discover.

One of the primary proclamations of authority in every religion is, *"It is written!"* To an illiterate population, the written word was a magical thing. Many esotericists over the ages have developed their own 'magical alphabets' to store their secret energetic magic. The written word in all its varied forms on this planet is just another form of magical alphabets used to harness our consciousness and keep us ever subservient to the authority of the written word. The illiterate person could not understand the magic of numbers or figures written on a piece of papyrus. To be able to do mathematical calculations only using some ink and paper went beyond their understanding. There was power in the written word! As the Gospel of John states in the first verse: "In the beginning was the Word and the Word was with God and the Word was God!" In this context, the Word is representative of who we know as Jesus. So let's break this all down from a different perspective.

In the first case, we don't know who this 'Jesus' was. In my previous writings I referred to sayings of Jesus because that is how the man is commonly known. But his name was never Jesus. He was born Immanuel - *that* was his name, so who is this character everyone worships called Jesus Christ? This may get kind of squirrelly in explaining, but I am going to give it my best shot.

I have already related the presence of the Anunnaki on this planet in and around Year 0 when this whole Jesus thing started. I have also presented a different explanation about what certain episodes in our past point to when viewed from a different perspective. From my previous works, if you accept what I have shared, we know that Immanuel was nothing like who the representation of this *Jesus* character marketed by Paul was. In light of that, we have to start questioning more deeply about all of this. I am going to have to take sort of a circuitous route to come back to the ultimate point I am trying to make here, but it will all dovetail before this chapter is finished.

In the constant ambitious egotistical conflicts of the ancient gods, one god would often kill or vanquish another god in order to steal their attributes and power. We have to look at this from an energetic standpoint, not simply a physical perspective. These ancient gods were very adept at manipulating and stealing energies. The religious practices just covered should illustrate that very clearly. When one god would kill another god, they would claim their energetic attributes, i.e. they would claim their individual power as their own. This is not too dissimilar a concept than that illustrated in the movie and TV series

Highlander where, when one immortal killed another, they would win their powers. The same theme was also seen in *The Chronicles of Riddick* where the motto of the Necromongers is, *"You keep what you kill"*. The major difference between reality and these cinematic adventures was that this process was not automatic when performed by the ancient gods. The claiming of attributes required specific energetic rituals or practices to attain the attributes of their dead foes.

Claiming attributes upon death of an adversary was a standard practice of the Orioners. The Anunnaki learned this practice from their creators, however the Anunnaki were more creative in that regard. In time, rather than kill an enemy and steal their attributes, the Anunnaki reveled in keeping their victims alive to witness how they corrupted or demonized their names for Anunnaki usage. In ancient Egyptian culture this practice of taking on the attributes of other gods is related through the hieroglyphic illustrations of gods and goddesses presented from previous pictorial renderings to having the traits or properties of other gods and goddesses mixed together in later pictorial renderings of the gods.

Let's take the goddess Isis as an example. In the oldest renderings of the goddess Isis, she is portrayed with a simple throne figure on her head, representing that she was queen. Through the centuries, this original portrayal of Isis took on different and more complex headdresses in later carvings and paintings. Eventually Isis wound up being represented with the horns of the goddess Hathor, wearing a bird-like headdress of the vulture, and with the lunar disc set between the horns of Hathor.

Modern scholars rely on the claim that it was more powerful priesthoods who gave these attributes to their gods and goddesses as they subsumed the weaker, dying cults into their own god or goddess's trappings. From the standpoint of strictly first cognition reckoning, this makes sense. However, this is not a correct assumption.

Just as in the *SG1* series, when one goa'uld killed another competitor goa'uld, they took all of their power and property, including their followers. The same thing happened with the ancient gods and goddesses on this planet. When one god killed another god, they got all their goodies, including their personal power through claiming their attributes, as well as claiming their herds of human cattle and other possessions. The attributes were not simply the pictorial representations of priesthoods subsuming weaker religions as modern scholars believe, it was an actual stealing of power that made the winning god or goddess more energetically powerful. This was standard practice between both the Orioners as well as the Anunnaki. Whenever one found a point of weakness in one of their adversaries, when they vanquished them in war, when they outright murdered them, or if they could manage it through deception, they always claimed their adversary's energetic attributes as a matter of form. This is how each particular god or goddess gained more energetic power.

The two most avaricious practitioners of claiming attributes since the Orioners were driven off the planet were the Anunnaki pair, Enki and Ninhursag. While they ruled in Egypt, Enki originally claimed the attributes of Osiris after usurping him and stealing his attributes after Osiris lost a war against the Anunnaki. Nin took on the role of Isis - both of whom were defeated in the same war about 5,000 years ago as we measure time. The story of this war will be more fully covered in Part 2 of this series. Once Enki and Nin established their superiority in Egypt as Osiris and Isis, then the systematic removal of the other gods and goddesses started in earnest. In time, Enki took on the role of the Egyptian god Amun, which is equally spelled Amon or Amen. Enki and Nin eventually ruled over all of Egypt with their alleged son Horus, claiming the attributes of all their adversaries every step of the way.

Having explained the real meaning about the claiming of attributes, whether the reader accepts the explanation or not, let's take another look at this whole Jesus thing again. When Christians and Jews close their prayers, the use the word Amen. We are told that the word simply means 'so be it'. But let's look at what closes the general Christian prayer - "We ask these things in Jesus' name, Amen." Let's use the word Amen as being nothing more than the variant spelling of the god Amun and revisit the prayer. "We ask these things in Jesus' name Amun." Kind of takes on a whole different meaning doesn't it without the pause at the comma?

Given what I just explained about the claiming of attributes of the ancient gods, how Enki was none other than Amun himself, who was first known as the Hidden God in Egypt and ultimately the invisible god in both Judaism and Christianity, then we can finally understand that the name Jesus is nothing but another name for Amun. So when people pray to this Jesus

172

character for their salvation or begging forgiveness, they are praying to Enki, who simply changed the name of his new energy harnessing program to Jesus. All the faith and defending and bloodshed that has gone on in the *name* of Jesus over the centuries has been for the sole dastardly purpose of feeding a vile Anunnaki tyrant all these energies created by fear and bloodshed in *His name* since this whole Christianity thing started.

Followers of the belief system are instructed to 'give it all up to god,' or 'let Jesus forgive your sins', or 'give yourself to Jesus,' never once having a clue what all of this cognitive dependency is about. They fight and kill to defend a tyrant masquerading as god. Because the Anunnaki thrived on bloodshed, warfare and human sacrifice, it doesn't take much logic to see Enki playing the role of Allah to the Muslims or Brahma to the Hindus. Hell, he gains power from the war and bloodshed from all religions who fight in his *name,* whatever that names happens to be within regional religions, the hydromancy through controlling their bodies and consciousness, and the energies stolen in all the churches, mosques, temples and synagogues worldwide. This guy and his sister have a virtual monopoly controlling the consciousness of the human cattle of this planet!

I kind of veered away from the primary topical matter of the chapter header, but there is none of the information presented herein that is unimportant or unnecessary. Learning about the adversaries of humanity is an important element in advancing our cognitive awareness. Knowing who they are, what they did throughout our most recent history, and what they continue to do to hold us all enspelled under their energetic control is the path to cognitive freedom.

To return to the point I was working to make with the written word. When the Anunnaki developed the written word on this planet, it was primarily designed as a form of holding spells in place in our 3D world. This is why using words is called *spelling*. Once established, they also saw the advantages for their priestly accountants to keep track of their personal inventories. In time, our species became totally dependent on the written word as the singular form of passing on knowledge as well as record keeping and keeping track of history. In essence, we all became *bound* to the word, and I use the word bound in the sense of magical, or programmed energy resulting in *spellbinding*.

We use this system of words and language as our primary means of defining our reality, yet words are totally insufficient to relate concepts from the second cognition. I have said repeatedly that our system of communication is wholly insufficient to relay these ideas, but that is the beauty of the Anunnaki magic. We all bought into the paradigm that words and language is all there is when it comes to communicating knowledge. We have been sold the magic of the written word as the primary method to describe our physical reality. The power of the word keeps us enchanted to this day. "Who told you that?" "Where is it written so I can look it up for myself?" Do these questions sound familiar? How about, "It is the written word of God," or "the Bible says", or "the Quran says"?

I brought up in *Demystifying the Mystical* how we are programmed by the very words we use. What I am sharing here is a deeper example of how the idea about *authority* in the words we read still holds our consciousness spellbound. The authority of the word started with the priests who were the only ones who knew how to write, who naturally had this knowledge passed down from their gods, and who created the written word to serve as a handicap to our cognitive advancement. To this day, we still look outside ourselves for the authoritative volumes that contain the words of our authorities. If it isn't *written*, it means nothing to many people on this planet. In academia one is expected to *cite their authorities* before a single idea can be given any kind of notice. We still give up our personal power to the presumed authority of the power of the word. What I am trying to impress on the reader is that word usage is not bad in and of itself, it is when we base our decisions on the *authority* of the written words of others while we operate in the first cognition that we do a disservice to our spirit selves.

I am going to give a prime example of this dependency on words. I could tell a truthful story, which I am in the process of doing, but every reader is going to demand an earthly source of written verification for anything I write. The only reason I am providing certain quotes from ancient sources is not because I require them, but because *you* do. Humanity has not yet developed the intuitive skills to know truth from the lies. Instead, we depend on the written word of some other authoritative source to validate anything anyone says. I have to provide these quoted sources because that is the only way first cognition people know how to operate when confronted with challenging ideas. They demand an alternative authoritative *expert* source, and the more the better. As it stands, I can't tell you the full story that needs to be told, because the reader demands hearing it from another source and, unfortunately, virtually all of those sources are tainted or nonexistent on this planet. People operating in the first cognition do not see this cognitive trap for what it is, so I have to walk between the raindrops and feed the reader certain pieces of information that they find acceptable *only* because I can cite other sources to back up my claims. This fact alone should illustrate how cognitively handicapped the entire human race is on this planet, and also why we can't advance as a species until we can get past this word-spell enough to trust our own intuitive instincts.

There is one final piece of this chapter on rituals I want to cover. Many of the rituals practiced by people in their religions are nothing more than hollow gestures these days. The practice in churches of walking the aisles with incense burning in censers had a specific practical purpose in the ancient world that had nothing to do with magic. The use of incense in Eastern religions has the same originating basis. I wanted to end this chapter on a lighter note, so I bring this to the reader's attention. The Anunnaki stank! They reeked with a nasty, dying, fish-out-of water smell that would gag a maggot. To compound this odor, the Anunnaki developed a special oil made from a certain breed of fish that they slathered all over the bodies to keep them moist when they were out of water. It was due to this being 'anointed' in fish oil that gave them the designation 'the shining ones', for in the sunlight, the Anunnaki shined when covered in all that oil, just as humans with suntan lotion seem to 'shine' when they are in the sun and covered with oil.

All one has to do to imagine this is to picture an 8-10 foot tall half-fish hybrid working in the hot, dry desert sun for half a day or longer to get a sense of their stench. The longer they were out of water for any length of time, the worse the stink got. The ancient priesthoods literally had to use incense to fumigate the temples during and after the presence of their fish-headed gods. Flooding the temples with incense was the only way the priests and congregation could keep themselves from puking from the smell in the presence of their gods. The modern practice by churches and temples of filling them with incense goes back to this simple ancient necessity. There is nothing magical about the practice, it is simply a hollow ritual whose true meaning has been lost in the corridors of time.

The word Christ comes from the Greek word Christós, which means anointed. If we take what I revealed about the name of Jesus simply being a name that Enki hid behind in order to create a new form of worship and cognitive tyranny disguised as religion, and couple Jesus (Amun) with Christ, then we finally have a total understanding of what the name Jesus Christ actually means - Enki/Jesus covered in oil. It is through this practice initiated by the Anunnaki that the entire ritual process of anointing originated in all its forms. I apologize for how this destroys Christian ego sensibilities, but it is what it is.

11. Screwing with Time

The books in this series are about advancing our personal cognitive awareness. They all address different aspects of how our perceptions control our consciousness, and in that regard, this volume is no different despite the difference in the subject matter. Each of the books in this series take on different aspects of our first cognition reality and put them under the microscope for closer cognitive scrutiny. In discussing the visitation of the Anunnaki near Year 0, we have to analyze just what was done to our perceptions as a result of that visitation.

Everything that has been presented so far in this volume was an exposé of things that actually happened during that time period, but that have been effectively erased from our cultural histories, and therefore our perceptual awareness. One of the most insidious of the occurrences around the Year 0 takeover of this planet by the Anunnaki is how our perception of time was screwed with. We have our perception of time now predicated on a seemingly singular event - the alleged birth of Jesus. Our calendar in the West, under Christian influence, has been designated until recent times as BC (before Christ) and AD (Anno Domini - the year of our Lord, or for some After Death). More recently we have seen this terminology change in the realm of non-Christian academics and scholars who altered BC and AD to BCE (Before Common Era) and CE (Common Era), much to the dismay and scorn of all Christians.

Here is the problem with our perception of time. It doesn't matter which acronyms you use, BC and AD, or BCE and CE, both systems of measure are still wrapped around that seminal event of Jesus' alleged birth, or the alteration of our system of measuring time starting at Year 0. We have all accepted the perceptual idea that time somehow stopped at that moment and that the clock of history reset itself due to some kind of divine entity being born. As first cognition human beings, we simply accept this resetting of time without question. We are left with the BC or BCE concept that the time before Year 0 was some kind of countdown before everything stopped, waiting on Jesus to be born. In our conscious awareness over the past 2,000 years, we have all come to accept this interruption of time, regardless of whether we leave Jesus' birth in the equation or not.

Time never stopped. But we have all accepted this resetting of our planetary historical measurement based on this seminal event. It has become part of our system of cognitive acceptance, at least in Christian societies. But here is something to consider. The Jews never reset their calendar at Year 0. Their calendar starts at 3760 BC and, for themselves, they have never changed that form of accounting time amongst themselves. We have to ask what it is they know that the rest of us don't?

This chapter is going to raise the alarms and accusations of anti-Semitism because I am putting a certain group of people under scrutiny that bear closer investigation under the subject matter of this book. I am not a racist in any degree, but those who don't want these matters investigated too closely will scream like stuck pigs over what I am about to discuss, and they are not all Jews.

I wrote in previous volumes in this series about how Alexander the Great developed the idea of syncretizing all the religions in the lands he conquered into a singular homogenous whole. I have taken Alexander's program forward and shown how Roman Catholicism, with its assimilation and stealing from Pagan cults was a mere continuance of that program, but now we have to raise some hard questions and put certain things under scrutiny in order to find answers to things that most people have either overlooked or refuse to consider.

All of our academic scholars have been tiptoeing around the questions I am about to raise because they fear the backlash of religious believers in the West. By tiptoeing around these issues, the truth is never discussed openly, if at all. Everyone is too worried about goring someone's religion ox, so these matters are quietly swept under the rug and ignored. This is one reason that academia is basically cowardly in the face of public opinion, they fear the repercussions of revealing the truth. It is time we collectively find the courage as a species to face these truths and admit what the truth is showing us and damned be the petty egos who can't rise above their religious dependency syndrome because the truth shatters their illusion of reality.

In the West, since the advent of Christianity, every bit of research up until recently was predicated on the belief that the Bible was actual history. All of the early archaeologists in Egypt were drooling at the mouth hoping to find the enigmatic Pharaoh that kept the Israelites enslaved for 400 years (whose identity the Old Testament conveniently fails to mention). Every archaeological dig was compared to the Bible as the historical authority through which everyone should measure and gauge the history of the world, and even today we have a branch of the science stupidly called Biblical Archaeology. Much of archaeology was originally formulated as a scientific way to prove the accuracy of the Bible and the history of the Hebrew people. Even our authorities in translating ancient Middle Eastern texts, like James Pritchard, titled his work *Ancient Near Eastern Texts **Relating to the Old Testament.*** Unfortunately, with the advancement of our civilization over the past couple of hundred years, we find less to support the alleged biblical timetable of events and the whole history of the Old Testament has come under critical scrutiny in the past few decades.

For close to 2,000 years people have believed the Bible as the word of God and that the Jews were his chosen people. To this day, anyone who wants to challenge the validity of the Jewish history is called anti-Semitic, simply for challenging the book as history. I am directly challenging the book as history, and I am going to give an alternative perspective of its origins.

Taking Alexander's mandate as continuing after his death, particularly considering that three of his generals divided up Alexander's domain and ruled all the areas around the Mediterranean, including Israel, up until Rome advanced into and conquered those territories, I am going to paint a different picture. I assert that the religious homogenization process was still ongoing at the time Nibiru arrived back in our solar system near Year 0. I will reveal in the next volume of this series how Enki and Ninhursag remained on Earth after Nibiru orbited into our solar system near 3800 BC. This fact alone places Enki actively working on his plan for a total religious takeover when Nibiru returned near Year 0. In light of this assertion, we have to view Alexander's mandate in a different light.

In 332 BC, Alexander went to the Oracle of Ammon at the oasis of Siwa in Libya. After this meeting with the Oracle, Alexander presumed himself to be a son of Ammon (Amun). No one knows for sure what words may have been exchanged at that meeting because we have no record of them, but I will strongly suggest that the mandate to start syncretizing the religions of the conquered territories was mandated by Enki, either directly or through the voice of his Oracle. We may be able to discount this idea until we look at the actions of Ptolemy I, the ruler that took over in Egypt after Alexander's death.

The Library of Alexandria was constructed by Ptolemy I Soter in the 3rd century BC. The library was put in charge of gathering all the world's knowledge. It is reported that Mark Antony allegedly gave Cleopatra 200,000 scrolls from the Library of Pergamum as a wedding gift, although some scholars believe this to be a myth. Given the circumstances of the time, with Enki ramrodding the show, I seriously doubt it is myth. The collection of written works of the conquered Alexandrian world continued in earnest over the next few centuries, with a particular focus on getting *original* works. If the Ptolemies couldn't buy the books, they were known to have boarded ships that came into the Alexandrian harbor and just plain confiscated them. Some estimate that there were over 400,000 scrolls housed in the main library, and an unknown amount of scrolls at a secondary library site adjoining the Serapeum (the temple of Serapis) located elsewhere in the city.

The Ptolemies specifically sought original works, and when they found them, the library held the originals while scribes made copies and returned the copies to the owners if they happened to be ship's captains, etc. If you stop and think about this a moment, can you think of a better way to start corrupting what history we had at our disposal at the time than taking original manuscripts and copying them with bullshit history to take its place? This is exactly what I assert happened. Enki had already decided that his homogenized religion would be headed by the Jews and the foundational idea for the Bible was already in his twisted mind. All of history before that time had to be rewritten or expunged in order to correlate it with his last and most famous brag book, the Bible. The histories and timelines for the Egyptian pharaohs had to be made to conform and coincide with the biblical timetable. The reigns of the Babylonian and Assyrian kings had to cross-foot with the biblical timetable as well as other events around the region such as wars with the Hittites and others. Once all this correlating was complete to where the Bible was to be the sole historical source authority for the next 2,000 years, the real history of the Anunnaki in our past had to be expunged, and then we have the mysterious and very convenient burning of the Alexandrian Library which I covered earlier. With the arrival of the Anunnaki 'hosts of heaven' preceding Year 0, can you honestly think that such a plan could not be put in place, or that it couldn't be enforced by these godly overlords?

During that particular time frame and for at least a couple centuries afterwards, we find the group we know as the Essenes living in the community bordering the Dead Sea called Qumran. This group is responsible for the Dead Sea Scrolls (DSS) - if not responsible for composing them, they were at least the gathering point of the many texts that formulated the new work called the Old Testament. The Essenes, according to the Jewish Historian Flavius Josephus, were in many cities in great numbers, so it is not just some local gathering if Jewish malcontents hiding in the desert bordering the Dead Sea as so many people believe.

Over the next couple of centuries, we also encounter the Gnostic sects operating primarily in Egypt, and they are the source of the material found in The Nag Hammadi Library. On the other hand, we have the followers of Paul with his evangelical tour working to shape the doctrine of Christianity to take control in Rome, whose doctrine very closely mirrors the cult of Isis, which will be covered in later chapters.

Where modern scholarship fails is in not tying all these groups together operating to achieve one singular goal - creating that homogenized religion that would ensnare the minds of all its followers under one religious umbrella. When we view Enki and his sister Ninhursag spearheading all this religious activity and the systematic expunging of ancient history, things really started to get interesting. I have already mentioned the competition for a patriarchal system of worship pushed by Enki, and the competitive system of goddess worship of Isis pushed by Ninhursag. In the end, the two systems were harmonized to a great degree and we find ourselves worshipping god as his own son and his sister-wife as the mother goddess of the Roman Church.

We know that there were many authors to both the DSS and the Gnostic texts. It is also known that there was a lot of sharing of these texts across wide regions of the Greek, then Roman world as these varied groups worked to come up with some solidified and homogenized doctrine. We are led to believe, by DSS scholars, that the texts of the Essenes at Qumran all originated from the hoary history of the Bible. We are all expected to believe that Judaism as we know it was pre-existent at the time the Essenes started their community at Qumran. I am here to contest that theory, and I think I am the only one who to contest it on the grounds elucidated below.

Other than a few random snippets of what eventually became part of the Bible, there is absolutely *no* ancient copy of the book that survives before the Dead Sea Scrolls. Oh, we have legends about how 70 Jewish scholars purportedly translated the Hebrew Old Testament into Greek because the Jews living in Egypt under the rule of Ptolemy II (309-246 BCE) could not read

Hebrew. This legendary tome is referred to as the Septuagint. It is also known that aside from this purported translation by the 70, that there were 7 or more other Greek translations in circulation that have since been 'lost' (how coincidental).

There is *no* extant copy of the alleged Septuagint that exists to this day any more than there is a single ancient copy of the alleged Old Testament. All we find are substantially later translations. I direct the reader to look up Septuagint on Wikipedia for a breakdown of the oldest texts that are claimed to be the Septuagint and you will see none of them are actually dated earlier than the 2nd-4th centuries AD. Only fragments survive, conveniently found in greater quantity in the Dead Sea Scrolls than anywhere else. The oldest surviving vellum copy in full is from about 100 AD, and there are scholars that claim that the Jews continued to edit the text for centuries afterwards. There is no textual evidence of the Septuagint existing before the first few centuries of the Common Era, which tells this author that the legend of its origins is simply another lie in this vast network of lies about the origin of Western religions. The composition of the book is even referred to simply as a legend, with no definitive proof to show the legend is remotely true. In *An Introduction to the Old Testament*, H. B. Swete, a British scholar stated:

"At some time between the age of the LXX and that of Aquila (ca. 125 A.D.) a thorough revision of the Hebrew Bible must have taken place, probably under official direction; and the evidence seems to point to the Rabbinical school

which had its center in Jamnia in the years that followed the fall of Jerusalem as the source from which this revision proceeded. "

The LXX is another way to refer to the Septuagint, which means Seventy. Given the framework I am about to present, I ask the reader to remember Swete's observation about the Old Testament being rewritten *"probably under official direction."*

The oldest surviving copy of what could be considered the Old Testament *is* the Dead Sea Scrolls, and their chronology has been hotly debated since their discovery. The DSS scholars all want us to believe that these scrolls are much more ancient than they actually are, for if they are in fact products of the 2nd century BCE to 3rd centuries CE, much like the Gnostic texts, which I contend, it means that Judaism and Christianity were developed at the same time along parallel lines to achieve a singular goal, and that all the accepted alleged ancient history of the biblical Hebrews goes right out the window. Not only that, by removing the alleged antiquity and historical belief in the veracity of the foundational documents of all three major western religions (the Old Testament), all three religions have to die an ignoble death because they are all founded upon an intentionally perpetrated fiction.

As stated previously, unearthing our history is like solving a cold case. Solving the riddle of organized religion which has ruled our perceptions for the last 2,000 years is a very cold case. We can never solve any cold case if we approach it with predetermined expectations or conclusions. In all cases regarding research into the Dead Sea Scrolls, all the scholars approach the scrolls with a predetermined conclusion - i.e. that the Hebrew history is real and that Judaism already existed for millennia before Year 0. They have all been trying to make explanations of how the Essene documents fit into this already accepted perceptual framework. In working to solve this riddle, I had to completely wipe the slate clean of all such preconceived notions and try to find the real picture hidden behind all the standards of misinterpretation. One of the most valuable documents I read in regard to solving this enigma was Robert Eisenman's *James the Brother of Jesus: The Key to Unlocking the Secrets of Early Christianity and the Dead Sea Scrolls.* This is a massive volume and not for the timid reader.

I don't agree with all of Eisenman's conclusions for, like all scholars in the Dead Sea Scrolls discussion, and being Jewish himself, his study is still founded on the belief of pre-existing Judaism during the time the Essenes were involved in compiling the scrolls. Eisenman goes to great lengths to show that there was serious opposition between Paul and his doctrine, and James, the brother of Jesus who was allegedly the head of the early Christian church in Jerusalem. Although the New Testament apologists over the years have worked tirelessly to show there was no friction between these two individuals, Eisenman makes very cogent arguments that there were very serious doctrinal arguments between them. Where Eisenman failed in getting to the absolute root of the conflict between these two individuals is in believing that 1.) James was a Christian and, 2.) that Judaism was already in existence at the time of their disputes, about 20-25 years after the crucifixion of Immanuel, James' brother.

Let's take the framework I have established about the Anunnaki hands orchestrating all this religious organization behind the scenes, that Enki was the catalyst behind pushing the finishing up of the religious syncretizing mission started by Alexander. Enki knew that in order for this new belief system to grow it had to have a history. From Old Testament accountings we are all familiar with the Chosen People myth of the Jews. But let's put this Chosen People thing in a different light. Let's assume that the Jews were *chosen* to spearhead the mission of writing the false history of the Jews as the basis for this new religion. The Jews may or may not have been chosen by their god in the ancient past like the biblical legend states, but the god Enki chose them to write both the foundational documents for Judaism as well as Christianity.

We have to wonder why, out of all the competing parties working on Alexander's project of religious syncretism, that only one group came out on top? And we also have to ask why a group that has been a minority of the population throughout our history got chosen for that task? That group is the Jews themselves. Let's look at all the angles and see what the reader comes up with for a conclusion, erasing everything but the evidence at hand. There is an open conflict between James and Paul, both Jewish and both with a specific and different agenda. The Pauline letters criticize Peter and James for the adherence to Jewish laws, while Paul is pounding the pulpit with all the Gentiles selling his product of salvation through grace and belief in James' brother, whose name has now been changed to Jesus and who has doctrinally become the son of God.

The conflict between these parties is predicated on each of them striving to set up two separate systems of doctrinal belief. James was working to establish Judaism and Paul was working to establish its Gentile competitor called Christianity. Both of these Jewish men were working for Enki in shaping the dogma that ultimately became the Bible. Regardless of the Christian apologists over the centuries trying to cover up this apparent conflict that is evident in some of the Pauline letters in the New Testament, no one has viewed this information without the tainted belief that Judaism was already in existence at that time. It wasn't, and there is *absolutely no physical evidence* whatsoever to prove that it was. The profound lack of evidence is enough to prove that Judaism didn't exist at the time the DSS were written.

Where the Bible and the alleged Jewish history are concerned, we are left with closed loop logic. The Bible proponents always point to the Jewish historian Josephus as the validating source for the Jewish history written in the Old Testament. Josephus's histories validate the Old Testament history of the Jews. One points to the other and there is no independent outside source that can historically support either one of them.

By his own admission in his books, Josephus was an Essene for a period of time, and he had also been a Jewish priest of some nature. If the group we know as the Essenes was in fact the Old Testament compilers, we have to notice just how convenient it is that one of their own ranks is the *only* source that can be turned to in order to validate the alleged Old Testament history. Do you see the convenient circular logic of all of this? Where is the external corroborating evidence outside these Jewish sources? *There are absolutely none!*

Another question that needs to be raised is that if the Old Testament was as old and hoary, and especially sacred to the Jews that their God proscribed them from altering 'one jot or tittle' of the text, then why is this religious sect, the Essenes, basically putting doctrinal crib notes on the margins of some of these most sacred of books? If the Old Testament was as old and as holy as we are led to believe, then what the Essenes were doing was a sacrilege! But if we view the Dead Sea documents as what they actually were, i.e. a rough draft, a work in progress, whose doctrinal issues were still being hammered out, then this issue of defacing a holy book reveals itself for what it is - one of the greatest frauds ever foisted on mankind in the last 2,000 years of our history.

So, on one hand we have James, who Eisenman I think correctly interprets, as the high priest of the burgeoning new religion, involved in a doctrinal battle with Paul who is carrying his brand of religion to the Gentiles, turning James' brother Jesus into God incarnate. Is there any wonder why they had this fight? Where Eisenman and others fail is in the presumption of pre-existent Judaism at the time the Dead Sea Scrolls were being compiled. There is absolutely *no* evidence to support this belief.

Now, let's go back to how our perception of time has been utterly screwed with. On the one hand, all history stops and starts again at Year 0, predicated on these two religions allegedly fulfilling each other. The Jews got to keep Judaism and the favor of their God, and the Gentiles were sold the rest of the goods - all orchestrated by the Jews themselves. It was not good enough to have a religion founded on a fictional history written by the Jews, the end result was for everybody else to worship a Jew as God!

There is nothing racist in these observations, but I can see no other way to view the circumstances in which we find ourselves after the last 2,000 years of tampered history. We can accept the first cognition song and dance about our currently perceived history, or we can pull off the blinders and see how we have all been duped by this cognitive charade. I don't lay blame for this at the feet of the Jews, even if they were the primary agents. I lay responsibility solely at the feet of the Anunnaki Enki and his sister, who had a larger role to play in this scenario than has yet been revealed.

Humans may be crafty and devious, but no human tribe can think on the scale of what this book is revealing. No singular group of humans on its own could formulate such a devious and dastardly plan that also had the power, patience and longevity to enforce its coming into being. We are talking about half a millennium or more of consistent focused attention on this goal. Human lives are too short to continue with a plan of such length and magnitude and see it come to fruition. It took an outside force with great intelligence coupled with great power and influence to pull off the biggest scam ever perpetrated in human history. What humans on this planet fail to realize is that our perception is limited in great part by our limited life spans. It is nigh onto impossible for us to conceive the idea that other beings elsewhere in the universe can live tens or hundreds of thousands of years. It is this kind of ancient intelligence that the Orioners and the Anunnaki bring to our perceptual table. It took a large force of entities to remotely bring about this corruption of our history and the complete disruption of our reckoning of time to fruition. I don't care how dastardly anyone may think that one group of humans or another can be to ever harness that kind of power, it is just not possible for Earth humans to think on this scale to achieve the ends I have revealed in this book. Not on a global scale, and it was global. What was done in India is even harder to imagine than what was done in the West, and that will be discussed in depth in the next volume.

We have to acknowledge that we have all been taken for a ride that none of us asked for. We are serving the designs of alien intelligence with an ego bigger than all humanity. We are talking about an ego who claims to be God Almighty, who is accurately portrayed in the Old Testament stories as being totally neurotic, bloodthirsty, who hates women and who plays favorites. Biblical scholars over the ages have worked tirelessly to reconcile this vindictive hateful God of the Old Testament with the New Testament ideas about love and forgiveness taught by Immanuel. Given what this series of books is revealing, it should be patently obvious that there can be no reconciliation between the arrogant and bloodthirsty Anunnaki, Enki, and the spiritually aware second cognition person named Immanuel.

For all intents and purposes, the Bible is nothing more than another one of Enki's personal brag books, like most of the Sumerian tablets or those of any other region where he played the role of God Almighty. All the hateful deeds recorded in the Old Testament performed by that vengeful God are Enki's tales of victory over any and all who opposed him in the past. "My way or the highway!" thus sayeth the Lord God Enki. When we can see Enki as the perpetrator, then we understand all the hate and vindictiveness of the Old Testament God. Leaving out the truth about Enki and his nature, we are only left with confusion about what sort of real God could remotely be like that. Putting Enki squarely on the biblical throne of God, then all this centuries long confusion and debate evaporates and a cohesive picture of the whole fraudulent song and dance of Western religion comes into view.

In light of this new perceptual perspective, then maybe we should look more closely at what I wrote earlier in this volume comparing the Anunnaki to the goa'uld of *Stargate SG1*. It's one thing for me to make that comparison and share my observations, but for verification we simply have to look to the God of the Old Testament for Enki's testimony to the accuracy of my observations. Look at all the plagues, murders, thievery, rape, slavery, warfare and destruction mandated by the alleged Hebrew God. If the reader is familiar with the *SG1* series, the correlation can't be denied. Granted, the show's writers may well have used the Hebrew god as their model, but hey, if the image fits. . . . The advancement of the Ori in the latter years of the series, the wars of destruction to kill any who refused to join the faith is exemplified in both Christian crusades and the expansion of Islam, not to mention similar wars in Hinduism. I ask the reader, wherein lies any difference?

Looking into the ancient Mesopotamian tales of their gods shows the state of incessant wars and murder between themselves, just as with the *Stargate* goa'uld. When we look at the Hindu Vedic texts about the wars of their gods, where can we find any difference? How much of presumed human history was developed or directed strictly by human hands? These are questions I ask the reader to ponder upon as this journey progresses. We have to admit that in the long run, the Jewish people suffered mightily at the hands of the Christian religion they helped develop over the centuries. Even if they were not coerced into playing Enki's game and were simply his human partners, the cost to their descendants has exacted a high payment, but viewed in light of how the Anunnaki fed off of the energies of fear and misery as they did, the Jews and their suffering were simply just another source of energetic food for Enki and Ninhursag. In that light, the Jews are no different than the rest of humanity on this planet. We have all simply been lunch for these fish-headed fucks.

Since our time was reset at Year 0, we have no genuine concept to measure anything where our reckoning of time is related. All of our historical reckoning before Year 0 has to come into question, for we don't know anything about how much time may have been expunged from or added to our history to perpetrate this massive fraud on our consciousness. Our archaeologists have used this corrupt timetable to reach all of their conclusions where it comes to archaeological dating. Can any of it be relied on at this juncture? How many of our archaeological assumptions are in error? How many centuries were there actually between BCE and CE when compared to the Year 0 reset? Were some of the centuries we consider BCE actually CE centuries, or vice versa? We have no way of knowing once our time clock was reset at Year 0. We are left taking the word of propagandists that any of the events happened when we were told they did. Is the reader starting to see the magnitude of this perceptual fraud on our conscious awareness?

I recently came across an article that stated that some scholars have raised the specter of a possible missing two hundred years between 2800-2600 BCE. This is not the same as the Phantom Time Hypothesis put forth by German historian Heribert Illig, and I am not giving credence to that idea at all, but if there is in fact some scholarly recognition that certain points in our presumed history do not cross-foot, then what I am about to share may account for any such enigmatic non-correlative centuries.

We all make the perceptual assumption that the alteration in counting time and it's restart at Year 0 is just a single-year rollover of our calendar. In all honesty, this is not an unfair assumption, for we have had no reason previously to view it in a different light or challenge it. But for the sake of theoretical argument, if such a 200 year gap, or non-correlation does in fact exist, then I ask those scholars who are noting this enigmatic shift in time to consider this possibility. What if all the events in the Old Testament that we feel seem to cross-foot with historical events from other lands, didn't really cross-foot from a historical standpoint? I mean, what if the Jewish Babylonian captivity didn't occur when we think it did, or that the invasions of the Egyptians and the Assyrians recorded in the Old Testament did not cross-foot with biblical time reckoning, that they didn't happen when we think they did? What if, in order to makes these events dovetail into the fictional historical timeframe of the Old Testament, that time had to be 'juggled' in order to make these pieces appear to fit together into the biblical chronology, when in actuality, they never did? If such an idea were remotely true, then we may have finally arrived at why our time was reset at Year 0, and if there is in fact a 200 year enigma in our ancient historical past, resetting the calendar to artificially synchronize historical events so they appeared to coincide with fictional biblical reckoning of time could take on a darker meaning. Such tampering with the timeline of our history would not only serve to confuse our sensibility of time, but would also give the false impression of the alleged accuracy of the Old Testament.

Every archaeological dig unearthed in the Near East and Egypt is predicated on calculating its historical context based on the fictional history in the Bible, for the most part. All of our calculations about the sequence of history are gauged by that book and have been since archaeology started as a treasure hunt cum science venture. If what I theorize is remotely true, then it means all of our academics are going to have to reassess everything they think they know about human history as well as its chronological validity. This is why the need for academic research by the experts is so necessary in solving these riddles of our past. Yes, this theory sounds ludicrous at first gloss, but all the evidence points to nothing being as we perceive it to be. If my theory is remotely correct, it means that everything we think about our presumed history comes into question, and that is not a psychologically comfortable place to find ourselves, layman and expert alike.

As human beings, we can't think on this level of dastardly deception. Oh, we have many faults and what we know of our recent history proves that we can breed some very unsavory and even evil beings, but what is being shown in this book goes beyond even human evil. This was a very well thought out plan for tyranny, and humans on this planet have been nothing more than the meat between the slices of bread called Enki and Ninhursag. We have never had a chance since our species was created, until now. It is through our awareness of these vile deeds that we can finally see the truth of a massive tyranny that controls or consciousness and choose to move beyond it into a higher state of cognitive awareness. As troubling as all the information in this book is, there *is* a way out, so I ask the reader to not give in to the idea that we are hopelessly roped into this fraudulent paradigm that holds our consciousness prisoner to the designs of alien intelligences.

12. Hollow Rituals and Initiatory Rites

I touched briefly on one of the hollow rituals still performed by many religions around the world through their continued use of incense in their rituals. I want to provide a little bit deeper explanation about hollow rituals and how they came about. This also ties into initiatic practices of the priesthoods and later magical traditions.

To illustrate a prime example of what came to be hollow rituals, I will point the reader to the movie *Mad Max: Beyond Thunderdome* for my example. During the film, Max finds himself in a wilderness community inhabited by children who survived a plane crash. The pilot of the airplane was named Captain Walker, and the children felt that when they found Max that he was the lost Captain Walker, who would ultimately fly them all to safety. The telling of the Captain Walker plane crash had basically turned into a ritualistic quasi-religious context for these children. The return of Captain Walker had turned into a prophetic belief to these children. The children had taken pieces of the airplane and were using them to try and communicate with the outside world based on copying what they remembered were the actions of the pilot before the crash. One would put on headphones and try to talk into a microphone, thinking that by emulating what they remembered seeing that they could somehow get help. This emulating of these actions they observed were hollow, fruitless rituals that never gained them anything, yet they still 'went through the motions' thinking that these rituals would somehow magically fix their desertion in the desert.

I use the illustration of this film because more people have probably watched the film than are familiar with what is called the Cargo Cults that sprang up after WW II, but that have purportedly existed longer than that. In the Cargo Cults that started after WW II, the indigenous peoples of the Pacific Islands went to the lengths of creating their own airstrips, building airplanes out of sticks or bamboo, and copying the actions of the GI's who were on the islands during the war thinking that by ritualistically duplicating their activities that they could entice their former benefactors to come back and bring their goods. Just look up Cargo Cults for more information on the subject.

Both of these examples just cited could be referred to as hollow rituals, the performance of which will yield absolutely nothing, but which the believers are firmly convinced have some supernatural power or benefit. In both of the examples provided, we find sort of a monkey-see, monkey-do development of forms of ritualistic behavior. Spiritual and supernatural con men have been around since the beginning of time. They have never hesitated to sell mystical ideas or rituals to the gullible or superstitious buyer. In many cases, some of these hucksters observed priestly rituals, watched the ritual motions of the priests without knowing the utterances provided by the priests, then sold these hollow rituals to someone willing to buy some kind of spell. This was usually sold with the huckster stating that it was exactly the same ritual practiced by any given priesthood.

Because such opportunistic hucksters have thrived throughout the ages, many have developed their own systems of magic and gathered followers to their ideas by simply inventing stupid ritualistic practices to give their hogwash an air of legitimacy. The practices of Neo-paganism and Wicca are exactly this kind of late-invented hollow rituals. The hucksters know they can pander to the human fascination for the mystical with certain segments of the population, which is why there are so many variants on the magical themes, which goes back thousands of years. The quest for and belief in the supernatural has bilked billions of people out of uncountable sums of money over the ages, and unfortunately, still does today as discussed in the previous volumes in this series.

All the ancient gods developed initiatory rites for their priesthoods for a number of varied reasons. Part of it was to determine whether the priests were trustworthy enough to handle the affairs of the gods, whether they were administrative affairs like bookkeeping and accounting, or whether they elevated to the position of High Priest and were trusted with parts of the god or goddess's energetic rituals. Initiations were part of the practice to insure that there was total devotion to the god or goddess. In some respects, initiation was also used as a weeding out process to determine those who were either not smart enough or devoted enough to the particular mission of the individual gods. If one did not exhibit the right motivation or dedication to serve their particular god, at best they would only achieve lower level duties within the priesthood. At worst, they would be removed from the ranks of the initiates and would be washed out, so to speak. If they became a threat in any capacity, they were simply killed.

The initiatory rites of the Freemasons is reflective of this ancient priestly practice, and the Roman Catholic Church has its own form of ritualistic initiations for their priesthoods, as I'm sure the Hindus do as well. I have little doubt that other religions are equally as regimented in selecting their high priests.

Many of these initiatory rites revolve around the donning of vestments, (or in the case of Masons, their Aprons and regalia - more trappings of power), specifically designed prayers and invocations designed to harness the energies of their gods and enslave the minds of their congregations, reinforce the power from their temples to their members, and performing ceremonies like Communion, baptisms and Christenings. By Anunnaki design, each of these rituals bring forth certain energies that they created but that are only accessible to the priests by using certain prescribed chants and/or invocations to their god that initiate the original encoded energy programs, coupled with ritual motions and gestures. These types of spells are formulas, or keys, utilized to access pre-existent energy programs. The spells are no different than a computer formula designed to trigger certain programmed functions to execute. The spells and rituals themselves only have power to access preprogrammed functions, and if those preprogrammed energy harnesses were not in place, the spells and rituals would do nothing.

The followers of religion will deny these claims and the non-religious scholars will consider this all superstitious nonsense, but one thing for certain, this God spell is plaguing our consciousness worldwide to this day. In our day of modern technology and science, we have to wonder just what it is that keeps billions of people around this planet adhering to their many religious convictions. Christians flatly refuse to acknowledge the pagan practices from which its origins sprang and the ancient stories of Enki and the Sumerian gods being grafted wholesale into their Bible. Protestants call the Catholics idolaters, yet they use the same book to bolster their own varied brands of the belief systems. There is really something wrong with this picture where you have people willing to die and martyr themselves over the ages and into modern times, lately illustrated with the radical jihadist sects of Islam we see today. We can only wonder how much the Anunnaki god of the Western world must be laughing his fishy ass off at our continued stupidity as he feeds on our faith, love, fear and martyrdom - in his name, Amun!

Other hollow rituals are sacrificial rituals, like giving something up for Lent, or any other form of sacrifice thinking that such exhibits of devotion are actually going to provide the sacrificer with some kind of blessing or another. The rites of sacrifice were designed to deprive humans of property, and subsequently their personal energy. The angst over sacrificing one's prized cow or horse at the behest of some priest creates personal anxiety in an individual, no matter how holy they think the act of sacrificial contrition actually is. The sacrifice itself is a hollow ritual, for it is through harvesting the anxiety from the contrite worshiper that we find the true meaning of sacrifice, whether it amounts to making oneself uncomfortable fasting for Lent, or sacrificing worldly goods. Mandating that the poorest believer contribute offerings to the church is but another hollow ritual that brings the believer no true benefit, but lines the pockets of the priests and makes the believer that much poorer, feeling guilty if they can't contribute their 10% to god. The whole religion thing is one of the greatest rackets ever designed, and it is an unfortunate statement against our species that we continue with these rituals of fear.

13. The Name Game

I didn't dwell too deeply on ritual practices in the last chapter because many of them have either already been revealed in previous chapters, or will be covered more specifically in the following chapters. If the reader wants to know more about ritualistic practices, then they are free to delve into ritual magic, the Hermetic tradition, Jewish mysticism or any number of the known rituals of the Masons and other spin-off secret societies like Aliester Crowley's Ordo Templi Orientis (OTO). The information is available for those curious enough to research such practices more deeply. As I stated, this book is not going to be a 'how to' manual for wannabe magicians.

I related the difference between how the Orioners claimed attributes after killing their enemies and how the Anunnaki adapted that primary practice to suit their own ends. I told how the Anunnaki used to keep many of their vanquished foes alive just so they could relish the anguish of those they co-opted in order to feed off of their misery at seeing what the Anunnaki did 'in their name'.

The Anunnaki and the Orioners were both artists when it came to deception and stealing and harnessing energies. Too many scholars find Greek and Roman human syncretism behind the harmonization of the many gods of the ancient world. What they have utterly failed to recognize is the practice of claiming attributes for being the energetic theft that it was. The very concept goes beyond the boundaries of our modern first cognition rationale and logic. The reason we find so many gods and goddesses being gathered under one ultimate banner in Western religions is due to a continual process of either killing or stealing the energies of other gods by two main perpetrators, Enki and Ninhursag.

Scholars just presume this rise to power and merging of the gods of the ancient pantheons is simply priestly syncretism and fail to see it for what it is. This is a purely human-centric first cognition interpretation. The way I learned to track Enki and Ninhursag through our known ancient history was by following their individual claims to power. After the expulsion of the Orioners, Enki was the Lord of Hosts, the god above all other gods. Ninhursag was not only the mother goddess, the virgin goddess, the goddess of war and sex, she is always found with her ultimate claim to being Queen of Heaven. Her bloodthirsty trail leads from Egypt all the way to India as the multi-faceted goddess Kali or Devi.

To give a few examples of this name game they both played, I want to focus on a few selections that can be tracked from Rome in or around the centuries either side of Year 0. There will be a few Google search options in this section, so it is advisable that one be near their computer for looking up the references for comparison purposes. Let's start with the name Sabazios as a search option for Wikipedia. If you call up the definition of Sabazios, you will see the primary symbol used in his cult, which is the right hand with the thumb and first two fingers pointed upward and the last two fingers folded down. Now, I ask you to Google *'papal hand gestures'*. When you look at the photos, you will see modern and more ancient Popes using this exact same gesture associated with the god Sabazios. If you use the Google search engine and type in *'Catholic image of Jesus'*, you should find a photo that says "Typical Catholic Image of Jesus". If you find this picture, you will notice Jesus also has his hand portrayed in the same position as the Sabazios idol.

This may all be coincidental, but I seriously doubt it. If you read into the Wikipedia definition about Sabazios, you find that the name was eventually altered to Sabazius. Sabazius was equated with Zeus as well as with Dionysus. He was also known as Jupiter Sabazius as well as the god of the Old Testament, Jahve Sabaoth. Although this particular Wikipedia definition says that this comparison was based on confusion by the Roman authorities of the Jewish god with Sabazius, I find this defense simply to be apologetics and doesn't stand on firm ground under closer scrutiny, as will be presented as we move along. You have to look up Zeus Sabazios being equated with Jahve Sabaoth under the Wikipedia definition of *Hypsistarians* (god fearers) to see that they were one in the same deity.

So here we have Zeus equated with Jupiter equated with Sabazios/Sabazius/Jahve Sabaoth equated with Dionysus and also equated with the Phrygian god Zagreus. Other aspects of Sabaoth will be discussed in later chapters. Wikipedia's explanations under *Hypsistarians* relates that within the Septuagint the Jewish god is referred to more than fifty times with the word hypsisto, meaning the 'Most High' God. The interesting thing is that the term only appears in documents from about 200 BCE - 400 CE. This is exactly the time we are talking about the return of Nibiru to our local solar system and the time frame that I assert was the formative period of the Old Testament, Judaism and Christianity.

There is more than coincidence going on here. The name *Zeus*, the Latin *Deus* and the Sanskrit *Dyàuspítah*, all originate from the ancient Aryan word *Dyeus*, (now called Indo-European migrating conquerors), which means Sky Father. See *dyeus* in Wikipedia. Within the text of the article we find that Dyeus Piter is also known as 'shining father'. Coincidentally, the Anunnaki also called themselves 'the shining ones' in the ancient Sumerian texts and I explained the meaning of the term when I discussed anointing previously.

You may be asking if there is any indication that all these different gods to all these different people were the same guy, and even if it was the same guy, are there any indicators that he was an Anunnaki fish hybrid? If we take Plutarch as a source, he states in *Isis and Osiris* that Dionysus was "called up from the water". We have to ask, if all these different gods were one in the same person, and they are all purportedly sky fathers, then why

208

is one aspect of this god named Dionysus, being *called up from the water*, unless what I am proposing is total fact?

In the Hindu religion we find the three primary gods/goddesses to be the same as the holy trinity in Christianity and the holy trinity in most of the pagan religions of old. Coincidentally, the supreme Hindu deities, Brahma, Devi (Kali) and Vishnu all have fishy associations. Look up the word *Matsya* to read about how Brahma and Vishnu were often portrayed like mermen, with a human upper torso and being a fish below the waist. Kali is often referred to as *"the fish-eyed one."* We have this same holy trinity of Father, Mother and Son all across the board through these religious traditions. This is not accidental or coincidence.

For the sake of consistency, let's take on one more ancient religion. Zagreus was a god associated with the religion of Orphism, which preached that the god Oceanus represented a fresh water river that totally surrounded the flat Earth. Oceanus's wife was Tethys, here again, a mother goddess. Not too surprisingly, Oceanus is also related to the Ourboros serpent that ever swallows its tail, and was also considered one of the Titans. Oceanus himself is portrayed with the upper torso of a man, sometimes with the head of bull, and with a serpentine fish tail. Once more, coincidentally, we have the primary elements of the creation mythology of the watery world that encircles the earth (Nibiru) and the fish god and his wife, the mother goddess, who are the rulers. Osiris and Isis are often equated with Oceanus and Tethys through the syncretic process.

In order to see the little bit of truth buried under all these myths, we have to make sure we don't get lost in the details of the religio-mythological tales that were specifically designed to misdirect and confuse our consciousness. As I hope the reader is starting to see, it is through getting lost in the details of these stories that scholars have failed to see the core story that hides behind the ancient mythological and religious stories of the Anunnaki gods. When you know what to look for, you realize that most of these mythological stories were concocted by the two main players in this cosmic drama in order to keep us all firmly rooted and subservient to first cognition tyranny. For many thousands of years it was a trio of a Father, Mother and Son who ruled these seemingly disparate pantheons of gods - Osiris, Isis and Horus - Brahma, Devi and Vishnu - Yahweh, Mother Mary and Jesus - Zeus, Hera and Hermes. The one advantage we have in tracking them is found in the fact that they just couldn't help bragging about themselves no matter which names they hid behind in many different lands. As for the being who played the son in these earlier trinities, he will be discussed in the next volume as his presence is not important in the Year 0 takeover. He was no longer on this planet at that point and no longer playing the game with Enki and Nin.

I am not going to track every role that Enki played during his long career of claiming attributes at this time because they are simply too numerous to count. The best way to find him is that he is virtually always defined as the Lord of Hosts or the head god of the pantheons he controlled, like the Greek god Zeus or the Roman Jupiter. He makes absolutely the same claim as the god of the Jews in the Bible and as Brahma in Hinduism, and he *always* claims to be the creator of mankind. Where we have all been deceived is in getting too involved in the mythical details of the stories concocted by these gods, and we fail to see the common factors that link all these intentionally designed myths together as a whole with the sole purpose of confusing our consciousness.

In order to track Enki and Ninhursag, we have to watch how the characteristics of the original gods or goddesses they co-opted changed after they claimed their attributes. In time, the two of them got creative enough to realize that they no longer had to vanquish enemies in order to get humans to worship them under the many and varied names they hid behind. Although they presented themselves in different forms as different gods and goddesses in the ancient civilizations, they eventually figured out that all they had to do was create a name out of thin air in order to get the same emotionally gratifying energies from the ignorant and fearful humans who were so indoctrinated with the god spell that they would worship anything if it could be marketed well enough and/or instituted by force.

Now, let's take a look at some of the roles Ninhursag played. She is most often portrayed as the queen of the gods, or more appropriately the Queen of Heaven. In our most recent pre-Christian history she was known as the goddess Isis, and it is through her role as Isis that we track her correlations with Juno of the Roman pantheon and Hera of the Greek pantheon. Ninhursag was already being syncretized as Artemis, who eventually was also equated with Isis. Hera, or Juno - who was considered the "great sister and wife of Jupiter" according to Apuleius, which is exactly the role Isis played in Egypt to Osiris, and this connection can be traced back to ancient Sumeria as Enki and his sister wife Ninhursag. Artemis was part of the Greek pantheon who was known as a virgin, as Isis was also known as a virgin and a mother. This virgin mother aspect found its way into Catholic iconography and belief as the Mother Mary.

Isis was also equated with Aphrodite, a goddess of love and war, and Aphrodite was known as Venus to the Romans. In ancient Sumeria, this same goddess of love was hiding behind the mask of Inanna, one of Ninhursag's earliest co-opted adversaries. I ask the reader to remember that the Dogon stated that the Nommo gods were hermaphroditic. It is not accident that the name Aphrodite is part of the word herm*aphrodite*. I will reveal the fact right now that Ninhursag was in fact an Anunnaki hermaphrodite just as the Dogon legends reveal about their Nommo gods. All of the Anunnaki were not hermaphrodites, but a great many were.

Hermaphroditism, which is rare in humans, was one of the more common side-effects that arose from the Orioners breeding animal and human hybrid species together. The cult of Aphrodite had its origins on the island of Cyprus in the Mediterranean. Curiously, a hermaphroditic counterpart to Aphrodite, Aphroditus, also originated on Cyprus. You can find images of Aphroditus through a Google search of that name. You will find Aphroditus with his/her skirt lifted and an erect male penis exposed. Modern scholars misinterpret these statues to represent transvestites or a representation of homosexuality.

Some of these statues are nude representations, and the last time I looked, they couldn't get boob jobs in the ancient world, so I say take the images for what they portray, not how modern scholars want to be apologetic for the statues, thinking they are simply a metaphor for transvestites or homosexuals. They represent exactly what they portray, hermaphrodites. More specifically they represent the true nature of Ninhursag as a hermaphroditic Anunnaki.

Aphroditus was purportedly a son of Aphrodite and Hermes. I bring this up to point out what is currently known in mystical circles as the Hermetic tradition. I will put forth the idea that Hermeticism originated with Ninhursag playing the roles of both Aphrodite and Aphroditus, and that the purported Hermes Trismigestus (the thrice great) of the Hermetic tradition was in fact Ninhursag. I will tie this all together as the chapters unfold. Read the information about Aphroditus on Wikipedia to get a fuller picture of what will be revealed as we continue.

If you visit the ruins of ancient Pompeii in Italy to this day you will find stone carvings of erect penises all over the place. If it weren't for the eruption of the volcano Vesuvius in 79 CE, we would not have any truthful rendering of how the cult of Isis and its practices of sexual ritual abounded in that era. Most of us have heard tales of Roman orgies. These orgies had direct connection to the cults of Isis and Dionysus (whom the Romans called Bacchus), and were part of the mystery traditions of the gods.

The ruins of Pompeii give us a microcosmic view of parts of the Roman empire of that era where the Isis cult thrived, most of the evidence of which has been systematically expunged elsewhere by the Roman Church and the subsequent rise of Christianity. This absence of such statuary in Rome and elsewhere shows the systematic removal of evidence that took place around Year 0 and for a few centuries thereafter on a very wide scale. All over the ruins of Pompeii one finds mosaics in dedication to Isis, and the city was filled with brothels and carvings and illustrations of the erect male penis. For more information, Google "Erotic art in Pompeii and Herculaneum" and read what Wikipedia has to offer on the subject.

The erect phalluses found all over the city ruins represent the god Priapus. As the Wikipedia information relates; *"Priapus was the son of Aphrodite and Dionysus, Dionysus and Chione, the father or son of Hermes, or the son of Zeus or Pan, depending on the source."* Despite the confusion, we have the same limited cast of characters I have already pointed out. Priapus is also associated with the Isis cult based on the legendary Egyptian tale of Osiris having his phallus cut off by Set, or Typhon. I will get to the Typhon aspect of the story in due course.

Another curious fact of these associations with hermaphroditism is found in the Orphic god, Phanes. In reference to Phanes, Wikipedia notes:

"Time, who was also called Aion, created the silver egg of the universe, out of this egg burst out the first-born, Phanes, who was also called

214

*Dionysus. Phanes was an **uroboric male-female deity** of light and goodness, whose name means "to bring light" or "to shine", a first-born god of light who emerges from a void **or a watery abyss and gives birth to the universe."***

[Emphasis mine]

As other parts of the Orphic story of Phanes relate, he was squeezed from a cosmic egg by a serpent. From the top half of the shell he created the heavens, and from the bottom half he created the Earth. Despite the mytho-religious elements here, these primary components also reflect the separation of the planet Nibiru (the heavens) from the Earth, just as related in the *Enuma Elish*. The 'uroboric' nature of Phanes is the worm of Ouroboros explained earlier that symbolically represents the orbit of Nibiru. The aspect of Phanes' name meaning 'to shine' should not be overlooked when viewed in light of the Anunnaki gods being called the 'shining ones' as alluded to previously. Phanes' name meaning 'to bring light' will have more significant meaning as we proceed. Once more, we find reference to these gods being hermaphrodites as well as being associated with Dionysus. Are we finding enough coincidences yet?

We have to look at how the stories and legends of these gods get intermingled and dovetail into one another. Alexander the Great conquered Egypt along with the known world of his time. It is not hard to imagine how the cult of Priapus could be grafted from Egyptian myths about Osiris losing his phallus to the god Set (or Seth) during the Hellenistic period of Greek rule

215

in Egypt, onto Hellenistic Isis cult beliefs about Priapus. It is not simple syncretism, it was a well formulated plan by specific design, as I hope to reveal.

You have to remember that Enki and Ninhursag were both working to harmonize, syncretize and compress all the old pagan religions they created and controlled into one universal religion. It was not, as modern scholars presume, at the whims of mankind or priesthoods that this was taking place. There were two distinct manipulators, and that is what I want to reader to be able to take away from this book. The ancient pagan religions had much that was not common across the board. The threads of the deception run very deep, and if one were to pay attention to the many differences in these ancient gods rather than look at the few relevant commonalities that thread them all together, then we completely overlook the truth - which scholars have done over the last 25 centuries - all except those who know these things and intentionally hold them in secret.

I realize that all this seems to be rather confusing, but I trust you are starting to see that we have a very limited cast of characters playing the major roles in all the ancient religions, especially during the syncretic period of about 300 BCE to 400 CE - the formative years of both Christianity and Judaism, as well as a developmental period in Hinduism that will be addressed in the next volume. The fact that Ninhursag was a hermaphrodite gave her the opportunity to play both male and female roles in this alleged history of the ancient gods, and even playing both roles together through the form of Aphroditus and the Orphic god Phanes.

Most of these ancient gods and goddesses did not originate from many real characters in later ages. Enki and Ninhursag covered a lot of ground over time and they portrayed themselves in many forms in many different lands. These two Anunnaki gods became proficient at both manufacturing and playing all roles in order to steal the power and religious devotion of all humans. By the time Year 0 came around, Enki and Ninhursag knew that all they had to do was produce a name to gain a following and ensnare humanity into their energetic traps for our consciousness. Ultimately, Enki created the name Jesus Christ - through which he could create another energetic food supply based on just another religious belief. I have already shared how Christians invoke their belief and close their prayers in the *name* of Jesus.

The calling on the name of a god is not just a Christian practice. The first line in the Quran starts with, "In the *name* of Allah. . . ". This is going to infuriate the Muslim world as much as I'm sure it infuriates the Christians and Jews, but the fact is that these people are all worshipping nothing but hollow *names* created by an artful and deceitful Anunnaki god named Enki and his hermaphroditic collaborator Ninhursag in order to harness our devotion, belief and fear in order to feed themselves with our energy.

If you doubt there is power in this name game, then you have to look at the ancient world where the Babylonian god Marduk had 50 names. In the Hindu religion, Shiva has 108 names. The Hindu goddess Kali has 1008 names. In seeing these numbers you have to realize that through every name the two of these Anunnaki tyrants used, they gathered power unto themselves. Whether the name was Zeus, Oceanus, Amon, Osiris, Oannes, Unas, Dagon, Ea, Enki, Marduk, Brahma, Vishnu, Indra, Jesus or Allah, all these names provided energy sources for Enki's taking. It matters not whether Ninhursag was known as Ninmah, Ninti, Sarama, Saraswati, Tethys, Demeter, Ceres, Inanna, Nanshe, Atargatis, Ishtar, Cybele, Asherah, Ceres, Juno, Aphrodite, Isis, Hathor, the 108 names of Durga, the 1000 names of Devi Parvati, the 1008 names of Kali, or Aphroditus and Phanes. Every name that gathered worshippers or was prayed to brought them power from the lowly humans who worshipped them under all these names. It is only through the explanations I am offering that these ancient name games have any real meaning. It is not simply religious syncretism on a human level going on here as scholars believe, and it was not spawned by the simple human need to worship something as so many psychologists believe.

Enki and Ninhursag were so power hungry that they were not only willing to start this name game, they wanted to cover all the bases for harnessing human cognitive energies and handicapping human consciousness under their god spells. Look at it this way, from a commercial standpoint, everyone doesn't buy the same product. In matters of religion, the same thing holds true, so the only way to rope every human consciousness into some sort of energy-paying belief structure, Enki and Ninhursag were very creative, creating every flavor of religion they could dream up in order to ensnare human consciousness.

I hope the reader is starting to understand the level of deception, tyranny and cognitive warfare that has been waged against human consciousness since our creation as a species on this planet. The only way out of this perceptual tyranny is by stepping into the second cognition and thereby removing your consciousness from their control. So long as we continue to give any of the first cognition power over our minds, the system these gods put in place still preys on our consciousness in one form or another. There is no point of reference in the first cognition that separates our consciousness from their dastardly designs, whether it be writing, science, religion or any other limited first cognition perceptual belief system. Even though these gods no longer exist, the systems they erected still command and control our conscious awareness within the first cognition and we willingly give up our personal power to this tyrannical energetic paradigm.

We have to not only be aware of what they did to our species, but the tools they used to keep our consciousness enslaved to insure their continual energetic food supply. These so-called gods only seem powerful because they kept us from our birthright to evolving into greater cognitive awareness through their continual deceptions and perfidy. They enslaved our consciousness and we are still slaves to that programming to this day so long as we remain firmly rooted in the first cognition. Their focus, despite all their knowledge about energy manipulation, was purely first cognition. They had no understanding of the second cognition, nor the power that spirit provides when we can overcome the slavery of the ego world.

They were just as subject to first cognition ego failures as the human race. They had knowledge about energy use, but they had no understanding of real power where spirit is concerned, and that was their ultimate downfall. All they understood was greed and the quest for personal power just like any other first cognition being, and they cared not who they stole it from or how they got it.

14. The Dependency Syndrome

It must be recognized that humans on this planet have never existed without the physical or mental mandate of worshipping these ancient gods, until our most recent centuries. The Orioners fed off the Anunnaki just as much as they fed off us and the other races they created in their genetic laboratories. The Orioners were by god in control! They had no need for priests or intercessors to take what they wanted from their genetic creations. The programming was already built into their genetics.

Because of this inherent power structure being in place for nearly 1 million years before humans on this planet ever existed, when we were created we were automatically drafted into this pre-existing tyranny of demanded worship. The earliest form of worship was not what we would call religions today. As cattle, we had no means to appeal to the Orioner gods. If a human in any way displeased them, chances were that the

Orioner gods would kill their families in front of their eyes, then roast them on a spit, strictly to create fear in all parties concerned and show their godly power over us. The religious belief that *God is in control* takes on a more realistic and dreadful meaning when viewed in this light.

The practices of human sacrifice and cannibalism were started by the Orioners. Humans who were ritually sacrificed were on some god's dinner table before the day was out. The sacrifices, as well as anything else these vile beings did, were designed to sow utter terror in the victims as well as the human society of slaves they ruled. The greater the fear the victims emitted, the more the gods fed on the energy, before ultimately feasting on the flesh of their victims. One only has to imagine the terror energy emitted while a person laid helpless under the knife of a priest, either in very ancient times, or during the sacrificial rites of the Mayans and Aztecs in our most recent history, to understand why such things were done where stealing energy was concerned. The same terror was realized by people being burned as witches while the mobs prayed for protection to their god.

The revelations provided in this book so far may seem farfetched and hard to accept, but we only need to turn to the Pyramid Texts and the tales of the last ruler of the Egyptian Fifth Dynasty, Unas, to see verification for many of the things I have presented about Enki's arrogance and delusions of grandeur; the close association with his sister, and claiming the powers of other gods through any and every means possible. What follows are a few select passages from the Pyramid Texts:

"Unas is he to eats their magic, who swallows their spirits.

Their great ones are for his morning meal,

their middle-sized ones for his evening meal,

their little ones for his night meal,

their old men and women are for his fuel."

[Some translate the last line as the old ones being burnt as an offering to himself.]

"Unas is he who eats men, who lives on gods, lord of messengers who gives instructions."

If you look up Unas in Wikipedia, you find alternate spellings of Wenis or Unis, and in the Hellenistic spellings either Oenas or Onnos. What you don't see offered in these name variants is Oannes, which is the name given by the Babylonian priest Berossus in reference to the fish god who came out of the Erythrian Sea as related in an earlier chapter. We have to wonder why this particular interpretation of the name Unas got overlooked. To prove my contention that Enki is Unas in the Pyramid Texts we only need to look at Utterance 211:

"Unas is conceived in the Watery Abyss, he is being born in the Watery Abyss".

The Watery Abyss is another reference to the Apsu, or Nibiru and you see many references to it throughout many mythological traditions, many of which will be revealed as we move forward. To illustrate the claiming of Osiris' attributes, from Utterance 213:

"O Unas, you have not gone dead, you have gone alive to sit on the throne of Osiris."

Through just this one utterance we see that Unas is claiming the throne of Osiris - i.e. claming the attributes of Osiris and inserting himself in that role. Lastly, we find the confirmation of my assertions about the Orioners being the creators of the Anunnaki gods:

"Unas is a god older than the eldest. Thousands serve him. Hundreds make offerings for him. A certificate is given him as a great power by Orion, the father of the gods."

The reference to *"Orion, the father of the gods"* should be enough to convince even the hard core denier that I am onto something that has been patently overlooked and intentionally written out of our history. In the texts Unas' sister is referenced as Sothis, which is the Egyptian name for Sirius, and is also symbolically associated with Isis, after Ninhursag claimed her attributes and took on her identity (which will be covered in depth later). In Egyptian lore, the 'heaven' of which Isis is queen is Nibiru which orbits to Sirius B at the other end of its 3,600 year orbital cycle. "Heaven" is equated both with Sirius as well as Niburu. If Unas was not in fact Enki/Oannes, then why is his sister associated with Sirius? If Unas was a mortal king as scholars surmise, then how can he remotely claim Isis as his sister? To all the academics who have refused to admit the existence of energetic magic, you are all invited to view the magical Pyramid Texts of Unas for exactly what they are, not simply superstitious metaphor. Given all that I have revealed thus far in this book, then Isis, the Queen of Heaven, ruling Sirius makes absolute sense. Continuing to demand that all these things are simply allegorical plays directly into the hands of the deceivers of mankind over the ages. Scholarly denial will not alter these facts nor will rigid scholarly disbelief change the truth we are being presented with in these ancient texts about magic.

To read the Pyramid Texts is no different than reading the bragging tales of Enki and the Anunnaki in ancient Sumerian, Babylonian and Assyrian texts. The tone and flavor of the braggadocio of Unas is a duplicate of similar brags by Enki in Mesopotamia, and is no different than the brags of Enki Almighty in the Old Testament, or Brahma in the Vedic texts. Modern scholars recognize that the Pyramid Texts are magical texts, but they utterly fail to see what the texts on the walls of pyramid of Unas in Saqqara, Egypt actually portray. The Pyramid Texts about Unas display the vitriolics of a lesser god, created by his Orioner makers, challenging those gods and claiming, "Look at me! Look at what I have done! I am just as good as you ever were, but I am even more powerful because I gained more power than you by defeating all of you, even the mighty Osiris! I am claiming the attributes of all you gods, the great Ennead (the Nine), my creators on Orion, and I am taking the attributes and throne of Osiris, eating gods and men to magically add to my power and steal their power." Yes, they are magical spells as scholars recognize, and that magic is real, folks. Take it or leave it.

For all intents and purposes, the Pyramid texts are a prime example of a god claiming the attributes of all the predecessor gods and goddesses in Egypt and elsewhere in one fell swoop. The utterances of Unas in the Pyramid Texts are exactly that. It is a series of spells for claiming attributes, strengthened and enforced by blood rituals and cannibalism. Egyptian scholars consider the texts to be funerary incantations having to do with the afterlife of King Unas, who they mistakenly consider to be a human king of Egypt, but when one understands the nature of Enki and how he paved his road to ultimate power on this planet, the spells reveal themselves for what they truly are. Scholars naturally assumed that the chamber on which these texts were painted was a burial chamber because parts of a mummy were found inside it, but there is no indication that this mummy is Unas, by their own admissions.

Further support of my contentions is found in the references to Horus in the Texts. In the most ancient Egyptian stories of the gods, there was no character or god named Horus in the original Egyptian ennead. The house of Osiris is always portrayed with Osiris, his wife Isis and her sister Nephthys. Horus doesn't appear anywhere in the most ancient accountings. It was Horus's invading army, the Shemsu-Hor, that ultimately overthrew the original Osiris and Isis and took his place with

Enki and Ninhursag as the ruling trinitarian gods in Egypt. This particular episode in Egyptian history will be covered in depth in the next volume.

Archaeological scholars utterly fail to understand these ancient texts because they do not have the connecting threads to understand them in the correct context. They assume they are regionally isolated human players and incidents, and most scholars consider them nothing more than religious mythology. They recognize the Pyramid Texts as magical incantations but utterly refuse to give credence to the idea that magic, or energy manipulation even exists. Zechariah Sitchin deserves credit in his work for at least seeing the Anunnaki influence spreading further than the borders of Mesopotamia, whether he understood the full scope or nature of their control or not. Modern scholars would be wise to follow in his footsteps and broaden their horizons when taking these texts into consideration, whether his ultimate conclusions were correct or not.

As Unas, Enki was rebelling at having been the messenger of the creator Orioner gods. He had, since his creation, been dependent on them for his claim to power. The Orioners expected and demanded subservience from all of their creations, and we humans are no different in either their eyes or the eyes of the Anunnaki usurpers who ultimately ousted their makers and took over this planet for themselves. The dependency syndrome of having a god or pantheon of gods to worship has been bred and brainwashed into our species since we were created. This syndrome of mental and emotional dependency on some sort of presumed higher power haunts our species to this day. The gods may have physically disappeared from our normal first cognition senses, but the psychological dependency they wrought is still rampant in our first cognition consciousness. Even without belief in religions, the concept of a higher source of power pervades every mystical and spiritual tradition on the planet.

This dependency is a *need* for some god or another, a *need* for a director of our lives and who we can purportedly look to for blessings to make our egos comfortable with the idea that someone or something greater than us is in charge. This psychological dependency was drilled into our ancestors by master geneticists who were tyrants and demanded such devotion from their creations. They herded us, they ate us, they demanded subservience, and they doled out their alleged blessings based on their immediate whims when it suited them. The religions of today are no less subservient even though the physical masters with the whips are no longer present to enforce our homage and subservience to them. The brainwashing has become so ingrained and so complete over all the generations of humanity on this planet that the simple fear of the gods is all that is needed to keep us in line. We enslave ourselves!

This whole god syndrome has kept our species ever looking outward, to some source or god outside ourselves as the provider of all our needs, whether they be needs begged for through prayer, or needs based on seeking an outside higher source of intelligence that can just fix or explain everything for us. This syndrome of always searching for answers outside ourselves is exactly what the Orioner controllers mandated of all their creations. The Orioners were never concerned about worship in the form that the Anunnaki developed as what we know as religion. The Orioners didn't care. They were ruthless psychopaths that ruled through utter fear and stark terror. The Orioners utilized this system of control through fear as a tyrannically enforced form of mind control that the human mind can barely grasp, and they used it against every race they conquered and every being designed and created in their genetic laboratories. When the Anunnaki came to power, Enki and Ninhursag capitalized on and redesigned this system into religions when they overthrew their own Orioner masters.

When I relate these things to other people, they always ask why no one or nothing stopped them? Why didn't god fix it? Why was it allowed to continue? Each of these questions reflect the psychological syndrome of dependency, that even when faced with such an ugly truth, we still look outside ourselves for some external higher source to resolve these problems for us. No matter where we turn in our varied cultures on this planet, this dependency syndrome is apparent everywhere, whether it is the reliance on a tribal elder as the authority, a Pope, an Imam, or a politician or academic. Every bit of this first cognition reliance on external authorities can be tracked back to the tyranny of the ancient Orioner and Anunnaki gods. The only way out from under that tyranny is moving into the second cognition and acknowledging the truth about the lies we have all been living as first cognition humans since our creation on this planet.

In order for the reader to gain greater understanding of these textual comparisons, many of these ancient texts can be viewed online through google searches. All of the Pyramid Texts are available for viewing simply by using a keyword search 'Unas - Pyramid Texts'. A goodly percentage of the ancient Mesopotamian texts about Enki can be found through keyword searches using 'Enki - Sumerian texts'. As I have emphasized throughout these books, do your own homework and follow your own intuitional guidance in order reach your own conclusions.

Unas was the last king of the Egyptian Fifth Dynasty, which is also when the more modern cults and legends of Osiris, Isis and Horus started, overlaying the real Isis and Osiris who they had vanquished in a war. If one wants a peek into the vindictive and greedy mind of an Anunnaki claiming the attributes of all his adversaries in one fell swoop, then just read the incantations in the Pyramid Texts to get a real life example.

15. Unveiling Isis

The allusion to the Veil of Isis comes from an inscription reported by Plutarch that was inscribed on a temple to Neith-Isis-Minerva at Sais, Egypt - *"I am all that hath been, and is, and shall be, and my veil no mortal has hitherto raised."*

Piercing the Veil of Isis has been at the root of Western Esoteric traditions such as Hermeticism, Gnosticism and Neoplatonism for centuries. Helena P. Blavatsky wrote a huge two-volume set of books entitled *Isis Unveiled,* which is rife with esoteric explanations, and it is Blavatsky's efforts, along with her disciple Alice Bailey and their invented traditions of Theosophy that have served as the foundation of the modern New Age craze in spirituality. As will be shown before this book is completed, all of these traditions hold a common core.

As I noted in Chapter 4, it is the Caesars who were the most devoted followers of the Isis cult that got the worst press in Seutonius' *The Twelve Caesars.* If we take the evidence unearthed from the ashes of Pompeii as any kind of guide to the accusations about their twisted sexual habits, then we have to ultimately give credence to much of what Seutonius revealed. What has been removed from the annals of Western history is how powerful the Isis cult was in the Mediterranean regions leading up to the establishment of Christianity. Had history taken a slightly different direction, the western world would be worshipping Isis today rather than the patriarchal god of the Jews. R. E. Witt has done a phenomenal job of presenting just how widespread the cult of Isis was in all its varied forms in his book *Isis in the Ancient World,* and for those with a deeper interest in the subject, I highly recommend reading his book.

To track Ninhursag through the annals of recorded history, to pierce the Veil of Isis, we have to go back to ancient Sumeria. Before allegedly being given the name Ninhursag, she had already been known as Enki's consort-wife Damgulanna (great wife of heaven) or Damkina (faithful wife). See *Ninhursag* on Wikipedia for more. She was the mother goddess Mamma or Mami, the goddess of birth Nintu, the 'Great Queen' Ninmah, and eventually took on the attributes of Inanna, who Ninhursag reshaped into the Sumerian goddess of love and war. Ninhursag is usually depicted with the omega symbol (Ω), which is also associated with the goddess Hathor. This symbol is generally represented in the hairstyle worn by both goddesses. The omega symbol also denotes the female womb and represents Ninhursag as a birth goddess. The Sumerian gods were allegedly "nourished by Ninhursag's milk." This aspect will hold greater significance when we move into her roles in Hinduism in Part 2.

I mentioned a lot of other names Ninhursag hid behind in Chapter 12. Each of these names came about from one of two different options, either she killed or claimed the attributes of a former adversary, as in the cases of Inanna and Isis, or she created the names as a form of worship to gather more energetic power for herself. I also voiced the idea that Ninhursag also played Hermes and Hermes Trismigestus during the period leading up to Year 0, both being at the root of the Hermetic mystery traditions. R. E. Witt also saw this connection between Isis and Hermes Trismigestus, so I am not alone in seeing the direct correlation between the two. For all intents and purposes, the Hermetic tradition is nothing more than the pursuit of Isian magical practices hidden behind the name of Hermes Trismigestus. The Hermetic traditions had a great influence during the Renaissance period and the later Reformation. To understand this influence, we have to have a deeper knowledge of Isis and what the cult encapsulated as its doctrinal basis.

The name Hermes Trismigestus means Hermes the 'Thrice Great'. To pierce this aspect of the veil of Isis we have to look to a couple of different things. First we need to look at the goddess Hecate, who is often portrayed as a goddess with three bodies, or three faces. See Hecate on Wikipedia for some illustrations. The mother goddess in Hindu religion, whether her name is Durga, Parvati or Kali is also a three-faced or three-fold goddess. This triple personality always represents Ninhursag the hermaphrodite where she can be male, female, or neither. See Triple Deity on Wikipedia for other correlations. With this correlation of the triple deity, then we can understand the reason for Hermes being the Thrice Great. It is all the same song and dance wrapped in the package of the presumably wisest magician that ever lived. This is whose magic is behind all of the Hermetic traditions and the explanation for the term 'thrice great'.

Unlike Enki, Ninhursag wanted to harness every energy possible from the cognitive endeavors of mankind. We have all heard the term to 'capture one's imagination', and at this present stage in our development, the term has become so commonplace that few people actually recognize what the term means from an energetic standpoint. We should view the term for what it is actually doing to our species from the standpoint of cognitive tyranny. Ninhursag knew that if she could 'capture' our imagination, in a very literal sense, that she could feed off of those energies and make herself stronger.

As Isis, she became the expert at capturing the imagination of throngs of humans. Isis was the goddess of the mariners, who sought her blessings before their sea voyages seeking her protection. As Hermes, she is the god of speech and, as I pointed out earlier about Aphrodite being part of the word hermaphrodite, Hermes is the name associated with the first part of the word - *herm*aphrodite. They are one in the same person insofar as the later Isis cultism is concerned. All of the evidence of Ninhursag's name perfidy and symbolism has been in our faces over the centuries. A curious note is that Hermes, in the Hindu tradition, is equated with the goddess Sarama - also known as the bitch of the gods. This association with a dog is part and parcel of Isis' association with Sirius, the Dog Star, despite how the religious legends of the Hindus have been tampered with to obscure this information. As we journey through this maze of deception, the correlative coincidences just keep piling up.

Like the Hindu goddess Saraswati, Isis was known as the goddess of wisdom, knowledge, music and the arts. The Isis cult was active in Alexandria in Egypt and, as Witt reported in *Isis in the Ancient World,* there was a temple of Isis adjoining the Library at Alexandria where medicine, science and philosophy were practiced and taught. Isis was the goddess of science, medicine, philosophy, pharmaceutics, fertility, seafaring and also known as the goddess of salvation in the afterlife. Her cult used baptism and sprinkling in its rituals as noted earlier, with the holy water of her cult purportedly shipped to her cult centers around the Mediterranean directly from the Nile river itself. Baptism with the life giving waters of the Nile was the guarantee of salvation of souls in the afterlife, which was later grafted wholesale into the traditions of all Western religions in one form or another. We see this direct association with the waters and purification also found with the goddess Saraswati in Hindu traditions related in book 10 of the Rigveda.

Ninhursag's cult of Isis catered to those from all walks of life, both the high and the low, although higher level initiates had to pay for the privilege. The concept of salvation served to turn our attention from thriving in this world to striving to make it to the afterlife, which both Enki and Ninhursag had a hand in developing in Egypt. Portions of the Pyramid Texts of Enki/Unas made their way into the Egyptian *Book of the Dead.* The pursuit of the afterlife and the fear of eternal damnation created quite the energy source for these two power hungry beings. It also turned into a very lucrative business concern with everyone paying to be mummified for the journey into the afterlife. The Anunnaki were never hesitant to make a buck where their religions were concerned.

Although the Isis cult seemed to be dropping many of the Egyptian hybrid animal-headed gods in her worship in these critical centuries (except Anubis), the concept of salvation and fear of consequences in the afterlife created great anxiety in humans, and still does to this day. The idea of eternal damnation was all that was needed to drive humans into the arms of Isis, and later, Christianity. This fear of the afterlife was created in Egypt once the Anunnaki took over there, and the concept was changed over and over to suit different audiences over the centuries. The religious concerns of people around the world and their making it safely into the afterlife can be laid at the feet of Enki and Ninhursag.

What few Christians realize is that before Christianity, the Isis cult was very active with baptism. Few Christians question the baptizer of Jesus, John the Baptist, or why he was even baptizing at all, especially since Christianity as we know it today had not yet come into existence. With the intentional expunging of the records and iconography of the Isis cult that happened concurrent with the rise and strengthening of Christianity, few if any Christians have made the cognitive leap to realize that John the Baptist had to be a priest of Isis, for that is the only cult that thrived in the Mediterranean at that time that was selling salvation into the afterlife through the ritual of baptism with water. The cult of Isis was widespread throughout the whole Roman empire and, just as later Christianity captured the imaginations of its followers with its promises of glory in the afterlife, the Isis cult had already laid the foundation for Christianity with the idea of salvation through water baptism.

Isis was also known as the Goddess of Magic and the Great Lady of Magic. In Egypt, she was also referred to as The Great Fish of the Abyss. If you follow the Anunnaki legends of Sumeria, you will always find magic in their tales. Enki was proclaimed as the Lord of Magic as well as in his later role as the Babylonian god Marduk. What humans perceived to be magic was simply energy manipulation, for the most part, although there may have been certain technologies that were also perceived as magical to our ancestors in our more ancient past. Our current cognitive system, predicated more on logic and reason since the Age of Enlightenment, patently refuses to acknowledge the practices of magic that I am revealing in this book. This denial has served the Anunnaki and their earthly servants very well.

I already related that the Pyramid Texts were a compendium of spells whereby Enki as Unas claimed all the attributes of his former godly overlords and adversaries. The Pyramid Texts are too lengthy to reproduce except through excerpts, so if the reader desires more insight into the spellcasting of Unas, they can read the Pyramid Texts themselves. During my research, however, I did come across what is called *The Invocation of Isis*. This particular invocation is exactly the spell used by Ninhursag to claim the attributes of Isis, regardless of how hard that is to accept with our given perception of reality.

I related in *Navigating into the Second Cognition* how certain inorganic beings used a form of feel good energy to entice people into fraudulent belief systems. The Anunnaki and other ancient so-called gods were just as adept at this type of energetic manipulation as are the inorganic beings. This is going to require a little explanation before I can share the invocation, so please bear with me.

Each god and goddess in the ancient past who set up any kind of temple for their worship used a form of prayer or invocation to open up the energies for their followers. Going back to the chapter where I explained rituals as a form of accessing energy, when a follower of a god or goddess invoked their names through prayers or invocation within their temples, it opened up an energy conduit that accessed the energy of the god or goddess. This energy conduit, established through the energetic temple within a temple harnessed through the shem stones, once opened, is what gave the follower that charge of feel-good energy, or sense of devotion - what some would call a sense of the 'divine presence' of the god. Each temple was imbued with this type of energy, and it is still found in religious edifices to this day, where the adherents feel closer to god in their respective god's house. Energetically speaking, nothing has changed where it comes to seductive energies housed in churches, mosques, synagogues or temples from ancient times to the present.

I came across this Invocation at the Wabash.edu website, which is the Wabash Center for the teaching and learning in theology and religion. I looked very hard trying the find the provenance of this Invocation, looking for ancient sources, etc., all to no avail. I finally found the Invocation located as part of the Golden Dawn Research Center after much scouring of the internet, but again, I found no other ancient provenance as to the source of this Invocation of Isis.

All of the books in this series are designed to help one transcend out of the limited first cognition awareness. When one succeeds in that effort, things open up on a greater cognitive scale. When I stumbled upon this Invocation of Isis, I knew intuitively what it was and what it represented. I have seen scores of prayers concocted by followers and Isis worshippers, from Apuleius in *The Golden Ass* to modern Wiccan and Isis cult prayers for the intercession of Isis in their ritual practices. All of these prayers or invocations are prayers *to* Isis, like any prayer to any god or goddess. What you are about to read is not an invocation *to* Isis, it is an Invocation *of* Isis. Just these simple two-letter words mark the distinction between simple prayers and quasi-religious invocations, and what the Invocation of Isis reveals itself to be.

In this invocation, you will note that at the beginning of the invocation, it is a prayer *to* Isis. The prayer part of the invocation is what opened access to the energies of the real goddess Isis, most likely in one of her ancient temples. Once that access was opened and the energetic *link* to Isis was established through the prayer, then the tone of the invocation completely

239

alters and instead of being a prayer to Isis, we see the claiming of Isis' attributes in the invocation when the prayer turns from praying to Isis to where the one praying is claiming to *be* Isis. It is through this alteration from the supplicant praying, then shifting to the form of identity theft, that Ninhursag deceitfully claimed the attributes of the original persona known as Isis. Because human scholars utterly discount the idea of energy manipulation as well as demanding that we believe that all the ancient gods sprang from the imagination of man, they are blinded to this type of energetic manipulation, or magic.

I beheld a great wonder in heaven, a woman clothed with the Sun, with the Moon at her feet. And on her head was a diadem of the twelve stars. Hear me, O Lady Isis, hear and save. O thou queen of love and mercy, thou crowned with the throne, thou hauled as with the Moon. Thou whose countenance is mild and glowing, even as grass refreshed by rain. Hear me, our Lady Isis, hear and save. O thou who art in matter manifest. Thou bride and queen as thou art mother and daughter of the Slain One. O thou who art the Lady of the Earth. Hear me, O Lady Isis, hear and save. O thou Lady of the amber skin. Lady of love and of victory, bright gate of glory through the darkening skies. O crowned with the Light and life and love. Hear me, our Lady, hear and save by thy sacred flower, the Lotus of eternal life and beauty; by thy love and mercy; by thy wrath and vengeance; by my desire toward thee, by all the magical names of old hear me, O Lady, hear and save. Open thy bosom to thy child, stretch forth thy arms and strain me to thy breasts. Let my lips touch thy lips ineffable. Hear me, O Lady Isis, hear and save. Lift up thy voice to aid me in this critical hour. Lift up thy voice most musical. Cry aloud, O queen and mother, to save me from that I fear most. I invoke thee to initiate my soul. ***The whirling of my dance, may it be a spell and a link with thy great light, so that in the darkest hour, the Light may arise in me and bring me to thine own glory and incorruptibility.***"

[Emphasis mine]

The part in bold print is where Ninhursag has started the role reversal when she asks that her "*dance be a spell to link with thy great light*" - i.e. the energy of the original Isis. The latter part of the invocation is the request that the Light of Isis (her attributes) arises in her (Ninhursag), and it brings Ninhursag the power of Isis through a form of energetic theft. The next segment of the passage shows how that spell was enacted through the energetic link, and how, through this magical invocation, Ninhursag becomes Isis by stealing her attributes and energetically *becoming* Isis herself. The invocation from here forward is Ninhursag not only claiming Isis' attributes, but also illustrates Ninhursag overlaying her own energies on top of and mixing her traits with those of Isis, inextricably linking the two energetic personalities into one new Isis.

"Isis am I, and from my life are fed all showers and suns, all moons that wax and wane, all stars and streams, the living and the dead, the mystery of pleasure and of pain. I am the Mother. I the speaking sea. I am the Earth in its fertility. Life, death, love, hatred, light, darkness, return to me, to me. Isis am I, and to my beauty draw. All glories of the Universe bow down, the blossom and the mountain and the dawn. Fruits blush and women are creations crowned. I am the priest, the sacrifice, the shrine. I am the love and life of the Divine. Life, death, love, hatred, light, darkness, are surely mine, are mine. Isis am I, the love and light of Earth, the wealth of kisses, the delight of tears, the bowel and pleasure never come to birth, the endless infinite desire of years. I am the shrine at which thy long desire devoured thee with intolerable fire. I was sung music, passion, death upon thy lyre, thy lyre. I am the grail and I the glory now. I am the flame and fueler of thy breath. I am the star of God upon thy brow. I am thy queen enraptured and possessed. High do these sweet rivers welcome to the sea, ocean of love that shall encompass thee. Life, death, love,

hatred, light, darkness, return to me, to me. Hear, Lady Isis, and receive my prayer. Thee, thee I worship and invoke. Hail to thee, sole mother of my life. I am Isis, mistress of the whole land. I was instructed by Hermes, and with Hermes I invented the writings of the nations in order that not all should write with the same letters. I gave mankind their laws, and ordained what no one can alter. I am the eldest daughter of Kronos. I am the wife and sister of the king Osiris. I am she who rises in the dog star. I am she who is called the goddess of women. I am she who separated the heaven from the earth. I have pointed out their paths to the star. I have invented seamanship. I have brought together men and women. I have ordained that the elders shall be beloved by the children. With my brother Osiris I made an end of cannibalism. I have instructed mankind in the mysteries. I have taught reverence of the divine statues. I have established the Temple precincts. I have overthrown the dominion of the tyrants. I have caused men to love women. I have made justice more powerful than silver and gold. I have caused truth to be considered beautiful. Come unto me and pledge unto me your loyalties as I pledge mine unto you. Oh mother Isis, great art thou in thy splendor, mighty is thy name and thy love has no bounds. Thou art Isis, who art all that ever was, and all that there is to be, for no mortal man hath ever unveiled thee. In all thy grace thou has brought forth the sun, the fruit that was born forth for the redemption of man. Oh Isis, Isis, Isis, graciously hear our cry unto thee, we mourn for thy blessings on us this day, every day, to nourish, to aid and to fill the emptiness within, that only you our beloved mother can satiate. Unto thee do we pledge our solemn oath of dedication, and for the power and glory of him the Unknowable One to witness our devotion to thee. For as we now receive thee into our hearts, we ask that you never leave us, in times of trial and joy, and even unto death."

Through the course of this spell claiming the attributes of the original Isis, you hear the voice of Ninhursag in all her many roles. She is bragging of her power and prowess just as Enki did as Unas. The original Isis had nothing to do with the Dog Star (Sirius), as she was originally an inhabitant of a planet that orbits Rigel in the Orion constellation. Both Enki and Ninhursag, in their many roles, claimed to have separated heaven from the earth. Through this one invocation, Ninhursag rolled all her different goddess personas into that of Isis. She worked to become all things to all people where her worship was concerned, and by claiming the attributes of Isis with this spell, she succeeded in that role.

A couple of other things should also be noted in regard to this invocation. It is curious indeed that the first sentence of the invocation should appear in Revelation 12 in the New Testament. Revelation 12:1 says: *And there appeared a great wonder in heaven; a woman clothed with the sun, and the moon under her feet, and upon her head a crown of twelve stars."* One other factor that most likely gets overlooked is the claim that she is *"who art all that ever was, and all that there is to be"*. This is no different than the claim of the Jewish god, with words put in the mouth of Jesus, that, *"I am the Alpha and Omega."* I have already shown Ninhursag's association with the omega symbol. To understand the Alpha part of this claim, we have to look to Plutarch, who stated plainly that the Greek letter Alpha was associated with the moon. Artemis was a moon goddess as well as Hecate, both of whom were other roles played by Ninhursag and subsumed into this new Isis. Taken in this context, the Alpha and Omega of Jesus' claim is a direct reflection of Isis found in the mouth of Jesus. The moon cycles are also corroborative of women's menstrual cycles, thus the importance of the moon equating with the Alpha symbol associated with the womb symbol, Omega. As we progress, we are going to see more weaving of Isis into the New Testament doctrine of Jesus.

Where questions of provenance of this passage exist, I can only state that no matter how skilled an adept is in the secret societies like the Rosicrucian's or the Golden Dawn may be, they could neither compose nor understand the meaning of this spell. This Invocation would serve no one beyond the person claiming the attributes of Isis and weaving her own personality in with the intent to overlay and co-opt the energy of Isis.

Another point that needs to be noted is that the original Isis was the daughter of Geb and Nut, not Kronos. The Greek goddess Hera, however, did claim to be a daughter of Kronos, which proves a character other than the real Isis herself is making this Invocation, to wit, Ninhursag. Kronos was one of the Titans - read that Orioners - who were ultimately vanquished from this planet by the Anunnaki. The claim to have been taught by Hermes should also not escape your notice.

We have all the clues in this Invocation to give it a validity that otherwise simple prayers of supplicants to Isis do not exhibit. It took balls to steal Isis' power, and no followers of the goddess would have dared such a thing as this Invocation exhibits. Whether we can definitively prove an ancient provenance or not, my own second cognition reckoning knows this Invocation is exactly what I present it to be. No other explanation makes any sense. You are going to have to appeal to your own intuition and see what you *feel* about my explanations and this Invocation.

Now that I have revealed the origin of the whole Catholic Mother Mary paradigm, revealed who people are really praying to when seeking Mary's guidance, I invite the reader to Google 'prayers to Mary' and read prayer after prayer to the fish hybrid Virgin goddess. We not only have to question why people have such dependent devotion with this religious paradigm, we also have to ask ourselves just what kind of narcissistic psychopathic personality would demand and feed off such devotion from any intelligent being. Reading these prayers in light of what you know now should make you ill, even if you aren't Catholic.

At this point I have to address what may seem to be contradictions between my presentation of certain sayings attributed to the man we know as Jesus and what I have just revealed. Every aspect of this series of books constitutes an unraveling of perceptual beliefs. I presented the sayings attributed to Jesus in *Willful Evolution* for the simple reason that those sayings are known and associated with that specific name. As I stated above, Jesus was never that man's name, his name was Immanuel. I presented those sayings in that book using the name Jesus because that is where most people's cognitive perception resides when talking about him. It is a name already known and accepted globally when trying to describe that individual and what he taught. I used the name Jesus for the sake of reshaping the perception of what he actually taught as second cognition teachings compared to the religious dogma that got attached to and overlaid his real message.

All of the books in this series are designed to advance human cognitive awareness. There is a method to how each of these volumes unfolds. In order to help people alter their cognitive awareness, they have to be met on terms with which they are familiar in order to present new concepts. There is no disingenuousness in my approach. Each book in this series, by both myself and Mrs. Beall, serve as a systematic presentation of information in order to help the reader work to unravel the perceptual lies that we have all accepted. In order to do that, I have to speak the lingo of the first cognition in order to get the reader's attention. The main thrust is to provide new perceptual interpretations within the framework of the reader's understanding. As the reader progresses through all the books in the series, they find themselves slowly advancing their own perceptual boundaries as each book reveals other layers of the cognitive deception that keeps our species bound in a world of limitations.

By revealing the cognitive perfidy created by Enki and Ninhursag, it may seem that I am offering contradictions when I use Jesus' sayings in one book, then turn around in this book and reveal that the name Jesus in itself is a cognitive scam designed to rope us into a system of mental slavery and dependency. Immanuel existed. His teachings as a second cognition human being are sound, but it takes keen spiritual discernment in order to make the determination between the true teachings and the dogmatic Anunnaki overlay designed to create that sense of religious and cognitive dependency. Had I tried to explain all of this in *Willful Evolution*, the information would most likely have fallen on deaf ears.

It is easy to sit back and say that I should have told you this all from the start, but given the number of pages already devoted to revealing everything we have in this series, you have to ask yourself whether you really would have listened to the message or not. The ego part of us is foolish enough to think that it is ready for anything, yet the information presented in this book should prove to you that you may not be as cognitively ready to accept these truths as your ego makes you believe. I have seen people go into a sort of cognitive shutdown when they receive too much information that simply overloads their cognitive circuits where this information is concerned. No one is ready for this information in one fell swoop, no matter how much the ego part of them tries to convince them otherwise.

16. The Gnostic Connection

The Gnostic texts are quite varied in their content, so it is not possible to homogenize all the disparate doctrines into one cohesive whole, although there are certain aspects that run through them that show certain threads of consistency. I'm not going into a total indepth analysis of the varied philosophies of the Gnostics, but I am going to illustrate certain correlations compared to what has already been related in this book to date.

As revealed earlier in the book, there was a massive collaborative effort to syncretize and homogenize the many disparate pagan doctrines from many lands after the Anunnaki arrived back on planet Earth near Year 0. Just as the Dead Sea Scrolls were being written and compiled, so too were the Gnostic philosophers formulating their doctrines, much of which found its way into the New Testament. Through examining the Gnostic texts, we find many connecting threads to what has already been revealed in this book. For instance, in the Gnostic *Book of Baruch,* we find a trinity that is comprised of two males and one female, just as in the myths of Isis, Osiris and Horus, as well as found in the Holy Trinity of Christianity. In that book *mētra* (the womb) is portrayed as a composite female being whose upper torso is that of a woman and whose lower half is a serpent. Take note of this fact as it relates heavily to the story of Typhon, or Set in Greek and Egyptian religious mythology.

From the doctrine of the Valentinians we find that their creation story relates:

"In the beginning were Darkness, Chaos and Water, but the Spirit indwelling in the midst of them, divided them one from another."

Ephipanius, Haer. 25, 5

Once again, in more mystical and philosophical formatting, we find the waters and the separation of them found throughout the ancient legends. The primary driving principle of the Gnostics in general is a being known as Sophia, who is equated with Wisdom. The ally of Sophia is Sabaoth, who has already been covered previously as Zeus Sabazius or Yahweh Sabaoth. As with Sophia, Isis was also associated with Wisdom, so for all intents and purposes, despite the philosophical-religious blind being erected by the intellectual Gnostics, we still find the core elements of all I have presented thus far. You can find this Wisdom, treated as a feminine noun, in what is known as The Wisdom Text in Proverbs 8 in the Old Testament. The reference to Wisdom is a direct correlation to Ninhursag as Isis, who is now masquerading as the Gnostic Sophia.

Citing Wikipedia in regard to Sophia as a World-Soul, we find:

"In this system the original cosmogonic significance of the Sophia still stands in the foreground. The antithesis of Christus and Sophia, as He of the right (ho dexios) and She of the Left (hē aristera), as male and female, is but a repetition of the first Cosmogonic Antithesis in another form. The Sophia herself is but a reflex of the "Mother of all living" and is therefore also called "Mother." She is the formatrix of heaven and earth, for as much as mere matter can only receive form through the light which, coming down from above has interpenetrated the dark waters of the hylē. . ."

With this correlation about Sophia being the female aspect to the male aspect of Christ, we can only wonder whether Jesus the Christ is not just another Aphroditus to Ninhursag's hermaphroditism playing the female counterpart as Sophia. The *"mother of all living"* and the *"formatrix of heaven and earth"* aspects of Sophia should be readily apparent aspects of Ninhursag showing up in just another spin-off religious doctrine. Certain Gnostic texts claim that Jesus was not a man in the mortal sense, but was instead only a spirit. Given what I have illustrated in the Name Game chapter, this is very likely closer to the truth than anyone named Jesus of the Gospels having ever lived.

The Dead Sea Scrolls told of a coming messiah, but the

name Jesus is never mentioned in those scrolls. Their god is the patriarchal Enki, the Lord of Hosts, the creator of all, the judge of the world. We find Jesus' presence in the Gnostic gospels, and in them, with what I have shared to date in this book, it seems most logical that the fictional character of Jesus was just another assumed male personality like Horus, Hermes or Aphroditus to Ninhursag's female aspect. The father god, Sabaoth, in the Gnostic texts is none other than Enki. What we find with the end result of the book known as the Bible is nothing more than myths about human actors created as a dramatic backdrop to give both Enki and Ninhursag bragging rights, all the while staying hidden behind the scenes of our cognitive awareness.

The Hermetic tradition is closely linked with the Gnostics and the rise of early Christianity. With what I have revealed so far, this should come as no surprise. We all know that in the end the vengeful god of the Old Testament won the day, and that the goddess Isis-Ninhursag-Sophia became marginalized as nothing more than the Holy Spirit or the Mother Mary. Since Enki won that doctrinal battle, the cult of Isis-Ninhursag was driven underground, with the Catholic Church fathers and their rabid, zealot destructive followers systematically removing nearly all the evidence of the Isis cult from human memory, except as an ancient Egyptian religion. All the doctrinal inserts developed by Ninhursag as Isis - the concepts of baptism, salvation, the advancement of science, medicine, philosophy and the arts were systematically removed and the tyranny of the patriarchal god drove Western humanity into the Dark Ages.

It was the appearance of certain Gnostic traditions that reared their ugly head in the Cathar religion, which the Catholic Church deemed heretical and the "Church of Satan", that the underground stream of Gnostic knowledge advanced forward. These same Gnostic traditions found their way into the Knights Templar, who were associated with what came to be called the Cathari Heresy, who were also eventually deemed to be heretics, and the Church once again tried to eliminate the doctrine of Isis.

The Templars devised their own code for communication, called the Atbash Cipher. The word Baphomet in the Atbash Cipher translates into the word Sophia, or the female Wisdom of the Gnostics. I ask the reader to Google the term "Baphomet - Eliphas Levi" and look at the image presented. You will see a goat-headed hermaphroditic form, with the lower torso also having goat's feet, and the upper torso shown with female breasts. The five-pointed star on the goat's forehead signifies Sirius, the realm of Isis-Ninhursag, as was stated in the Invocation about Isis wearing the star of the God on her forehead. Note the positions of the fingers on both hands and you will see the same gesture used to illustrate the cult of Sabazios. The crescents pointed to have a dual representation, superficially they stand for the sun and the moon, light and darkness, but the hidden meaning is representational of the orbit of the planet Nibiru which orbits into our solar system from above the ecliptic plane to below the ecliptic, giving rise to the true meaning of "As above, so below" in all the esoteric doctrines.

The goat features are representational of Ninhursag in the role of Pan, the god of lust. The torch on the goat's head is associated with Hecate and represents the torch of Illumination, or Wisdom. The caduceus represents Isis' support of the sciences and medicine, and the entwined serpents are also representational of the star Sirius in more ancient traditions, not to overlook the association with the double helix of DNA. The twin serpents can also be found in the ancient Sumerian god Ningishzida, who the scholar A. L. Frothingham capably associated with Hermes in his paper *Babylonian Origin of Hermes the Snake-god, and of the Caduceus* published in 1916 and available for free download from JSTOR for those interested in seeing a deeper, more scholarly presentation of the matter. The scale-covered torso of the Baphomet illustration is representational of water, and the reader should well know what that signifies at this point. According to esoteric traditions, one arm is female and the other is male, signifying the hermaphroditic aspect of the Baphomet goat. Overall, we find most of the aspects of Isis-Ninhursag gathered into this one esoteric image.

Also pay attention to the fact that Ninhursag claims to be the *grail*. When we look to the legends of the Holy Grail, we find that the Grail romances were popular during the era of the Templars. The public mythology is that the grail is a cup or plate or chalice, but if we look at the grail as the chalice of birth, i.e. the womb, then the Holy Grail is Isis/Ninhursag. The Cathari religion worked to elevate the position of women to the priesthood in absolute opposition to Roman Catholic patriarchy, which is one reason they were deemed heretics. There has been speculation that the Cathari Heresy had its associations with the Holy Grail mythology. If we look at the role of the Fisher King in the story, we find a wounded king, who was wounded in the groin or leg, who has become ineffectual and basically unable to move or do anything but fish. It doesn't take much to see this wounded king as Osiris, who allegedly had his phallus cut off by the diabolical Seth of Egyptian religions mythology. In the role of the Fisher King, the allegorical person of the wounded king and the fisher king are separate personages, either a father and son, or grandfather and grandson.

The reason that one can potentially link the Grail romances to the Cathars is in the allegorical criticism of the Roman Church. If the Cathars were indeed an underground stream of the heretical Isis knowledge, then the wounded king in the story is representational of the father god of the Roman Church, known through esoteric traditions as Osiris, the wounded king - wounded in the groin by having his phallus cut off by Seth. The son is the fisher king, who spends his days fishing. This fisher king could easily be allegorically equated with Jesus, the alleged 'fisher of men'. As the story goes, it is only through some form of magic that the king can be healed, which is also an allegorical allusion to Isis and her power of healing magic. Given all these allegorical interpretations, it is not hard to believe that the whole set of Grail legends are associated with Isis and with the Cathars. The Cathari belief system also held echoes of Gnosticism, and its sister religion, Manichaeism, in its dualistic principles. There is still dispute as to whether the Templars were closely associated with the Cathars, but as will be revealed, there is more in common between them than not.

From the Templars we next find the trail of Isis and the esoteric traditions in the Reformation movement against the Church of Rome. The word Baphomet comes directly from Templar secret coding of the Atbash cipher, so denying a Templar association with Wisdom-Sophia-Isis is virtually impossible. We next move forward to the Reformation and take a look at Martin Luther's Rose to find nothing more than the stylized pentagram redesigned into a five-petaled flower. Look up Luther's Rose on Wikipedia to see the flower. We can also track the underground stream of knowledge through the Rosicrucian's and into the secret societies like the Alumbrados, another form of heretical secret societies that was prosecuted in Spain by the Inquisitions, and who had definitive Gnostic origins. At the center of the symbol of the Rosy Cross of the Rosicrucians we find the same five-petaled rose that became Luther's symbol. Curiously enough, Ignatius Loyola, the founder of the Jesuit Order (The Society of Jesus), was brought up on charges of being a member of the Alumbrados before he was ultimately set free. This same organization, the Alumbrados also operated under the name of *Illuminés* in France in 1623. Again, see Wikipedia under Alumbrados for more.

The Black Virgin is often equated with representing Isis, although the Catholic Church to this day denies that connection. Curiously, when Loyola developed his rules for the Jesuit Order, he is reported to have spent an entire night venerating the Black Virgin at the Abbey of Montserrat, and he therefore dedicated his life to Mary. Further, he is reported to have stopped at every shrine of the Black Virgin along the way to Rome seeking to have his Order sanctioned by the Pope. The high priests of Isis were noted for wearing black robes. I find it quite coincidental that the Jesuits wear the black frock with the little white collar, which is highly indicative of the Baphomet image and the light and dark aspect of esoteric traditions and, as R.E. Witt pointed out in *Isis in the Ancient World,* this frock mirrors that of the high priests of Isis in the ancient world.

Osiris was considered the Great Architect, and it is in the Freemasonic traditions that we pick up the thread of the Isis cult found in their reverence for the Great Architect, the grand designer of the universe. The Masonic Great Architect is none other than Osiris, playing the secondary role to Isis in their secret worshipful ceremonies. The Masons have a high affinity with Isis, which is found in *Mozart's* opera *The Magic Flute.* Mozart was a known Freemason and *The Magic Flute* had heavy Masonic and Anti-Catholic symbology and heavy Enlightenment philosophy influences. After the storming of the Bastille, a statue was erected of the goddess Isis, called "The Fountain of Regeneration" in 1797. Isis came to signify the goddess of the French Revolution.

The goddess Hecate is portrayed in statuary as wearing a spiked crown, very similar to that found on the Statue of Liberty. She is also portrayed holding two torches. The symbol of Lady Liberty can be directly tracked back to Hecate and her being subsumed by Ninhursag-Isis. You can find illustrations of lady liberty from the period of the French Revolution, so it is pretty undeniable that the statue sitting in the harbor in New York is none other than Isis-Hecate.

In Albert Pike's *Morals and Dogma*, he presents the idea that the Masons worship Lucifer, but in order to understand this, we have to first comprehend their doctrine. To Pike, Lucifer is a representation of Venus. I have already shared the correlations of Ninhursag with Venus. The Lucifer of the Freemasonic tradition is a female entity, the "Light Bringer", exactly the same personage as the Gnostic Sophia and the Wisdom goddess Isis. We also can't forget the Orphic hermaphrodite Phanes, who was also a 'light bringer'. To the patriarchs who wrote the Bible, Ninhursag-Isis was the great Satan. She was the Devil incarnate, a female who designed the fall of man, in opposition to their patriarchal god, Enki.

There have been many accusations over the centuries about certain sexual rites held in secret in Freemasonic Lodges. Stanley Kubric made the film *Eyes Wide Shut* to bring such orgiastic practices to light, although he didn't mention the Freemasons by name. It is curious that in the ritual scenes in the film that most of the participants were wearing black robes, just like the high priests of Isis and the frocks of the Jesuits. The sexual practices associated with Isis worship were already noted above. How many coincidences have to pile up on this investigative trail before we all finally realize what we have been subjected to in this war between two gods who both seek to rule this planet by controlling our consciousness? When we see the three faces of Hecate and other goddesses, both in the Middle East and into Indian Hindu beliefs, all we have to realize to solve these great 'mysteries' is to recognize the three part nature of

Ninhursag the hermaphrodite - the male, the female and the androgyne.

The personage that Christians worship as Jesus is simply another Enki-Ninhursag name creation that her tyrannical Anunnaki brother Enki co-opted for his own uses. The Old Testament of the Bible with its concocted stories portrays the true neurotic nature of Enki and his way of ruling through fear. The New Testament was purportedly a kinder and gentler approach to ensnare the consciousness of mankind, hiding behind the mask of the benevolent Mother Goddess. Both forms of tyranny have been nothing but a trap for human consciousness since the Anunnaki took control of this planet from their master creators in Orion.

This is the legacy these fish-heads have left humanity with over the last 2000 years. All of humanity is caught in their snares of religious deceit, destruction of records and evidence, forced religious indoctrination through warfare, and blind subservience to a hybrid race of beings who can't show themselves in public because they are technically monsters by our system of cognitive reckoning.

One of the most argued points in regard to Freemasonic symbols is that of the G in the center of the compass and the square. Some say it stands for God, others claim it stands for Geometry. G in Hebrew is the letter Gimel, which has the numerical value of 3. In order to solve the true riddle of the letter G and its high significance in Freemasonry, we only need to take the number 3 and equate it with the triple goddess to realize that the G stands for Genetrix - the Queen of Heaven, all that is, all that ever was, and all that shall be - Isis/Ninhursag. Between these two power hungry gods and the multitudes of religions they spawned (pun intended), we finally perceive the pincers that have squeezed the cognitive life out of our species for the last 5,000 years.

I realize that the information in this chapter may seem to feel rushed in its presentation, but the fact is that tens of thousands of pages have been written over the centuries by and about all these organizations. Thousands of researchers have been trying to make the connections between many of these secret societies and what ultimately threads them together, but they have all lacked the essential key to ultimately solve the puzzle. People have tried to figure out just what the *secret* is that the secret societies are keeping secret and why they must be so secretive about it. What I revealed in this chapter is the connecting thread that ties all these organizations together and exposes exactly what the deadly secret is that they are protecting from the profane masses and the 'uninitiated'. This explains why they are bound by blood oath not to reveal the inner workings of the temple.

I used the analogy of ice cream flavors earlier in the book to describe all the variant sects and religious cults. With their secret traditions and knowledge about manipulating energies, the high level adepts of Masonry and the other religious and secret societies over the ages have continually developed new flavors of religious ice cream to not only ensnare human consciousness, but to make themselves individually more energetically powerful by creating these religions and mystery traditions, thereby energetically feeding on the beliefs of the followers of the new doctrines themselves. We find the same old magic wrapped in new clothing for new audiences, peddling the different flavors of religious or esoteric ice cream to insure that no human can escape the energetic traps for our cognitive energies. If one flavor won't sell, they will develop another one that will. If it isn't religion, it is mysticism, but regardless of the wrapper, it is all the same *underground stream of knowledge* designed to ensnare our consciousness to their perverted wills and keep our species subservient to their hidden fish hybrid gods.

I have no need to rehash every correlation between these different secret societies, whether they be Rosicrucians, Freemasons, neo-Gnostics, Theosophists, Jesuits, Opus Dei, Satanists, Hindu Brahmins, members or initiates to Crowley's OTO, or any of the several other secret societies that abound around the world. These are the secrets of the high priests and the highest adepts of any aspect of the 'craft'. The path to alleged 'high magic' is fraught with a slow and continual erosion of personal impeccability. The more a person can be corrupted and lose any sense of moral values, the more the doors open to the highest levels of initiation. This is the price exacted to become a high initiate into any of the secret societies. One must be willing to molest children, involve themselves in tyrannical sexual rituals and, often, resort to murder in order to attain the title of adept within the craft of Freemasonry.

People decry the pedophilia found in the Catholic Church by its priests, but the fact is the priests are fully aware of who their god truly is and what that god's road to personal power demands. It is a road that demands total destruction of any sense of personal spiritual impeccability, and that is why they keep this secret the grim secret that it is. It is a road to corrupted power that only evidences itself as tyranny over the minds of others. Every Mason in the Blue Degrees, those who are putting on the benevolent front for their Brotherhood, is ignorantly hiding and protecting the dirty deeds of their higher-level brothers. What is shown in this book is at the root of the Craft, no matter what kind of bullshit benevolent front they present to you, whether it is priestcraft or craft of esotericism. The higher you progress in the Brotherhoods of the Craft, the more you have to erode your own moral compass in order to become an Adept to the Craft. This is the only road to high magic and these are the corrupt hybrid gods all this magic serves. This is not the fanciful meanderings of some lunatic. This is the reality of the world in which we live. The sooner you recognize it the sooner you can move your consciousness beyond this system's chains of control over your consciousness.

When the Masons and priests perform their cornerstone rituals, performing energetic magic in order to harness the energies of the moon, the planets and the stars, is it truly any wonder why these organizations hold such power and control on our planet? None of what they do has anything to do with Satan or the devil. Christian detractors of the Masons are so blind to their being controlled themselves that they are willing to fight to the death to defend their beliefs in what they think is their god. Muslims are no different in their beliefs with jihads. Every ounce of human conflict can be laid at the feet of Enki and Ninhursag, and it is their psychosis that rules the mind of humans to this day.

Through the use of energetic power collected in the *mes* of their robes, badges of office, their architecture and even through our placing *authority* in the written word, our consciousness is held captive. We willingly give up our personal power to their institutions and their false religions, their system of authoritative academic control and their systems of politics, which are all ultimately nothing more than servants to the ideas handed down to us by these psychotic fish hybrids. It is well past time that we reject, refute and deny any more of this power over our minds and our species. These systems of control can only control you so long as you continue to allow it.

These systems are all predicated on fear and compliance. There are those in power, the global elite, who have been privy to these secrets for more than 5,000 years. It is not shapeshifting lizards from Draco, it is not little Grey aliens, it is human beings that are doing this to the rest of us, and the only reason they have gotten away with it until this moment in our history is because they held the energetic edge to adversely affect our consciousness. They create false flag illusions, like the infamous Illuminati, to keep people always searching for some dark conspiracy and keep us looking at Satan or the aliens who are presumably controlling this planet. The fact is that we control ourselves by continually buying into the first cognition fear bullshit. If we weren't so cowed by thousands of years of psychological manipulation through fear and secret energy manipulations they would never have gotten this far.

Yes, there is a dark conspiracy, but this book shows just how dark, how ugly, and just how far back this conspiracy goes. Our consciousness is continually and intentionally sent on wild goose chases trying to piece this thing together, and this wild goose chase is orchestrated by people who are in the business of controlling our perceptual reality on behalf of their controller gods. They tell us what to think, what is real and what is not real, what god thinks, how we will pay if we don't follow god's rules, and they continually play us against each other through any and every means possible. They are masters at sowing dissent and we are so foolish as a species that we keep taking the bait and playing the game of divisiveness perpetrated against our consciousness. They have divided and conquered human cognition, and so long as we continue to take the bait and defend the lies, we are simply their pawns.

17. Explaining Other Mysteries

Many of the myths and legends left to us are truth hidden behind allegory and religious mythology. Behind many of these myths we can find the truth if we know what to look for and can remove our own perceptual barriers of refusing the admit the truth we find. We are fortunate indeed that the Enki and Ninhursag were the braggarts they were, for it is through their consistent desire to rub our faces in what we didn't understand that I have been able to track their presence through so many ancient religions and myths.

I stated earlier that the Egyptian god Set, or Seth, was the same as the Greek god Typhon. I also suggested that Seth was Ninhursag playing a male role as that fictional god in Egyptian mythology. Here is my reasoning behind making that assessment. I have already written how the Orioners were a totally male-dominated, misogonystic breed. Even though Ninhursag was a hermaphrodite, she favored her female side the most because the female gained more manipulative energy by playing the constant victim in a male dominated universe.

Because the entire Orioner system of governance was so misogonystic, she never stood a chance to gain any real power under their thumb, and she was a very angry entity over this constant marginalization. In order to understand the symbolic mythology behind the myth of the death of Osiris (two deaths actually), you have to understand the psychology and anger behind Ninhursag in creating the mythology.

I am going to have to foreshadow a little bit of the next volume to relate this story. During Nibiru's orbital swing into our solar system near 3800 BC, Ninhursag had been living on Nibiru, ruling as the Queen of Heaven, while Enki had remained here as Lord of the Earth. A war had started here, which Ninhursag got wind of while Nibiru was out near the far swing of its orbit near Sirius. When the planet arrived in our solar system, Ninhursag was all geared up for total war against the Orioners and the other enemies of the Anunnaki. When she finally arrived, the Orioners had already staged a strategic withdrawal back to Betelgeuse, so she was left with her anger over not attaining her vengeance against the Orioner overlords.

The original Osiris was part of the warring faction against the Anunnaki forces, and once he was captured, Ninhursag did her best to usurp his authority by concocting the myth of his death and dismemberment by Seth. Playing the role of Seth in the religious mythology, Ninhursag developed the myth of dismembering Osiris and fabricated the search by Isis for her husband's 14 separate dismembered pieces. As the religious legend goes, Isis found all of the pieces except Osiris' phallus, which had been swallowed by a fish. The story, in allegorical form, tells how a very angry Ninhursag, masquerading as the god Seth, basically emasculated the god Osiris in rebellion against the system of Orioner partriarchy, and the story of the fish swallowing his phallus is representative of Ninhursag the fish taking on the male energy of Osiris, since Seth was the mythological perpetrator of the crime. If we don't understand the psychology of rage that was Ninhursag over the whole patriarchal Orioner system of control, this myth loses all its meaning.

The issue with the phallus with both Osiris's alleged imasculation as well as the cult of Priapus needs to be recognized as a continuation of the Orioner misogynistic patriarcal programming. Even though Ninhursag herself revolted at the misogyny, she was not averse to tapping into that power to suit her own power-hungry need for control.

It is through not only understanding the psyche of the Anunnaki, but Ninhursag in particular, that we start to see how and why these mythologies were created and the actual messages they are hiding from us in plain sight. When we can see the consistency of legends through different religions, such as the correlation between the Orphic god Zagreus being cut into 7 pieces and Osiris being cut into 14 pieces, then we can readily see the instigators behind all these myths. Enki and Ninhursag both played their own variants on a set of repeating themes, and that is the best way to track them down through all these ancient legends and myths.

Once we understand Ninhursag's rage at being a marginalized female under the yoke of Orioner male domination for tens or hundreds of thousands of years, then we can also start to understand how Enki, as the Lord God Almighty of the Old Testament, damned all women on this planet by laying the blame for evil on Eve in the West, and other women in India. By believing this mythological female demonizing, humanity to this day marginalizes our own women in the same manner that the Orioner gods marginalized their own women, and their Anunnaki step-and-fetch-its on Earth. Lord Enki, simply perpetuated the sexist hatred. Until we can understand the origin of this sexist form of divisiveness, we can't move past the mythology that divides men and women on this planet to this day. It is less pronounced than it used to be in modern Christianity, but it is very prevalent in the Enki-created religions of Islam and Hinduism. The misogonystic patriarchal system of the Orioners still haunts our species to the present. It is prevalent in every religion that only allows male priests instead of women, and it is the priestly classes that continually perpetuate the sexist hatred.

Going back to the Invocation of Isis presented earlier, we need to pay particular attention to her claim that she created all writing. Before the Anunnaki takeover, there was no system of writing in place with humans on this planet. All we find is ancient petryglyphs that, to this day, no one has deciphered. Given what I explained in a previous chapter about the control of writing and how it controls our consciousness, this claim takes on a more profound and sinister meaning. I find the claim by Ninhursag of creating writing and the separate tongues in order to sow confusion substantially more convincing to believe than the biblical story of the Tower of Babel, which has no corresponding historical reference outside the Bible of which I am aware. So far as our academics conjecture, writing started in Sumeria, in the very heartland of Anunnaki control. I leave it to the reader to decide which story is more plausible, the Tower of Babel or the claim by Isis/Ninhursag that she invented writing and brought it to humanity.

As previously asserted, the Anunnaki were bred from a form of telepathic fish on Nibiru. So far as we know, there may have been more than one breed of fish on that planet with this ability. Through genetic hybridization with the Orioners, I will suggest that they never lost that telepathic ability, and as such, they had no need for written language in order to communicate. If this is so, then the only reason writing and the varied languages were invented on this planet and given to the human races was as a form of controlling our consciousness and sowing continual confusion between Earth humans. They ruled all humanity through the principle of 'divide and conquer'.

We all know that when one language is translated to another language there is always something lost in the translation. If you consider beings who wanted to insure control over an intelligent species like Earth humans, then creating different written languages would most assuredly serve as a very powerful control mechanism to keep our species ever apart from each other. The chances of all humans ever banding together to challenge the authority of the Anunnaki on a large scale would be virtually nil. This, I suggest, is exactly why writing and different alphabets were created, to keep humanity firmly under their control with our species always at odds with itself over the variance in languages. It is the most sublime form of divide and conquer ever devised. The Anunnaki did not create the diversity of languages for they were all shaped and formed by the offworld participants on this planet. The only created the systems of writing to harness the use of those languages through the written word. This will be discussed in greater depth in the next volume.

You might ask how it is that they would know so many languages. The fact is that they didn't need to know them. Being telepathic they would have complete understanding of what was being communicated to them via thought transmission, alleviating the need for knowing language at all. The best proof of this that I can offer is found in the ancient myths of the gods, especially Isis, who communicated to her followers through dreams. This process in the cult of Isis was called incubation, and it was achieved when a believer slept within the temple and Isis communicated her wishes or answered the adherent's questions in the dream state of her followers. If you look at the tales of the Old Testament prophets, they often receive their messages in 'visions'. How would one describe telepathic communications passed on through pictures other than as a vision?

I reported how the Anunnaki and other hybrids were created in Orioner genetic laboratories. In time, Ninhursag herself started working with the Orioners and learned a lot about genetic manipulation herself. The Sumerian tablets tell the tales of her false starts allegedly creating the human race on this planet. Although she did not create the primary human species on this planet, she still did a lot of genetic manipulation with human hybrids and ultimately mastered genetic manipulation. We have numerous ancient stories in mythology about part-human hybrids, the Minotaur and the hybrid animal gods of the Egyptians as the two best known examples. These stories have a basis in reality when we consider Ninhursag playing genetic roulette with many species. While doing research for this book, I wondered whether or not I would be able to find any earthly references to support my contention that she was in the business of creating a lot of genetic misery and mayhem. I found the confirmation with the goddess from Greek mythology named Echidna.

Echidna was purportedly half-woman and half-snake and meaning in Greek, "She viper". As Wikipedia tells:

"She was the mate of the most fearsome monster Typhon. She was known primarily for being the mother of monsters, and many of the more famous monsters in Greek myth were said to be her offspring."

"Echidna's family tree, varies by author. The oldest genealogy relating to Echidna, Hesiod's Theogony (c. 8th – 7th century BC), is unclear at several points. According to Hesiod, Echidna was born to a "she" who was probably meant by Hesiod to be the sea goddess Ceto, making Echidna's father (presumably) the sea god

Phorcys, although the "she" might possibly refer instead to the naiad Callirhoe, which would make Chrysaor Echidna's father. Pherecydes of Leros (5th century BC) has Echidna as the daughter of Phorkys, without naming a mother."

I already showed how the Greek Typhon correlated dirctly with the Egyptian Seth, and the extreme likelihood of both of them being male manifestations of Ninhursag. Through her hermaphroditic nature, it takes no stretch of the imagination to see her playing both husband and wife to herself in this mythological context about Typhon and Echidna. Note, once again, the birth from sea creatures, which has held consistent throughout this book when tracking the Anunnaki. Continuing with the story of Echidna in Wikipedia:

"According to Hesiod's Theogony, the "terrible" and "lawless" Typhon, "was joined in love to [Echidna], the maid with glancing eyes" and she bore "fierce offspring": first there was Orthrus, the two-headed dog who guarded the Cattle of Geryon, second Cerberus, the multiheaded dog who guarded the gates of Hades, and third the Lernaean Hydra, the many-headed serpent who, when one of its heads was cut off, grew two more. The Theogony may also have given Echidna as the mother of the Chimera, a fire-breathing beast that was part lion, part goat, and had a snake-

headed tail, though possibly the Hydra or even Ceto was meant as the mother of the Chimera instead. Hesiod next mentions the Sphinx and the Nemean lion as having been the offspring of Echidna's son Orthrus, by another ambiguous "she", read variously as the Chimera, Echidna herself, or even Ceto."

It is questionable whether all of these creatures were genetic hybrids at the hands of Ninhursag's experimentation, but there are other examples of her handiwork found in ancient Mesopotamian illustrations where we find creatures like man-headed dogs, etc. Genetically manufacturing two or three-headed dogs, whether by intent or by accident of genetic roulette does not go beyond the realm of possibility. The pantheon of animal-headed gods of Egypt are simply another allegorical representation of Ninhursag's genetic manipulation capabilities with Egyptian religion wrapped around it. She could never stop crowing about her achievements, whether it was through allegory of religion or her ultimate claim to have created mankind in whole as the Sumerian mother goddess Ninmah.

When we consistently see Ninhursag cast in the mother goddess role, or as a goddess of birth, with a long chain of offspring, the likelihood of her truly bearing children in a biological manner is pretty thin. With her genetic manipulation capabilities, it was not beyond her to 'birth' many kinds of genetic monstrosities or monsters in the laboratory to intimidate the human cattle. We can either accept this reality that has been intentionally mythified and has become a consistent part of Ninhursag's braggadocio, or we can continue to accept it as simply being myth and deny the evidence provided to us. If we can accept that Ninhursag was in fact heavily experimenting with hybrid genetics, then her role as Mother Goddess everywhere she appears makes patent sense, for her multitudinous monster offspring were nothing more than manufactured beings, just as the Anunnaki and our species were the 'offspring' of their Orioner genetic creators. It was also through laboratory creation of these monsters that Ninhursag can lay claim to being the Virgin Mother. She could spawn whatever she needed in her genetica laboratory without ever having to conceive a natural born offspring on her own, and this explains the enigma of the Virgin Mother premise in its entirety.

I can't speak for how the reader is going to accept all of this, but as for me, I have to go where the evidence leads. Aside from her true genetic creation of hybrid monsters, once the reality of some of these monsters had crept into the human psyche by observation of their existence, later fabrications about other monsters that never actually existed was all that was needed to keep ignorant humans in line through fear of monsters and things that go bump in the night. Our species has provided a continual food supply to these psychopathic monsters, and we still do it to ourselves to this day.

Another example of one of these hybrid creations is found in the Babylonian creature that belonged to Marduk (Enki) called a *Sirrush* (see Wikipedia). It is this creature that is alluded to in the biblical Book of Daniel, and which Daniel purportedly poisoned. This is all predicated upon whether you believe any biblical character named Daniel ever existed. As for the Sirrush, I have an easier time believing in its physical existence more than I do the fabled prophet Daniel. Our past is riddled with demons and monsters, and it should be apparent by now that the worst monsters of all were the Anunnaki hybrids themselves.

I have extensively covered the story of the Babylonian creation epic the *Enuma Elish* and what the story actually means. The reader should find it odd indeed that the same story is found in the Old Testament in Genesis 1:6-7:

> *"Then God said, "Let there be an expanse in the midst of the waters, and let it separate the waters from the waters.""*

> *"God made the expanse, and separated the waters which were below the expanse from the waters which were above the expanse; and it was so."*

I ask the reader to define what this *"expanse in the midst of the waters"* is, if not the long orbit of Nibiru between our sun and Sirius B as I have described and we see recounted over and over as a repeating theme in so many ancient myths? Let's look to Psalms 148:4:

> *"Praise him, you highest heavens and you waters above the skies."*

Absent the explanations I have given in finally solving the creation story, what the hell does *"you waters above the skies"* possibly mean? It is only in the context of the explanations provided in this book that these mysteries are no longer mysteries but in fact make perfect sense, no matter how farfetched the idea may be at first glance or how uncomfortable this truth makes us. Given everything that has been revealed in this book, and Enki's specious claims to have created the heaven and the Earth, then can the reader in all honesty say that Yahweh of the Old Testamant is not one in the same person as the Sumerian Enki?

Let's look to some more confirmation of the collaboration between Ninhursag the Mother Goddess and church iconography. For example, let's take the modern Christian fish symbol that we see on bumper stickers all over the place. Note that the fish symbol is perfectly proportioned. This proportionate representation is what is called the *vesica piscis.* Wikipedia defines *vesica piscis* as:

> *"The vesica piscis is a shape that is the intersection of two circles with the same radius, intersecting in such a way that the center of each circle lies on the perimeter of the other. The accurate geometrical construction is described within the prominent place of the first Proposition, of the first Book of Euclid's Thirteen Books of Elements (c.300 BC). The name literally means the "bladder of a fish" in Latin."*

Damn, there's that pesky fish stuff again! If you look at the symbol you will find that it not only looks like a fish when placed on its side by extending a couple of lines, but that standing upright it looks like and is a representation of the vaginal opening. Wherever you see the *vesica piscis* symbol in Roman Church iconography, or in stained glass windows in many churches worldwide, it stands for the womb of the Mother Goddess, the Mother of Jesus - Ninhursag. It also carries sexual overtones of the Isis cult and many other goddesses of love and represents the vulva almost globally. One of the Hindu titles of the Great Goddess was *'a virgin named Fishy Smell, whose real name was Truth*." Have I provided enough information about these fish beings yet to solve this ancient cold case? One other aspect of the Christian fish symbol is that it is also representational of the Eye of Horus in a more simplified form.

With all the information presented in this book so far, let's take a look at a few other enigmas and misconceptions that modern humans have made in regard to ancient Egypt. We have a tendency to cast modern interpretations onto our ancient past, and with shows like *Ancient Aliens* speculatively leading the way, we have all sorts of ideas about ancient aliens visiting us and we make the assumption, based on our own levels of technological advancement, that they had to exclusively use a higher level form of technology to lord it over our ancestors. In light of these assumptions about technology, let's take one simple example that seems to infect the modern mind in regard to a certain set of carvings in the temple of Hathor in Dendera, Egypt

- what is commonly known as the 'Dendera light bulb'. I have already firmly established the connection between Hathor and Ninhursag in The Name Game chapter.

As humans, we have a tendency to cast images and ideas of our known world onto the past seeking correlations for things about which we have no real understanding, and we place points of modern comparison on them to try and comprehend their meaning. The Dendera light bulb is one of those images that admittedly resembles a modern light bulb, so we leap to erroneous conclusions in regard to these images based on our own system of technological advancement and preconceived ideas. If this book has taught you nothing else, it should be patently obvious that we know very little about our presumed history, academic experts included.

The first assumption that must be overcome is the idea that those assumed light bulbs carved in those temple walls are meant to be construed as clear glass. The carvings are a two-dimensional set of renderings designed to tell us a hidden story. There is nothing but our assumptions that gives us the idea that whatever is being illustrated is clear glass. Simply because we have invented a device called a light bulb, and because these carved images vaguely resemble a light bulb, we make the erroneous leap of logic that it must be a light bulb. There are those who have used these temple carvings to actually make a light bulb that resembles the pictures, but this does not substantiate that what we assume was a light bulb was in fact a light bulb of ancient technological design.

Because we are dealing with magic when we are unraveling the mysteries of the Anunnaki, we have to view all things in regard to them less technologically and more magical in orientation. We see a 'cord' in the carvings that connects to the ends of these oblong tubes, make the association with a light bulb, and assume that this represents an electric cord to light the bulb. Once we make this assumption we blind ourselves to any other possible explanation to account for what it could mean in the alternative. I am going to offer an alternative explanation for the Dendera carvings which makes more sense when dealing with the Anunnaki and their knowledge of hydromancy as explained previously.

If you look up "Dendera light bulb - illustrations" through Google, you will see a lot of images of the carvings. I ask the reader to note that in all the carvings, the serpents are illustrated in full, from head to tail. This fact alone dispels any idea that the serpents represent any kind of filament connected to the base of the fixture. So, if this is not a light bulb, we have to discern what it is and what it represents in the alternative.

The Dendera light bulbs were in fact containers made of clay. There is no way to represent the material, whether glass or clay, in a two-dimensional carving that tells us what it is. What we see in these carvings were actually tanks filled with water. If the reader doubts this assertion, then you have to come up with an explanation about why the serpents are always suspended seemingly in midair within the bulbs and not lying on the bottom of the enclosures as gravity would dictate if it were a snake, and if they were not floating in water. The fact that they are always shown suspended in the middle of the 'light bulb' suggests that they are floating. The serpents inside were electric eels, and when in use, there was more than one serpent in the containers.

The eels were originally stored in level containers and moved to these tilted tanks in order to agitate the eels, which caused them to generate electrical charges into the water. What we assume to be an electrical cord is in fact a tube for draining the charged water from the tanks for Ninhursag's use in her ritual acts of hydromancy. Ninhursag had discovered, quite by accident, that when a tank is tilted in the manner illustrated in these temple carvings, it upset the eels and created stress, which caused them to generate electric charges. After this accidental discovery, she had the tilted tanks manufactured specifically in order for her to harvest the electric eel-charged water for her magical purposes.

Eels are very sensitive creatures, and do not survive long after prolonged durations of stress, so her harvesting of these electrical energies was performed on an as needed basis. Because eels were so fragile and also extremely hard to come by, she learned how to use and preserve them as much as possible.

The figures we see under the bulb fixtures were her slaves who pounded on the bottom of the tanks in order to further agitate the eels, thereby getting them to emit more electric charges into the water due to the stress factors of being moved from a level tank, and then dealing with the pounding noise generated by those pounding on the bottom of the tanks. The figure at the end of the tank with the hose plays no role in the process and is most likely window dressing to the carving in order to confuse the meaning of the illustrations.

The two-dimensional wall carvings do not show the openings in the tops of these tanks through which the eels could be transferred in and out by using fish nets. Because clay is porous, the tanks were most likely coated on the outside with bitumen to prevent leakage, which was readily available from sources on the Dead Sea, and which is still mined from the surface of the Dead Sea to this day. It is historically proven that the Egyptians imported bitumen from the Dead Sea. Coating these tanks to prevent leakage was one use of that bitumen.

We see other illustrations of the light bulb carved in the walls where the bulb is positioned in an upright position, giving further cause for our misperceiving these tanks as light bulbs. These electric eels were hard to come by, and Ninhursag cared more for these eels that she did her personal guards. The upright carvings are illustrative of smaller tanks which held either a pregnant eel before birthing, or for containing the baby eels as protective enclosures. These smaller tanks were sometimes made of glass as they were not required to hold as much water, so the fragile glass could be used to view the contents and deal with the lower pressure that the large tanks would have shattered under. These containers also had holes in the top for accessing the eels with nets. In a two-dimensional carving, there is no way to illustrate the openings at the top of the tanks in either style illustration.

Ninhursag had numerous tanks of this nature in her temple at Dendera in order to have access to as much charged water as her magic hydromancy spells required. I have already covered all the points about hydromancy and the claiming of attributes. One god whose attributes she claimed was the god Thoth (Tehuti), the Egyptian god of wisdom. This claiming of Thoth's attributes as the god of wisdom grafted onto Isis as the goddess of wisdom as well as the Gnostic Sophia, and is most likely where she stole the energy of 'wisdom' to begin with.

If you Googled pictures of the Dendera Light Bulb, look for the specific illustration where an individual is standing at the end of the light bulb holding what appears to be two knives. Scholars interpret this figure to represent the god Thoth based on the baboon-like tail depicted. Despite the baboon-like tail on this figure, I ask the reader to focus on the head of this entity. There is no way that this head can be remotely reminiscent of a baboon's face. No matter how you squint or eyes or turn your head, that is a fish face, pure and simple. By this one example alone, I assert that the Thoth figure is in fact representational of Ninhursag performing some ritual associated with her eel-filled tanks of electrically charged water. All the pieces of this puzzle fit seamlessly together once one has the correct key to interpret the carvings, and there is nothing technological involved with this interpretation. The Dendera tanks are *not* light bulbs except to our vivid modern technological imagination which is ever seeking comparisons through which we make our cognitive determinations. As for the fancy djed pillar with the arms holding the tank, they are simply an ornamental stand with no real magical or technological value.

The Egyptians were fine artists and they most assuredly knew the difference between a square-snouted baboon in profile and the profile of a fish. There can be no sound argument that the face on this character performing the ritual doesn't have a fish face, and the fact that this is so, lends great strength to my assertions about the tanks. There is nothing about this carved face that remotely resembles a baboon. The fish eyes are even placed wrong for a baboon, but they are accurately and intentionally positioned for a fish.. The fact that Ninhursag even allowed this truth to be hidden in plain sight in this carving is evidence of her own arrogance in thinking that no human would ever figure out the true meaning of these carvings. It is simply an in your face sneer at human cognition - i.e. that we would always be too stupid or too brainwashed to ever figure it out.

I am not saying that is what Ninhursag looked like in actuality, but that the fish face is an allegorical representation of her, and she was so arrogant in her own twisted sense of power that she most likely mandated that this particular carving be rendered that way. There is no was to remotely think that this was accidental. We have to ask ourselves in light of this illustration why scholars have not made this same observation about the fish face on the figure holding the knives as I have. It is undeniably obvious, and I have never seen this observation made by Egyptologists, although I have admittedly not read everything published about these carvings.

The other mystery I want to address is the alleged sarcophagus in the Great Pyramid. This alleged sarcophagus has no lid, either intact or found in broken pieces in the King's chamber. Scholars are at a loss to explain why the lid is missing. The fact is that there never was a lid. It is not a sarcophagus at all, it is an abzu tank. In Stephen Langdon's book *Mesopotamian New Year Mystery Texts* there was a composition he presented called *The Death and Resurrection of Bel-Marduk.* I have already drawn a direct correlation between Enki and Marduk being the same person.

Using these same texts, Zechariah Sitchin concluded that Marduk was once imprisioned in the Great Pyramid. From other non-textual sources I know this to be true. The actual basis for this imprisonment will be discussed in Part 2. With that information in hand, that Marduk was indeed held captive in the Great Pyramid, then his imprisoners had to insure he at least had an abzu tank to make him live a long and miserable existence. If this assessment is the truth, and I firmly believe it to be true, there was never any pharaoh entombed in the Great Pyramid, only an outlaw Anunnaki locked in the purported King's Chamber with nothing but an abzu tank to keep him company. For that matter, there has never been a single mummy ever found in any pyramid, which puts the whole pyramid as a tomb concept into question. Academics really need to stop knowingly lying to the public about these things just so their egos can claim a sense of superiority over the rest of us and keep the world ignorant of the truth.

18. Putting the Ribbon on the Box

What I have revealed in this book is the factual story of our history. Most people are going to be unwilling to even entertain such ideas, let alone recognize it all for the truth that it is. We have had a repeating pattern of tyrannies perpertrated by these two outlaw gods and their earthly henchmen for more than 5,000 years of our history. They have used similar stories over and over again to capture and ensnare our consciousness. Before closing this volume, there are some loose ends that have to be addressed to put the final bow on top of this package of truth.

I ask the reader to note the direct correlation in the decription of Set-Typhon in the Osiris mythology to the 'womb' analogy in the Gnostic *Book of Baruch*. Viewed in this context, the infamous Set who chopped up the body of Osiris was none other than Ninhursag playing the role of the male villain in that fabricated mythology. Like the Jewish religion, Set demanded sacrifice of an unblemished red heifer, the same demand made of the Jewish priests in the Old Testament. Many scholars have seen the Jews involved with Set worship well before this author.

The cult of Set outlawed the eating of pork, just as Judaism did, and subsequently, Islam.

During my own years of spiritual deveopment and having been on the receiving end of energetic hits many times over the years, I stumbled upon an interesting discovery in regard to pork. Orion hit energies have a very distinctive and unpleasant feel to them. Characteristically, they leave one with a massive, intense headache at the base of the skull as if you were hit with a ball bat. These hit residuals are usually accompanied by feeling sick at your stomach, often accompanied by diarhea, and feeling generally out of sorts. Quite by accident I discovered that eating pork dissipates these hit residuals. I found this out by having to eat before I went to work and I was heavy into bacon and eggs for breakfast at the time of this discovery. It took me a while to notice, but eventually I figured out that eating bacon reduced the headaches and nausea and I bounced back more quickly after the hits and the effects of the energetic hit faded much more quickly. I also experimented with other forms of pork, like ham and sausage, to see if it was only bacon that would lessen these hit residuals. I discovered that any kind of pork product does the trick. Upon this discovery, I finally realized why there is the prohibition from eating pork in both Judaism and Islam. Enki and his associates wanted to make damn sure that if they ever had the need to energetically hit one of their followers, that they would not have the remedy to lessen the impact of the hit by eating pork. Eating pork basically dissolves the spells produced by energetic magic and they wanted their followers to not only feel the displeasure of their god, but made damn sure they could get no relief from the hit by eating pork!

With the rise of both the Osiris and Isis cult at the end of the Fifth Dynasty of Egyptian rulers, we find the pantheon of the hybrid animal gods moving ahead. Illustrations of some of Ninhursag's human-animal monstrosities can be found in Black and Green's *Gods, Demons and Symbols of Ancient Mesopotamia*. All the hybrid representations of the Egyptian gods served a dual purpose, on one hand they created confusion in the consciousness of the Egyptian followers of the cults, on the other hand, and most importantly, they illustrated Ninhursag's prowess in genetic manipulation - one of her trademark bragging rights.

Over time, the god Anubis overshadowed the alleged son of Isis, Horus, to take third place in a holy foursome. Anubis as the Jackal-headed god represents Sirius, Ninhursag's 'heaven'. We followed the dog thing into India with the goddess Sarama. Isis was often portrayed riding on a dog. The goddess Hecate was also associated with dogs, and I'm sure more research will reveal other goddesses with the dog affiliations - all subliminal references to the Dog Star, Sirius. The priests of Isis wore masks of Anubis in their religious processions and their religious rites.

Although what we know as Judaism today is totally a patriarchal representative religion, the Jews also worshipped a goddess in their temple, who they called the Asherah, also known as Ashtoreth, or Ishtar - other goddess associations with Ninhursag. For a comprehensive study of this goddess aspect of Jewish worship, the reader can read Raphael Patai's *The Hebrew*

Goddess. As with all other roles Ninhursag played, the Asherah was the consort to Yahweh and was also considered the Queen of Heaven. There are some scholars who have reached the same conclusion that I have, for different reasons, that the patriarchal religion of Judaism didn't start until about the second century BCE. Until that point in history, Jews worshipped the many gods and goddesses as much as anybody else. It is no accident how the religion of Judaism originated in that timeframe from the 2nd century BC to about 400 AD when Enki made his seat of power in Rome and the Anunnaki were all over this planet making sure all these pieces of these religious and historical tyrannies got put into place.

Isis is often associated with and equated with the cow. Part of this can be seen in the attributes of the goddess Hathor and the cow's horns atop the headdress of Isis in the post-Fifth Dynasty illustrations. It is through this correlation that the concept of the sacred cow found its way into Hinduism. The aspects of the Hindu religious overlay will be covered more extensively in the next volume.

We have been sold a bill of goods where all world religions are concerned. The rise of modern science at the hands of Sir Isaac Newton has its basis in Newton's studying ancient alchemical secrets of the Isian or Hermetic traditions. Regardless of what science has turned into, it finds its foundations in the mysteries of Hermeticism and Occultism. All of modern academic studies are right out of Isis' playbook during the centuries she was competing to establish her religious superiorty, encapsulating science, philosophy, medicine and religion all under one banner. The close-minded thinking of academia is as much a trap for our consciousness as any religion. The academics are virtually all as rigid and unbending in their perspective as any religious adherent. All sides are right in opposition to all other sides. In this respect, human consciousness has become completely locked down and controlled by beings who thrived on our professed knowledge, which is in actuality, only sublime ignorance and a form of tyranny over our cognitive evolution.

Ninhursag may have lost the battle with Enki in the religious fracas near Year 0, but with the passage of time, her principles and desires have come to fruition through her philosophers and academics over the centuries. All of the sciences may not be contained under the umbrella of religion as she worked to do under the name of Isis, but the end result amounts to the same thing where our cognitive advancement is concerned. Science has become a religion unto itself, it just hasn't admitted that fact. Academia is as lost in its perceptual denials and illusions of intellectual superiority as any religionist who denies anything but the belief in their god.

I have illustrated how the magical traditions of both Enki and Ninhursag have served to harness our consciousness through building their energetic mind traps in their temples over the ages. There is just as much energetic tyranny found in Catholic edifices as there is in Freemasonic Temples, Jewish Synagogues or Islamic and Hindu religious structures. The priestly and secret society uses of the trappings of power, whether they be found in priestly garments or judges' robes, Masonic aprons, rings and signets, staffs or symbols, is how they have energetically controlled our societies for thousands of years. It's high time we break free of this type of energetic and cognitive tyranny once and for all and advance beyond what even these tyrannycal fish-heads could ever foresee.

Those in the know have been intentionally abusing these energies against the rest of humanity in order to keep themselves and their institutions in power for thousands of years. The Popes, the Jesuits, the Rabbis, the Master Mason high adepts, the Brahmins, the Hermeticist adepts like Aliester Crowley, Helena Blavatsky, Alice Bailey and a cast of thousands have done this to all of us. They are each individually and collectively a major part of what is wrong on this planet, for their highest adepts know the truths presented in this book, and they patently refuse to admit to any of it. If one does some research into certain cultic religions, they will find Freemasonic connections behind all of them. Wicca, Scientology, Mormonism, 7th Day Adventism and the New Age movement all have Masonic fingers behind their origins. Prior to establishing the Masonic organizations, we have the Isis underground stream of knowledge which can be found behind the Reformation and the rise of Protestantism.

This has been a rigged game from the start, and it isn't just the Anunnaki gods doing it to us. It is other human beings who *served* those gods over the centuries since Year 0, and who keep the rest of humanity enslaved through their knowing perfidy and continued use of these energetic practices into the present. They want us all to bow at the pedestal of the gods, either through religion or the worship of science and academia as supreme. We are all servants to this system and the perpetrators all know their own perfidy. The information in this book is the terrible truth that has been kept from all of humanity. The Pope knows, the Rabbis know, many world leaders know, and the secret societies know at the highest levels of their organizations. Now you know.

These agents have used practices of energy manipulation handed down to them by the ancient so-called gods to control the rest of humanity. They separated illusionary magic from the real energetic magic in order to be able to deny that magic exists, while they actively used the real magic behind the scenes. In that regard, they sold the world a contrived bill of goods by defining our perception of magic in strictly those terms. Unfortunately, it is this designed and intentional misdirection about magic that our societies have bought into when it comes to our perception of magic, and the academics are the worst deniers of all.

Science refuses to acknowledge such practices are real as we all bow to the altar of science. Science dictates what our reality is and is not. The academics are the enforcers of the religion of science. No matter which way we turn, true history and reality have been kept out of the grasp of our consciousness - until now. What is presented in this volume solves some of the biggest mysteries of the ages, and now the secret is out. It's not all about rocketships and alien technologies as Sitchin and the cast of *Ancient Aliens* would have us believe. It has been a control more sublime and dastardly than humans can scarcely comprehend.

It is up to you, the reader, to decide what to do with the information presented in this book. I have painted the picture. I have given you a multitude of sources to support my contentions in solving this cold case. If you have done your part, you have done the Google look ups and seen the images that tell the story that has been intentionally kept from humanity at large by the most energetically powerful institutions on the planet, the Vatican, the Masons, the Banks, world Religions, the universities and our very own governments. In solving these mysteries I have not had to bend one ounce of available information to bring the picture into clarity. All the pieces fall together seamlessly on their own once one sees them assembled with the right keys of information to understand them. All the sources are from earthly references. The question is whether you can reach the wisdom to see this as the proof it is, or not.

This book is an important step on one's path to greater cognitive awareness. Until we can take off the blinders that have been intentionally put over our perceptual eyes and see these truths, we will stay slaves to this system of false beliefs, mysticism, supernatural gods and pure materialist science. I had much of the information in this book in my hands 18 years ago when I composed a previous book. With the advent of the internet and the availability of data and pictorial support, it was wise that I waited until now to release the material, because what is presented here is more fully dynamic than that first book was.

This book is going to cause a lot of controversy in many circles. It is going to get a lot more people disconcerted when they realize that this is all real and that their perception of reality is not what they perceived it to be. As with the other books in this series, it is very likely going to result in people having serious bouts of cognitive dissonance as they come to terms with the facts presented in this book. It is well past time that the people of the world know why this planet and all of our societies are as messed up as they are, and we have to wonder why we continue to give our service to all the concocted religious practices around the world. The sooner religions pushing the afterlife and reliance on all the false gods die out, the sooner we, as a species, we can focus on fixing ourselves and our home world and stop continually looking for the mystical way out to the happy hereafter.

This book is simply a snapshot, an overview of our past, which the varied fields of academia have been picking at for the last three centuries or more. The full story requires substantially more focused investigation than what this volume presents, and that is why our scholars need to get involved in looking more closely at this alternate version of our history. They are, after all, the experts, and being the experts they have an obligation to delve more deeply into these things rather than just sitting on their academic laurels defending their first cognition perceptual faith. The information in this book is going to be as equally disconcerting to their consciousness as it is to the lay reader, if they can find the courage to accept the evidence presented in this book. Yes, this book challenges all of our perceptions. It upsets the perceptual apple cart of our reality, but that doesn't make it untrue, and that is the most disconcerting part about this information. It is downright scary, but we have to move our consciousness beyond fear and simple denial because the truth makes us uncomfortable.

We have no shortage of hard evidence on this planet that needs to be genuinely evaluated, legitimate DNA studies on those elongated skulls, to name just one. With the new interpretations provided in this book, genuine inquiring academics and lay scholars should have more than enough new insights to provide them research possibilities for decades. It's well past time that we quit just shrugging our shoulders and saying 'it's a mystery' and put the necessary effort into seeing these mysteries as things that *do* have a valid explanation.

The heretic academics presently involved in solving these ancient mysteries need to get past their fascination with seeking supernatural explanations as well as simply focusing on ancient technologies to explain what the ancients reported about magical practices. We have to expand our arrogant and limited human-centric species perspective and recognize once and for all that we are not alone in this universe and never have been since we were created as a species. When we can advance our cognitive abilities beyond the programmed concept of magic being basically sleight of hand performances using magic wands or illusionary magic, then we can finally start to grow into an energetically informed species. We need to transcend all of these perceptual illusions, and within these illusions I also categorize hard physical science materialism, for all of these avenues keep our perceptions harnessed strictly to the 3D realm of what is known, acceptable and psychologically comfortable. The way out is the second cognition and finally facing the truth.

Continuing to embrace the lies will only keep our species mentally enslaved in the first cognition and subject to the neurotic whims of our creators, which we so forcefully defend. By transcending this mental tyranny, we can finally take control of our own destiny as a species and evolve into something that even these creator gods could never comprehend. The invitation is delivered, the door is open, do you have the courage to walk through it?

19. Afterword

There are two main areas of focus in this book. The primary area the reader will probably focus on most is the information presented that shows our perception of reality to be hopelessly askew. The secondary, and probably overlooked message in these pages is that of personal empowerment and cognitive advancement.

There are many human 'agents' of the Anunnaki working against the rest of humanity on this planet. These human controllers and their origin will be collectively revealed in the next volume. What the reader needs to focus on most in this presentation is how this information gives one the foundation for understanding and not get caught up in the paradigm of fear that acknowledging this information initially brings with it. Contrary to every system of first cognition beliefs on this planet, we are not powerless in the presence of some faceless god, nor even powerless against the Orioner and Anunnaki system of control. Only our fear keeps us as slaves to this system.

Our perceptions of reality are utterly and totally controlled, but we can never escape this system of control until it is finally revealed. Researchers over the years have seen large pieces of this conspiratorial puzzle, but they have not been able to see the overall picture. Some of the best research I have found has been done by Christian researchers identifying much of this global conspiracy and the people involved over the centuries, but they are so blinded and controlled by defending their own faith that they utterly fail to realize that their religious beliefs are as much a part of this system of control as what they are seeking to reveal.

People need to realize that the global conspiracy is not just about Banksters and Gangsters, Satanists and crooked Politicians, Freemasons and the Vatican. The conspiracy, this undeclared war against humanity, has been waged against the consciousness of the entire human race, and the pieces of the conspiracy that are being revealed to the public are only small segments of a darker and more dastardly agenda that keeps us all cognitively enslaved. It is the entire system of current global consciousness that is the enemy of us all, not just a few segments of our societies who are the controllers of our perceptions. Yes, there is an overarching group of conspirators on this planet who control every avenue of human perception. The system of control is in academia, it is in the political systems, it is broadcast every day through news venues (both written and video), it is in every religion, it is exercised through publishing houses that censor the truth by refusing to print it, and it permeates the financial systems which keeps everyone but the controllers struggling to simply survive under this financial tyranny. This system of control is continually reinforced by excommunicating the heretics, by labeling valid researchers as 'fringe nuts', and by the defenders of everyone's personal perception of reality. Whenever we buy into their perceptual lies, they win.

Our perceptions and beliefs are controlled through fear and emotional and psychological manipulation. The people in charge of keeping the entire world divided and subjugated so they can continue to control us are the perpetuators of this system of cognitive tyranny, and they are very knowledgeable in the science of manipulating the human psyche through perceptual and emotional control. The general public worldwide is intentionally kept in the dark about the truth. Government agencies cover up the truth as a matter of routine. Investigations into any kind of alien presence is besmirched and belittled by those in control who know the truth of what is presented in this book and who have a vested interest in keeping this all secret. They can only control us through ignorance, fear and emotional manipulation. Through using these psychological weapons against all humanity, they keep the Anunnaki system of control in place and keep themselves in the positions of controlling this planet.

The controllers rule us through not only keeping the truth from humanity, but by using disinformation as a weapon to misguide genuine researchers down blind alleys, continually chasing their tails trying to unravel the truth, when very little truth can be found in our entire global history. The chase to find the enigmatic Illuminati is a prime example of one of those blind alleys, and the controllers are laughing their asses off at our continual energy expenditure chasing phantoms. Where most researchers have failed in ultimately figuring out the root of these issues comes with each of them defending their own personal perceptions. Each and every one of them brings biased baggage to the investigative process, seeking to solve the riddles of the tyranny, but demanding to keep their own perceptual illusions in place while doing so. I cite the Christian researchers as a prime example, but academics are just as guilty as bringing similar baggage to their theoretical projections. By bringing this perceptual baggage to the equation, demanding to challenge everything but one's own perceptual beliefs, it leaves every researcher half blind to solving the mysteries that surround us.

The main reason why I succeeded in unraveling many of these mysteries where others have failed is specifically because I left all of this personal perceptual baggage at the door. I approached solving these problems without any preconceived notions about what our perceptual reality presents to us. In other words, I trashed everything I thought I knew, erased the chalkboard, and started from scratch. Without having any perceptual territory to defend, I removed my own blinders and did a reassessment of the evidence, just as anyone solving a cold case would do. For the reader to advance their own cognitive abilities, they have to approach this information with the same mindset. They have to take the information for what it presents, not by trying to fit it into their pre-existing perceptual box, but through expanding their own perceptions in order to see the larger picture. This one aspect alone is why people haven't figured these things out. The picture is larger than any of our present first cognition perceptions allows and every researcher has failed to solve these riddles of our past because they all possess that individual perceptual box into which they try to fit all their conclusions.

To ultimately advance as a species we have to destroy these perceptual boxes to expand our cognitive potential. Revealing the very troubling aspect of our history presented in this book is part of that process of eroding the perceptual lies we have embraced for the last 6,000 years of our history. Denying the truth presented in this book because it doesn't fit into the current frame of your perceptual reality does not make the information untrue, it simply means that you choose to deny it. Denial is what drives our consciousness at this time. The controllers are counting on your denial of the information presented in this series of books for one simple reason, if you continue to deny the truth, they can continue to control your perceptions by continually force-feeding us their contrived lies about human history.

The controllers can only control us through divisiveness. They use race, religion, politics, abortion, gender, sexual orientation, culture and nationality to sow these constant elements of division. They can only continue to control the planet so long as we keep bowing at the altars of their perceptual lies. So long as we continue to allow our consciousness and our very emotions to be manipulated by this system of control, they will continue to control us. Each individual on this planet is ultimately responsible for freeing themselves from this cognitive tyranny. No one is going to do it for you, you have to do it for yourself. You are now armed with the knowledge of the weapons they use to control the consciousness of an entire planet. How much of this control are you willing to continually subject yourself to?

I don't want the reader to cave into fear because of the information contained in this book, regardless of how troubling the information is. Your own personal fear is what impedes your consciousness from advancing into a higher level of cognitive understanding. Each of us has to overcome this fear paradigm in order to free our own consciousness from this system of cognitive tyranny. If you are reading this book at all it suggests that you at least have an inquiring mind and that you are seeking answers. This observation alone should tell you that you are not just another one of the robots who not only stays rooted in this system of tyranny, but who will, in their profound ignorance, die to defend it and keep it in place. You have to ask yourself whether such a system is worth dying to protect or not.

In order to advance as a species we have to be brave enough to acknowledge our humble origins. There is no sin in acknowledging our origins, only in refusing to accept them. We are at a crossroad for human cognitive evolution, but we are never going to advance so long as we continue to maintain our ego-oriented, human-centric mentality. The universe is a vast and wondrous mystery. To think that we are the only intelligent created beings in this universe is logical foolishness. To continue to think that we are the only living incarnate intelligent beings created by some supernatural god, who the angels allegedly became jealous over and warred against this god is simply ludicrous. We have to swallow our species pride and come to the realization that, as a species, we are not as special as our individual egos makes us believe. Despite our ignominious origins, we hold great potential when we can free ourselves from our perceptual self-delusions. The ultimate question is, are you individually ready to do that?

References

Friedrich Nietzsche § 55 of *The Antichrist*

Michael D. Swords, PhD, Biochemist; Professor Emeritus, W. Michigan University; *UFOs: The Secret History (2010)*

Seutonius - *The Twelve Caesar*

Zechariah Sitchin - *The Earth Chronicles series*

John B. Davis - *A Dictionary of the Bible, 1942*

Unger's Bible Dictionary

The Enuma Elish - L. W. King, Translator, 1902

Donald A. Mackenzie - *Myths of Babylon and Assyria, 1915*

Epic of Atrahasis

Michael Tellinger - *Slave Species of the Gods, Video presentation on Youtube*

Robert K. G. Temple - *The Sirius Mystery*

Berossus - *Fragment from Alexander Polyhistor*

Jeremy Black and Anthony Green - *An Illustrated Dictionary: Gods, Demons and Symbols of Ancient Mesopotamia, 1992*

James B. Pritchard - *Ancient Near Eastern texts Relating to the Old Testament, 1950*

H. G. Wells - *The Outline of History, 1920*

The Nag Hammadi Library - James M. Robinson, General Editor, specifically *The Paraphrase of Shem* translated by Frederick Wisse

David Ovason - *The Secret Architecture of Our Nation's Capitol, 2002*

Holy Bible - KJV

W.G. Lambert - *Enmeduranki and Related Matters*

R. E. Witt - *Isis in the Ancient World, 1971*

Demotic Magical Papyrus of London and Leiden

L. Ron Hubbard - *Battlefield Earth*

Stargate: SG1 TV series

Samuel Noah Kramer - *The Sumerians, 1963*

Endall Beall - *Demystifying the Mystical, 2015*

Endall Beall - *Philosophy for the Average Man, 2015*

Endall Beall - *Willful Evolution, 2015*

Endall Beall - *Navigating into the Second Cognition, 2015*

Mrs. Endall Beall - *The Energy Experience, 2015*

H. B. Swete - *An Introduction to the Old Testament, 1914*

Robert H. Eisenman - *James the Brother of Jesus: The Key to Unlocking the Secrets of Early Christianity and the Dead Sea Scrolls, 1998*

Flavius Josephus - *History of the Jews*

Plutarch - *Isis and Osiris*

A. L. Frothingham - *Babylonian Origin of Hermes the Snake-god, and of the Caduceus, 1916 - JSTOR access*

Albert Pike - *Morals and Dogma, 1871*

Raphael Patai - *The Hebrew Goddess*

WIKIPEDIA References

Ea
Enki

Ninhursag
Berossus
Oannes
Orion (mythology)
Unas
Nommo
Apkallu
Abzu
Rakshasas
Hypsistarians
Christós
Ptolemy I
Library of Alexandria
Septuagint
Cargo Cults
Sabazios
Sabazius
Sabaoth
Dionysus
Zagreus
Phanes
Dyeus
Zeus
Brahma
Vishnu
Kali
Devi
Durga
Sarama
Saraswati
Matsya
Ourboros
Okeanos
Tethys
Typhon
Echidna
Hermes
Hermes Trismigestus
Hermetic tradition
Marduk
Ningishzida

Aphrodite
Aphroditus
Priapus
Pan
Hathor
Hecate
Isis
Sothis
Sirius B
Osiris
Sophia as a World-Soul
Cathars
Atbash cipher
Alumbrados
Vesica piscis

INTERNET LOOK-UPS

Fish god images - Jeremy Green
Inanna and Enki - Sumerian text
The Erra Epic - Sumerian text
Elongated skulls - images
Fish creatures - Papal mitre - images
Osirion
Papal Hand Gestures - images
Catholic image of Jesus - traditional image of Jesus
Erotic art in Pompeii and Herculaneum
Unas - Pyramid Texts
Enki - Sumerian texts
The Invocation of Isis
Baphomet - Eliphas Levi - image
Baphomet - Atbash Cipher theory
Christian Madonna - Isis - images
Dendera light bulb

The Evolution of Consciousness Series

Book 1

A Philosophy for the Average Man: An Uncommon Solution to a World Without Common Sense

Book 2

Willful Evolution: The Path to Advanced Cognitive Awareness and a Personal Shift in Consciousness by Endall Beall

Book 3

Demystifying the Mystical: Exposing Myths of the Mystical and the Supernatural by Providing Solutions to the Spirit Path and Human Evolution by Endall Beall

Book 4

Navigating into the Second Cognition: The Map for your journey into higher Conscious Awareness by Endall Beall

Book 5

The Energy Experience: Energy work for the Second Cognition by Mrs. Endall Beall

Book 6

We Are Not Alone – Part 1: A Challenging Reinterpretation of Human History by Endall Beall

Book 7

We Are Not Alone – Part 2: *Advancing Cognitive Awareness through Historical Revelations*
(Currently in the process of being written) by Endall Beall

Book 8

Psychology of the Gods: *A Modern Analysis of the Behaviors of the Gods and the Psychological effects their Behaviors have on the Human Psyche*
(Currently in the process of being written) Mrs. Endall Beall

This series of books is still in the works but some of them are already available at:

www.Amazon.com and www.barnesandnoble.com and www.booksamillion.com

About the Author

The author of this book has concerns for the direction humanity is taking at this time. Everywhere we look we find turmoil. The author is a person with insight into the way out of this turmoil through advancing our cognitive awareness. The information provided in this book is more about the reader and the advancement of human consciousness than it is about the author. The author doesn't matter when compared to the information presented in the book.